New Play Development

Facilitating Creativity for Dramaturgs, Playwrights, and Everyone Else

New Play Development

*Facilitating Creativity for Dramaturgs,
Playwrights, and Everyone Else*

Lenora Inez Brown

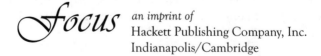 an imprint of
Hackett Publishing Company, Inc.
Indianapolis/Cambridge

A Focus book

Focus an imprint of
 Hackett Publishing Company

Copyright © 2015 by Hackett Publishing Company, Inc.

18 17 16 15   1 2 3 4 5 6 7

For further information, please address
 Hackett Publishing Company, Inc.
 P.O. Box 44937
 Indianapolis, Indiana 46244-0937

 www.hackettpublishing.com

Cover design by Deborah Wilkes.
Composition by Aptara, Inc.

Library of Congress Cataloging-in-Publication Data

Brown, Lenora Inez.
 New play development : facilitating creativity for dramaturgs, playwrights,
and everyone else / Lenora Inez Brown.
     pages cm
 Includes bibliographical references.
 ISBN 978-1-58510-724-7 (pbk.)
 1. Playwriting. 2. Plays-in-progress. 3. Theater—Production and direction.
 4. Drama—Technique. I. Title.
 PN1661.B76 2015
 808.2—dc19

                                                        2015012429

The paper used in this publication meets the minimum requirements of American
National Standard for Information Sciences—Permanence of Paper for Printed
Library Materials, ANSI Z39.48–1984.

∞

CONTENTS

For my family.
Thank you for all of your generosity, love, and support.

Expand your vision.
See as others see, for there is more than
what is immediately apparent.

—Rev. J. Mark Hobson

ACKNOWLEDGMENTS

This book would not have been completed were it not for a number of people lending support throughout this process. I want to thank my publisher Ron Pullins for believing in the first book so much that he welcomed this second book. His comments and suggestions throughout the planning process helped this book immensely. Many creative processes encounter difficulties and the writing of this book was no different. First, my father passed away suddenly and it was no longer possible to meet my initial time line. Ron never pushed or doubted that I would return to this work. Thank you for that time, Ron. Second, Ron retired from publishing and merged Focus Publishing with Hackett Publishing. I want to thank the Hackett staff for embracing this work fully and helping it through its final stages, especially Deborah and Laura.

There are people I turned to for support throughout this process. These amazing individuals set aside their plays, syllabi, dissertations, and crying children to field a telephone call, read a passage, listen to an idea, or offer an insight. I so appreciate your time, generosity, and words of encouragement. Thank you: Carla Stillwell, Dr. Holly Gerzina, Chuck Smith, Larissa Fasthorse, Dr. Penny Smith, Mead Hunter, Anne Marie Cammarato, Kirsten Greenidge, Hilary Mason King, Nate Speare, Mark Charney, Dean Corrin, Dr. Rachel Shteir, Karen Zacarías, David Burke, Rose and Bob Gaier, Paula Brazil, Nedra Starling, Pat Turner Cunningham, Anthony Clarvoe, Dr. Robert Neblett, Andre Burton, Chris Bodendorfer, and Tanya Palmer. I also want to thank Carla Fioretta, Kimberly Kilby, Brenda Redmond, and Rani Affandi for their love and support.

I also want to thank Joyce Brown and Vatella Call for making many things possible.

Finally, I want to thank my family. Their support and love knows no bounds: Elizabeth, Warren, Pam, Poplar, Leonie, Dr. Yvette Jackson, Howard Gollub, Dierdre Watson, Daya Doolin, Helene Clarke, Jeanette Gianetta, and Jackie Hoyer. Mom, if it weren't for you . . . and Dad, miss you every day. Love always.

PREFACE

Prior to completing *The Art of Active Dramaturgy*, many colleagues and friends asked when I would write about play development. I resisted answering because at the heart of this question was the assumption that working on new plays meant knowing little about working on set-texts. Truthfully, it's nearly impossible to work on new plays without understanding set-text dramaturgy. Yes, there are differences, but approaching a new work without appreciating and embracing set-text dramaturgy opens an artist up to disaster. The first book, *The Art of Active Dramaturgy*, takes a dramaturg—and anyone who uses dramaturgical skills which, in theatre, is everyone—through the process of approaching work on a set-text and then builds upon and applies those ideas to new work. The approach seemed balanced and covered the basics.

Then I finished *The Art of Active Dramaturgy*.

During conversations and lectures focused on *The Art of Active Dramaturgy* at KC/ACTF regional festivals, I found myself addressing topics that *Active Dramaturgy* touched on, but did not explore in-depth. The same happened while consulting with theatre companies working to establish or focus their play development programs. They knew *The Art of Active Dramaturgy*, but had questions that fell beyond its scope.

Even though the roots of new-play dramaturgy depend upon understanding the principles of set-text dramaturgy, the greatest difference is that the work is new. As such, there are no guarantees that the play succeeds in total or in part. The individuals who choose to work on new work must have a bit of the intrepid explorer about them; each new work explores unknown territory, and to see a new work into existence requires a great deal of bravery and perhaps even a bit of *chutzpah*.

Anyone who takes on the challenge of new work—actor, director, designer (of every ilk), dramaturg, stage manager, or producer—needs a strong comprehension of the play's critical elements and how they work. A new-play artist must also possess an ability to envision a clear goal, understand how to achieve that goal, and remain flexible in the execution of that goal every step of the way. Artists devoted to new work have an incredible faith in the play—its voice, language, and story—and follow its lead to build whatever's necessary to realize fully the dramatic world.

To facilitate creativity means to change the question or questions used to fuel or shape the process of doing. To shift the focus means to take the givens and perceived truths and transform them by refusing to accept them at face value. The overreaching concepts in this book work to develop the skill set needed to push one's creativity in general, and specifically to develop new plays. This book also identifies and articulates ways to approach new work by building upon the philosophies and practices introduced in *The Art of Active Dramaturgy*.

The four major areas of play development for directors, active dramaturgs, and playwrights are:

1. Developing a flexible eye, or knowing when to go with the flow and when to let go;
2. Keeping an eye on the big picture while discussing the small moments;
3. Rewriting or filtering comments in favor of simple, elegant solutions;
4. Remaining objective or listening to the play and others without losing perspective.

A need for precise thinking under pressure within a limited time, with comments delivered in clear, focused, pointed yet supportive language, defines the new-play dramaturgical process. To realize the needs of a developing play, the active dramaturg and those who use dramaturgical tools in their work, often prepare questions based on observations made during manuscript reads, rehearsals, or creative conversations, and deliver these questions and observations during ten and twenty minute breaks. What's more, the active dramaturg's insights and notes must incite artists to consider adjustments or rethink ideas and make the process of rewriting appear to be a less gargantuan task than it truly is.

Understanding the elements of a play, the difference between plot and story, and the rules of the play versus the rules of the world will help active dramaturgs negotiate the four major play development areas with ease and create a game plan for development that works.

A dramaturg, or anyone who adopts the dramaturgical role, helps clarify and prioritize the development process. An active dramaturg thinks a few moves ahead to consider when an idea will be heard and how that will affect the writing so that any shifts or changes in text will be elegant and keep with the play's voice and vision.

The one role a dramaturg does not assume is that of writing instructor. New-play dramaturgy looks to deepen the story without making the writing more complicated. Using simple open questions that look to add specific details and explore those details adds nuance to new work.

An active dramaturg facilitates the play development process as well as the play's next evolution. This may mean selecting a dramaturg so in sync with the writer that she understands the writer's vision and can identify ways to connect the themes and ideas within the play, and can also challenge the writer so that the play evolves and grows. Too often, however, collaborators consider the definition of artistic synchronization to mean someone who embraces the play so fully that the artist and writer appear to be the same person. To have a love fest or a fantastic working relationship does not mean everyone agrees with each other—sometimes such mirroring equals a recipe for disaster. The goal is to form a creative team that can collaborate well, provide pushback in ways that generate or inspire unexpected solutions, and still respect and encourage each other throughout the process.

Play development is tough for everyone involved and even tougher for the active dramaturg, because much of the dramaturg's work product is invisible. In other words, to the untrained eye, it often appears as if the dramaturg and the active dramaturg do nothing during the workshop. If they choose to, those collaborating with the active dramaturg can see the impact this artist has on the process and the final product. In the end, it is the active writer's words that are heard, the actors who enliven the world, and the director's vision that is seen. The active dramaturg's efforts remain unseen to most audiences and even colleagues, but it is often those intangible qualities that bring about the clarity of imagery and story that audiences and artists hold onto when acknowledging the effect a work has.

All dramaturgs, and anyone using dramaturgical skills, approach play development with a similar level of optimism and passion. However, the active dramaturg's ideas and questions encourage a new way of seeing that sometimes causes their contribution to be met with opposition or for the dramaturg's critical comments to be seen as negative.

Change is difficult.

Committing to shaping work so that it moves beyond expectation is similarly difficult. It is my hope that *New Play Development: Facilitating Creativity for Dramaturgs, Playwrights, and Everyone Else* will help demystify the development process and illuminate the philosophy behind many of the active dramaturg's questions and critiques so that creative teams—and especially playwrights—will better understand and embrace the challenge to deepen the creative collaboration that an active dramaturg offers.

In spite of its challenges, dramaturgy and play development remain the most exciting theatrical work there is. Understanding the process and philosophy of developing new work ensures the health of the field, its artists, its writers, and everyone who takes on a dramaturgical role in action if not in word or title.

How to Use This Book

This book is divided into four parts, each of which addresses a major topic governing the act of developing a play or the mindset that helps to best frame the experience.

Part I: Building the Game Plan   This section focuses on the foundational thoughts an active dramaturg needs to collaborate well and to lead and manage the development process, and identifies language that defines the active playwright's process.

Part II: Active Dramaturgy, Active Playwriting, and the Workshop   This section introduces the workshop process and its evolution (which may differ from the play's evolution). In addition, Chapters 4–7 discuss how those collaborating can remain flexible throughout the development process and still progress forward. These chapters also deal with the challenge of filtering comments and remaining objective so that the work gets done.

Part III: The Dramaturgy Variations: Developing Play Development Skills   This section does more than provide skill-building exercises for all artists interested in play development. This chapter also outlines how to apply the skills within a workshop setting. Most of the exercises can be done in a group setting or, for an extra challenge, individually. When done individually, one truly develops the ability to separate the analytical self from the creative self.

Part IV: Thoughts to Consider   Certain issues may influence play development and production but do not always inform the actual workshop process. Three of these concerns involve: cultural or ethnic diversity in the theatre and cultural competency; how the field labels and discusses playwrights; and the tendency to confuse the dramaturg's role with a teacher's. These aforementioned issues may never be put to rest, but anyone interested in play development must acknowledge that avoiding these discussions has had (and will continue to have) an impact on new work, the field of dramaturgy, and playwriting.

INTRODUCTION

One of Sherlock Holmes' greatest skills is his ability to solve any puzzle or mystery. His encyclopedic collection of esoteric material serves him well and, when combined with his keen sense of observation, allows him to see order where others see chaos and to pursue a distinctive line of questioning while others fall back on pedestrian methods. Sherlock Holmes always appears as a marvelous master of thought.

One of the greatest weaknesses of Arthur Conan Doyle's works, however, is the absence of clues the average reader needs to solve the cases. The written tales avoid revealing key elements in the story—in ways a layman might follow—ensuring that Holmes' solution surprises and beguiles.

At times, those observing active dramaturgy within a play development workshop find it as mysterious and surprising as following Sherlock Holmes—impossible to pinpoint what was done where, when, why, or how, because so many vital clues seem to be missing. Should a successful result emerge (and what defines success in a workshop?), the active dramaturg either appears as amazing as Holmes or as invisible as Dr. Watson.

In truth, there is nothing mysterious about an active dramaturg's role in the development process and nothing esoteric about the tools and information used. An active dramaturg in new-play development—or anyone using dramaturgical skills and tools during a new-play workshop—follows a methodology as tried and true as Holmes': observe, pose questions that help the process even when they appear quite obscure and off topic, and constantly consider the alternatives (taking care to note that more than *two* possibilities constitute an alternative).

Even so, the active dramaturg's work during the development process remains invisible, leading some to balk at the active dramaturg's questions just as doubters resist Holmes' observations—until the results prove successful.

Why then, one might ask, engage in play development? The process can be long and drawn out with only the slimmest hope of achieving a full production, which is how most define success following a development process. The reasons the process tends to last long varies: sometimes opinions differ regarding the play's story and its growth, and sometimes the artistic team fails to function as a unit, with each artist vying for an individual point of view, making the development process challenging at best and a battle of wills at worst. Even if the play moves smoothly through development, the theatre or organization producing the work may begin to express its own ideas based not on the work, but on the theatre's preferences, and subtly—or not so subtly—ask for changes at the expense of the writer's vision. Sometimes the process serves an individual's creative expression or vision at the expense of a coherent or thematically engaging piece. In other words, if led and managed poorly this process of developing a new work can quickly become a test of wills and egos rather than the exploration and development of an idea, talent, and creative world.

Although the aforementioned possibilities are not ideal or examples of strong play development, any of those options can and do infiltrate (to some degree) even the most model development process.

Why, then, engage in play development?

Because there is an opportunity to create a work that speaks to where society is now and to facilitate the artistic growth of many (and, specifically, the playwright). Because playwrights write plays—living, breathing works of art that require actors to enliven the words that exist on the page, and workshops facilitate a writer's growth.

Another undervalued reason to engage in play development is to ensure a story and dramatic vision the active playwright, the creative team, and the play can agree upon. Yes, the play has a say in development. For, as discussed in *The Art of Active Dramaturgy*, the play is akin to a person with a unique voice, vision, world, and reason for existing. Playwrights are initially the most intimately connected to the play's genesis. By the end of an excellent development process, the play will reveal its individuality, assume a distinctive place within the writer's *oeuvre*, and go on to have a life of its own.

Another reason why: play development is the theatre's version of research and development. Without new plays, the theatrical world remains staid, without innovation, and fails at its primary obligation—to provide posterity a record of how society lives now (or a voiceless past). This call and obligation exists for all voices, all experiences, all visions and all manners of telling story. Theatre artists—the creators and the producers—must engage and support all equally even when the presumption is to serve one audience.

Understanding the seven critical elements helps readers first engage with a play without bias and then helps establish a framework for thinking about, questioning, and then discussing the play with the writer and other members of the creative team. *The Art of Active Dramaturgy* includes a lengthier discussion on how to engage with a manuscript without bias and a discussion of the seven critical elements. Below is a brief summary.

A Review of the Elements and Reading a Manuscript

To read a manuscript or new play, the active dramaturg begins by approaching the work with an open mind and without bias. To read openly, the active dramaturg must first acknowledge what regularly happens for that reader during a first read. When reading a play, some hear voices akin to a radio play and others see images as if watching a film. When a play encourages the active dramaturg to experience the play differently (see images if sound usually predominates or vice versa), the active dramaturg takes note.

Similarly, the active dramaturg acknowledges dramatic styles or tropes that prove most exciting and adjusts the response accordingly. It is as if the play were a person. If you prefer those who wear glasses, you will gravitate toward them at the exclusion of everyone else in the room. Just as you would work harder to meet someone wearing glasses, the active dramaturg reads with greater intent those plays that fall outside their comfort zone.

As much as an active dramaturg works to read without bias or at least an awareness of bias, the active dramaturg does read with three distinct expectations in mind: to discover the play's rules, its world, and its voice.

The Play's Rules   Every play has a unique set of rules that are established by how time shapes the world, which events make the world work or throw it off balance, and how linguistic styles affect the play's musicality. Actively looking for the play's rules rather than how it conforms to preexisting styles and structures makes new discoveries possible. The play's rules correspond closely to plot. (Brown, 5–6)

The Play's World   Contrary to expectation, the rules of the play are not the same as the rules of the world. The play's rules establish the way events unfold. The rules of the world govern how the world the characters inhabit regulates itself. The play's world corresponds closely to story. (Brown, 6)

The Play's Voice   The play's voice is comprised of the seven critical elements, and these elements combine to create a unique work of art. As noted in *The Art of Active Dramaturgy*, "the play's voice is like a piano chord. . . . When played independently, each note has a distinct sound or aural character. When played together, each note still exists but the ear registers one full, balanced sound" (Brown, 8).

Play's Plot   The plot looks at what happens in the play. To understand the plot, look to the basic points that anchor the play's action or story. (Brown, 11)

Play's Story   The play's story is the compilation of events that reveal how or why the plot unfolds as it does. Story also includes the ideas and nuances that enrich the plot. (Brown, 14)

Play's Voice and Its Components   To find the play's voice in either set or new texts, dramaturgs focus and reflect on the entire play and how the seven critical elements combine. The seven critical elements—story, time, character, language, image/metaphor, active themes, and form or pattern—are a play's basic ingredients that combine to create a distinct work of art. (Brown, 7–8)

Time   Time remains the play's most common way to organize story and plot. Understanding how time orders events and action helps reveal the play's voice and rules. (Brown, 15)

Character   An active dramaturg's allegiance lies with all characters, not just one. Noticing how each character's individual journey connects and propels the story forward informs the story's tension and story progression. (Brown, 18)

Language   How characters speak—with words that dance or move haltingly through a scene—determines the language of the play. Active dramaturgs look for writers who disappear behind the character's true voice, for these writers have mastered language. When characters are true and clear, the writer's hand disappears, revealing rich dialogue that drives the plot. (Brown, 19)

Image/Metaphor   Metaphors exist as ways to ground and discuss the ever-changing human experience. Active dramaturgs consider which metaphors and images jump to the fore or resonate below the play's surface to shape the play's voice. (Brown, 20)

Active Themes   Active themes connect language and metaphors to characters and plots; they may also locate a play within a particular political or social framework. Themes are big ideas that impact each character and the play's world. (Brown, 22)

Form or Pattern   Time, language, metaphor, character, and themes all combine to create a distinct pattern or form for the play's story. Many analytical texts use the term "structure," which risks reinforcing old ideas. Writing plays by the numbers often produces uninspired, even turgid writing; just as analyzing a play according to pre-determined formats can lead theatre artists to miss exciting new works. Using the term "form" to refer to how the critical elements combine allows the writer, active dramaturg, and other artists to freely observe new twists and unique solutions. (Brown, 24–25)

Challenging Moments   A challenging moment, scene, or event within a play occurs when a moment presents a problem without an immediately apparent solution. Challenging moments present opportunities for exploration within new works rather than immediate cuts or rewrites.

In the end, those reading and looking for scripts to develop at workshops and festivals are looking for innovative, distinctive writing and hoping to develop a long and healthy relationship with the writer.

Even though workshops facilitate the writer's process, play development often serves the play first, the playwright second, and the artistic team (actors, director, and active dramaturg) third. Most often, theatres and play development institutes see the purpose of the workshop as an opportunity to help a specific story come to life on stage. Even when the theatre or organization expresses a long-term goal to establish a relationship with a playwright, it is often the play—its specific dramatic story—that brings the group together and helps solidify the first steps in the relationship.

The assembled artistic team often uses the workshop to explore the possibility of a longer collaboration. The group may hope that the team will remain together in some fashion for many productions to come, but forging a single collective team throughout the play's evolution happens less and less in the regional theatre systems (expense and the desire to use local talent and staff are often key factors) and more in the independent production and Broadway models.

Open, Closed, and Neutral Questions

Active dramaturgs and those who use dramaturgical skills begin to approach new work with open questions. The greatest challenge throughout the development process is balancing what is currently needed with what *will* be needed and what of the original (or preceding) draft remains a part of the story. As discussed in *The Art of Active Dramaturgy*, "When working on a new text, the rules and facts of the play may change with each rewrite or adjusted line. As a result, the active dramaturg (or anyone helping the text grow) needs to acknowledge and address the play's current and future state" (Brown, 40). "The active dramaturg's arsenal of questions includes five words . . . *who, what, when, where,* and *how.* We tend to avoid *why* because this leads to defensive responses" (Brown, 37–38).

The open question remains the active dramaturg's strongest tool and requires the greatest amount of practice to perfect. A vague question stalls or destroys the play development process. A poorly timed neutral question can lead a playwright to rewrite according to the collaborator's wishes rather than the play's. A journalistic question can cast a combative pall over the collaboration. The open question encourages the active playwright to explore the work within the play's parameters and never forces the writer to defend the work.

The observations and reflections made after reading the manuscript (or scene) shape the open question, which focuses on the play's world or story without making assumptions. When an open question focuses on a specific character, the active dramaturg does so to illustrate how the character might more deeply connect to and expand the play's world.

Active Listening

The flipside of an open question is the ability to listen actively to the response. It's tempting to simply hear what is said, but in doing so a dramaturg may miss nuances that reveal a writer's biases, concerns, joys, and challenges with the process. When done well, active listening leads to strong understanding and will clarify communication rather than promote assumptions, which benefit no one.

To listen actively, listen for language that repeats, is judgemental or overly vague, or that resonates with the play but never actually appears in the play, and use these observations to shape a conversation that encourages the writer to be more specific. Look for ways to connect these observations to the writer's passions, their initial reason for creating the play, and even fears. Avoid listening for what *you* want. If you and the writer agree, wonderful; if you have a particular vision that is based on your biases, let that limited point of reference go. Be open and listen to where the writer comes to the story. Sometimes a writer's experience level will place them well behind most of the creative team; at other times the opposite is true. Although every process stretches a writer and the other artists on the creative team, the process should avoid pushing an artist so fast that they become exhausted and burn out.

Because play development allows the writer time to hear the work in its current state and provides the resources (human, technological, or financial) to explore and evolve the script, the writer gains greater familiarity with the play's world and how to best express its rules, quirks, and truths. The length of time devoted to play development can be as short as one intense workshop or take more than ten years of workshops, readings (public and private; staged or at the table). Active dramaturgy's goal is to keep the time spent in workshop to a minimum, not ten years.

Active dramaturgy yields results more quickly than typical dramaturgy when the writer is an active and willing collaborator. Nevertheless, it remains difficult to pinpoint the active dramaturg's contribution since so much of it is intangible. Sometimes collaborators can point to an excellent question or a great note, but most of the active dramaturg's process is intangible, making it easy to discount and devalue the artist's contribution. Those who appreciate active dramaturgy know that managing the process—keeping track of the various elements of creating and supporting a new work—requires a rare skill set. Demystifying the philosophical approach active dramaturgs use within the workshop and rehearsal process (while working on new plays, specifically) invites a greater understanding of which dramaturgical skills and approaches add to the development process.

Without explanation, active dramaturgy proves as elusive (though less nefarious) as the master criminal Moriarity because so few watch active dramaturgs in action. If someone does watch an active dramaturg work, often one sees a person who takes notes, listens to a question or two, and participates in a three-minute notes session while the actors take a ten-minute break. But as Holmes cautions, "To see is not to observe, the difference is clear" (Doyle 162–163). In other words, the observer sees a little bit of intense work, but fails to observe the preparation needed to execute the exchange.

In short, to the untrained and outside eye, the active dramaturg's process can seem unclear and vague.

Similarly, Holmes' process is unclear at the end of some of Doyle's books. True, the Baker Street resident is a fictitious character who achieves clarity through his use of questions and innovative and insightful thoughts, establishing him as an excellent role model for those who seek ways to lead rather than manage old patterns. When active dramaturgs and those who use dramaturgical tools are seen as leaders who create spaces where others can be more creative than they imagined and achieve their goals more quickly using tools everyone can access, they are seen as vital to the development and theatrical process.

Developing new work can be an even lengthier task than solving a mystery, and the process of helping a play evolve into a stronger version of itself can prove more confounding than any case Holmes and Watson ever attempted. However, just as Sherlock Holmes finds a way to enjoy the challenge of matching wits against the unknown, an active dramaturg knows that through a development process fueled by vigorous thought, careful observation, and a flexible game plan, a clearer play will emerge.

With that, let's begin our exploration into active dramaturgy within a play development setting. Let us explore how to develop an eye for innovative writing, create a game plan for the play's evolution and the workshop's time frame, pose questions that promote vigorous thought, and discuss how the ideas and concepts impact the real world.

As Holmes said to Watson when they began the exciting journey of discovery in *The Adventure of the Abbey Grange*, "The game is afoot!" (Doyle, 164).

PART I: Building the Game Plan

Chapter 1: The Foundations of the Game Plan

Play Development and the Search for Innovative Writing

Sherlock Holmes loves a good mystery. He enjoys the excitement and intrigue associated with challenging questions that take him and Watson into *terra incognita*. Holmes knows what he must uncover, and he has some sense of how he will discover the truth—through questions and investigation, and keen powers of observation. He doesn't accept every case because he prefers those without a typical set of clues. He looks for the problem that is extraordinary in its challenge and demands a unique if not innovative solution. The case that grabs his interest presents opportunities to wrestle with unknowns and feels akin to a challenging game. The intrigue Holmes seeks isn't rooted in the stuff of melodrama and soap opera, but the elusive thought piqued by provocative questions and unusual relationships. Even as he travels through virgin territory, he has a strategy in mind, one that is simultaneously fixed in its process and flexible in its execution and design.

"Strategy" can have a negative connotation when it's defined as a method to control others (or a situation) so that one person wins. However, when applied to the work of play development, "strategy" means that it is best to approach work with the playwright's needs and wants at the center, and to devise a way to shape the process that proves beneficial for the writer and the play.

Like Holmes, the active dramaturg has a process for approaching the development of new work that is both fixed and flexible. Open questions fuel an active process rooted in observations (gleaned from reflections) that respond to how the play realizes its critical elements. Just as Holmes encounters various witnesses and must distinguish between a genuine clue and a red herring, the active dramaturg must separate conversations that talk about solutions from those that present active options to pursue. To talk *about* a dramatic moment during the workshop is to explain the problem or add detail to embellish. During a workshop, such language presents a false sense of moving forward. To discuss a moment means exploring options that will activate and propel the play forward. Active dramaturgs work to cultivate discussions so that the active playwright has options when rewriting.

To best frame the play development investigation, the active dramaturg must remain flexible and rely on the active playwright's vision for the play, which will adjust either a little or a lot throughout the workshop.

> Active playwrights create worlds. Characters live in worlds. The strongest plays have fully realized worlds inhabited by characters, be they fully or partially realized.

The most crucial aspect of the game for Holmes is challenge. Holmes defines challenge as a problem that presents an opportunity to stretch the mind while assisting others, which coincides well with the active dramaturg's idea of challenge. Similarly, Holmes defies each obstacle the challenges present by engaging more fully in the process of thinking, questioning, and applying strategy until he achieves success. In short, Holmes finds challenge fun. Sadly, most shy away from this positive type of challenge because it is tough. That said, when challenge is simply an opposition for no rational reason, it is right to avoid it.

The Goal of a Workshop

To discuss success within the context of a play development workshop may seem misplaced because a workshop inherently means to engage in the act of doing, and most revere the development process for its ability to support constant discovery without necessarily fixed outcomes. Even so, identifying the hallmarks of a strong, successful workshop remains key in light of the numerous ersatz

> Balancing or tuning the play's voice signals a successful workshop.

processes that result in no substantial change or revitalized artistic vision. In brief, an unsuccessful process looks like this: throughout the rehearsal, the room feels alive with welcoming, engaging conversations, and even a few rewrites appear, but the collaboration yields results that no one uses after the workshop.

Many mistakenly believe the goal of a workshop or the hallmark of a workshop's success includes achievements like completing an act or score, or writing the play's ending. The workshop's true endgame, however, is to find the play's heart or story by crafting an active sentence for the play, and to connect the moments, scenes, or dialogue to this sentence. A successful workshop means that the active writer leaves with a vision for the play, a plan for writing (or rewriting), The Sentence to focus the rewrites, a desire to embrace how it may morph, and an enthusiasm to continue discussing the play. Balancing or tuning the play's voice also signals a successful workshop. Every step of a strong game plan operates with these points in mind.

The Sentence Defined

To facilitate a dynamic play development process, the active dramaturg leads the active writer through a process to discover The Sentence that best captures the play's action. Some might call The Sentence the play's thesis statement; to others, it is the play's journey, which is akin to a character's journey. Like the active statement that an actor crafts to identify a character's journey, The Sentence frames the play's action (story and plot) from the first moment to the last. The Sentence needn't revolve around one character, but it should articulate the story the play seeks to tell in a single thought, simply expressed. The Sentence articulates the story the play seeks to tell and addresses at least two of the play's major themes, which connect to the journeys of at least two-thirds of the play's characters (both major and minor).

The Sentence

- An active statement that articulates the play's action in a way that impacts at least two-thirds of the characters
- Helps shape the creative team's conversation
- Helps focus the creative team's conversation
- Helps focus the development process

The Sentence is active, straightforward, and often difficult to formulate. Why? Because a play depends on numerous details, character stories, and thematic ideas coming together. To express each of these ideas through a clear frame proves challenging because The Sentence strips everything away and identifies a central idea connecting each of the play's thematic lines or at least the play's major action. The Sentence activates and connects story and plot.

The Sentence also articulates the active idea that shapes every scene and a majority of the characters. As such, The Sentence serves as the touchstone for the entire development process, for it functions as either a metaphorical clothesline upon which all scenes and moments hang upon or a ladder where each character, moment, and scene exists as a rung. For these reasons, The Sentence resonates as more than the primary lesson or takeaway for the play. The Sentence serves as the play's crucial organizing principle.

How to Craft The Sentence

Hollywood regularly distills every film, especially action movies and thrillers, into simple trailer statements or sentences. These often imitated trailers begin with the phrase, "In a world where . . ." The second phrase introduces the character's (or characters') response to the setup. The third part presents the obstacle that the character faces and will inspire the film's main action. The Sentence embraces this simple philosophy but encourages the writer to articulate the dramatic ideas in a creative, active, non-formulaic manner.

> ### The Sentence of the Play #1
> #### Hamlet
> The play's sentence could be: **To right the wrongs committed against Elsinore and its people**. This sets up the play's opening: the night watch and the ghost's haunting suggest that things are not right in the state of Denmark and the town/castle of Elsinore. This sentence continues to frame the action through the play's end when Fortinbras enters to find all Hamlet's family and key supporters dead. The Fortinbras line is in a position to reclaim the land that, according to Fortinbras, belongs to his family and was wrongly taken. At the beginning, the audience believes that Hamlet will set out to right the injustice and the wrongs festering within the kingdom. Throughout the play's action, however, the story reveals that Old Hamlet brought about the air of evil and mistrust, and that Fortinbras, not Hamlet, spends the entire play focused on these political injustices as he traverses the Danish countryside; whereas Hamlet is focused on his family's betrayals.

The Sentence and Play Development

Using The Sentence throughout a play development process helps shape the conversations and work. The greatest difficulty for most is identifying the key sentence. For example, if a character's journey fails to connect to The Sentence, either The Sentence or the character's journey must change. Or, if a major theme lives outside The Sentence's focus, most likely The Sentence needs to change. In truth, The Sentence can and will evolve as the story moves into focus. This is fine. At some point the right Sentence will emerge. A changing sentence indicates a deeper understanding of the play—its themes, characters, and vision. The sole caveat: remember to adjust the elements of the story as The Sentence changes. This constant evolution will lead to specific changes rather than endless and general rewrites if the active writer, active dramaturg, and artistic team continue to focus on one thing: clarifying the story.

> In general, The Sentence is simple and direct with few subordinate clauses or heavy grammar.

Collaborators flounder or encounter outright resistance (or a thinly veiled look of contempt) from the writer when critiques are based on their assumption of the play's goal or intention. These missteps make a successful collaboration difficult and stem from one crucial mistake: failing to ask the writer to describe the play's action succinctly. Asking for clarity of thought does not minimize the play's scope and importance; it simply asks the active playwright to participate in shaping the process by articulating the through-line for the dramatic work. Using The Sentence removes the need to employ overly guarded or obtuse language when discussing the play. Every open question posed, reflection obtained by using the critical

The Sentence of the Play #2
Hamlet

The play's sentence could be: **To navigate the challenge of placing family loyalty and needs before that of the State's**. This sets up the play's first challenge: managing the new relationship with Claudius, Hamlet's uncle-father. It also sets up the second challenge: the ghost's appearance and his directive. Laertes has a similar challenge from his send-off to his return after his father's murder. Fortinbras also takes up the family versus state mantle. How the women fare proves even more complex. It's possible that Gertrude must marry a Hamlet in order to remain Queen. Ophelia must grapple with state politics and dating a royal. When Hamlet, a royal, murders her father, an advisor, she must accept the state's decision to not prosecute Hamlet. Throughout the play's action, the world reveals that individuals lose a great deal of self-esteem and power (even mental stability) when subjugating one's self to the interests of the state. Even Fortinbras reflects on the impact sacrifice has and will have on him.

elements, or successful dramatic moment may be discussed in relation to how poorly or how well each supports The Sentence throughout the play.

The Sentence doesn't seek to reduce or minimize the story but to identify the action that drives the play forward and propels the characters through a journey comprised of tangential or central plot lines. A good play is concerned with more than one idea. Using The Sentence as a frame and a starting point for all subsequent questions, comments, and other creative choices makes it easy to see how various comments and observations impact or respond to the work. Often, identifying The Sentence can help reduce the play development conversation to mere minutes because everyone is on the same page. When ideas inspire new perceptions or a fresh take on an old insight, collaborators simply need to ask, "How does this point connect to The Sentence?" or "Should The Sentence itself change?"

Clarifying The Sentence

Many mistakenly believe The Sentence states what the play is about or the topics the play covers. It does not. The Sentence pinpoints key moments of action and gravitates toward active storytelling. Second, The Sentence is concise. A play may embrace many ideas, but focusing on what a play is about often leads to generalities and a long unwieldy sentence. Focusing on what the play is about can lead to general conversations about states of being (such as happiness), or general themes (like bullies are bad). Only when dealing with a play with multiple subplots (think Shakespeare) might The Sentence expand to two or three sentences, though with a little effort even these multi-act plays may be summarized with a strong, single sentence.

Charting the evolution of The Sentence and how it impacts the active dramaturg and any conversations the active dramaturg and active playwright have with various members of the artistic team may help demonstrate The Sentence's effectiveness.

Consider a fictitious work that features barnyard animals vying for power and freedom and contending with their world's boundaries—a fence, a river, and a road.

The Sentence first begins as:

> *This play explores what it's like when considering options.*

This sentence indicates what the play's themes might be, but states nothing explicitly. Quite simply, this sentence expresses what the play is *about*, which is why it comes across as vague and fails to help the play appear unique (at its root, any play deals with options). The questions this sentence provokes are many. For example: Is the play presenting life and death options for the barnyard animals? Or, what are the farmer's options regarding keeping or selling the farm? Is the play following the animals as they consider a way to rebel to save their lives or rebel to solve the humans' problems? Without a good Sentence, the options are too varied and it's difficult for a director, dramaturg, actor, or designer to begin shaping a specific world that realizes the playwright's work. However, posing open questions that illuminate the writer's ideas and aid in developing the play will ultimately help the writer create more specificity and dynamism within the work. If the active dramaturg crafts open questions that bring out more detail and eventually define this Sentence's "options," The Sentence and the play will begin to evolve. When the conversation with the writer includes too many closed or vague questions two things could happen. One, the writer becomes overwhelmed by the number of times the word "options" is repeated and realizes the entire piece or sentence needs to change in some way; or two, the active writer thinks of numerous literal answers rather than the solutions the play needs. In either case, the development process begins to involve options or character journeys that are unintended and not in line with the writer's vision.

The play development that accompanies an overly vague Sentence may see a number of rewrites as various ideas are explored. Great scenes could be fashioned, but the overall story would remain bloated and perhaps heavy on exposition. Forward progress won't be made because the roadmap for the play and what the writer wants to see in action remains as fuzzy by the end as it was in the beginning.

Unless . . .

The Sentence morphs into:

> *This play explores what it's like when a chicken considers options.*

If the writer considers some of the questions posed by the dramaturg or other lead members of the creative team and uses them to identify a central character, or set of characters, and their wants, The Sentence will evolve into something more specific and active. Suddenly, The Sentence helps the play begin to take on a personality and reveals the play's possible voice (or quirkiness) by identifying a central figure. By grounding The Sentence in a central character, the way the "options" will be considered will change, for a chicken thinks one way and a pig, another. True, it would be nice to know what the options are, but the possibilities are winnowing. This version of The Sentence tells us that the options concern the chicken only. The rest of the barnyard animals figure into the story, but less so, and each animal may respond in ways that echo or challenge the chicken, creating possibilities for tension and conflict.

Certainly adding a specific character helps, but the vagueness of the options still remains. The writer runs the risk of losing the ability to lead the play development process and discover the answers best suited to the play. However, because the writer has now identified a central figure through whom much of the action flows, and other characters for the chicken to interact with or respond to, the play can begin to develop a singular focus even though it runs the risk of hitting one note and losing its focus early.

Unless . . .

The Sentence morphs into:

> ***This play explores what it's like when a chicken considers crossing the road.***

Suddenly the chicken has a clearly defined obstacle: crossing the road. There's a risk that this idea could result in a great comic skit and not an interesting play. However, if the active writer, active dramaturg, and creative team begin to explore the various obstacles and benefits of breaching this particular boundary something interesting might evolve. What's more, it's now possible for other characters to consider this central idea—the chicken crossing the road—and their responses to the chicken's dilemma can slowly (or quickly) take the play in other directions. Also, the phrase "what it's like when a *chicken*" makes it clear that what the chicken does, sees, or hopes for will be placed in contrast to other characters; the play is not looking at what's unique to chickens. A variety of perspectives and insights, if followed, guarantee a multifaceted play.

Even so, there is still the possibility that the play will remain cerebral and concerned solely with philosophical ruminations, rather than with pursuits that lend themselves well to dramatic action.

Unless . . .

The Sentence becomes:

> ***This play follows the journey (life) of a chicken unable to cross the road.***

Suddenly the play's story is clear and full of action, dilemma, tension, and breadth. When the active playwright presents this active sentence, it is clear how the active dramaturg and other members of the creative team can respond to the play and focus their observations and comments. The team can now look to see whether the play's moments serve the chicken's journey and conflict: an inability to act; specifically, an inability to cross the road. The specificity of this question means that The Sentence is working to focus the moments and scenes so that they respond directly to the chicken's inability to cross the road. If the play's moments do not support the personal search for action, perhaps they support the journey of a chicken's life? Again, this question stems directly from The Sentence, which ensures that the scenes and moments tie into the dramatic action while embracing other life challenges the chicken experiences with her friends on the farm. Actors can make choices that connect to this major through-line and add color and depth to this vision, and so can designers and directors. Active dramaturgs can use the specific obstacles that prevent the chicken from crossing the road to help the writer use form and time to enrich the story and establish a unique dramatic world. In addition, this version of the sentence does not telegraph the ending. The chicken may gather the strength

> The Sentence avoids giving away the end but does help the team get there.

to cross the road by play's end either on its own or with the help of other animals or farmhands, or she may never succeed, but discover something else along the way. The insertion of "unable to cross the road" alerts everyone to the chicken's consistent, but perhaps not permanent, state of being.

The Search for Innovative Writing

Those who embrace the principles of active dramaturgy and active playwriting when developing or producing a new work must have a willingness to experiment, explore, and set high standards. Setting a high bar does not mean expecting perfection, but it does suggest an unwillingness to embrace mediocrity or what has been done before *as* it has been done before. Untold examples of new work modeling tried-and-true structures exist, and have garnered the writer (and artistic team) success at the expense of truly innovative work. Success, often defined in monetary terms, can mean spoon-feeding audiences what they think they want or repeating what is now well past its prime. The challenge with remaining ahead of the curve rather than producing the expected or the current fad is to identify the moment when the storytelling style shifts from new and avant-garde to predictable and hackneyed. There are times, however, when a new story works best if supported by a tried-and-true form or plot. When the ideas and character struggles are too challenging or explosive, and are then coupled with an explosive and daring form, the play's story and message may not reach any audience.

Active dramaturgs and those who use dramaturgical principles work daily to develop an audience's sensibilities so that the audience remains adventurous and open to new theatrical styles, but also appreciative of strong, old fashioned storytelling structures that facilitate bold new ideas. Active dramaturgs ferret out innovation to ensure creative, artistic, and yes, financial satisfaction for all. The challenge is to champion innovation in whatever shape it takes so that audiences and artists embrace it fully and so the final result leads to good fortune for all—however one may define fortune. The challenge for active playwrights is to push new forms when appropriate and to embrace traditional forms when the narrative proves too explosive.

The question is, how does the writer use a formula to tell a story? Is formula used as a default to simplify the process, or to frame challenging ideas so that they are easier to grasp? As ironic as it may seem, at some point every storytelling form becomes formulaic for one simple (if not sobering) reason: formulas can and do work.

It's true.

Law and Order's nineteen-year run (in spite of multiple casts) is a testament to the fact that formulas work. Even though you can set your clock to the entrance and exits of the cops, attorneys, the obligatory twist, last minute collaboration, and final confrontation, the stories hold the viewer's attention. Even in reruns, the ripped-from-the-headlines story almost always seems new or timely. Why are the repeats so successful and engaging? Because the writers focus on the facts and rarely embellish the storytelling with extraneous character details. The catch with *Law and Order* is that these are not facts recounted baldly—these are facts supported by the essential details that round out the who, what, when, where, and sometimes why. Essential details avoid rigid interpretation; instead they embellish a fact by grounding it.

Excellent writing for the stage does much the same thing—it provides audiences and creative teams the facts or essentials needed to define the story's truth. Such writing leaves room for performers to build nuanced characters that speak to every generation regardless of when or where the play is set. Too often, however, writers choose or are urged to elevate their story with details or flowery additions rather than the specifics that pierce the story's heart.

> As noted in *The Art of Active Dramaturgy*, the more general you are when you begin the more general the work remains; the more specific or detail oriented you are, the more universal or timeless the work becomes.

As noted in *The Art of Active Dramaturgy*, the more general you are when you begin the more general the work remains; the more specific or detail oriented you are, the more universal or timeless the work becomes.

Writing or Discussing an Idea versus Writing or Discussing the Truth of the Idea

When developing work, many dramaturgs often give notes, but use vague language. The questions either lack strength or the openness needed to fuel creative thought that moves artists toward clarity. The following questions will not help most writers focus on generating essential facts:

"We need to know more about the character, how is she bad; how does she love?"

"We need more humor in the second act or what we're calling the second act."

"What can we have to better understand this world and these people?"

Whether offered as responses to dramas, comedies, or plays about people of color, the aforementioned comments give the appearance of collaborators communicating, in truth, these questions lead to artists talking around the issues and each other.

Discussions where artists talk *about* characters lead to discussions that circumvent identifying the critical points or the play's facts rather than how to use those facts to propel the action forward. An active dramaturg either uses open questions to generate a discussion that unearths ways to move the play forward or pinpoints where facts serve as exposition only so that these facts might inspire action in addition to setting the scene.

Poor adjustments and questions lead writers to write to the idea and not what's needed to craft an active, forward-thinking adjustment. When writing the idea (as with performing or directing the idea), one engages in the general outline or impression of what embodies an emotion, thought, or personality. When developing a play, everyone seeks to have the rewrites focused on writing the truth of the idea.

To write the truth of the idea means to identify and articulate the unique aspects for that world, character, or moment. To write the truth requires a commitment to rigorous detail, rich prose that activates situations and characters and propels them to do something specific and exciting. For example, a character isn't just rushed; a character is late to pick up a child from daycare. Or, a character isn't just hungry; a character has picked up his favorite barbeque after a long day of traveling in the car, and the temptation to sneak a bit is too great. The joys and concerns such specific distinctions bring will pervade many lines of dialogue and moments of performance.

This attention to detail or commitment to truth may lead to the decision to fashion a new form for the story, or place a new story within an old form. If the choices are active or leave room for active interpretation on stage, the prose will avoid sounding leaden or weighing the scene down; the writing will be on the verge of innovative.

Many who read manuscripts—original works or adaptations or translations—look for plays by those who write truths rather than the *ideas* of truths. Yes, an ability to use language, time, metaphor, and imagery in unexpected ways remains paramount, but in the end, a story that evokes new understanding and relationship to the world through laughter, tears, heady ideas, or a combination of all three attracts more attention. So, if the process of rewriting suggests that the story is so explosive an audience and cast need it shrouded in a more recognizable form or formula, that's fine. If the character's story comes across more clearly and reaches more people, then excellent. Take time to ensure that the unique insights remain lucid and exciting.

Simpler Not More Complex

When executing rewrites or incorporating change, many mistakenly opt for more over less; not more specifics or substance, just more—details, words, ideas. Active dramaturgs and active playwrights look to enhance a project's effectiveness by honing in on what accomplishes most, works best, and retains the voice of the character and the play without overwhelming the script. Any artist can add detail to a scene, but the strongest artists with the clearest vision, pinpoint the crucial moments that need specificity and use the fewest crucial elements to elevate moments of the play to greatness.

Balancing Simplicity with Original Intent (How to not lose voice and its elements when rewriting for simplicity)

Focusing on The Sentence helps active writers retain a hold on the play's story, especially when a number of people are involved in the development process. Without a clear understanding of the play's drive or its journey, the goal can remain a mystery throughout much of the process. Also, without The Sentence to frame the conversations, the writer runs the risk of leaving the development process either resentful or despondent because the play the writer set out to write has been lost. Even a play that appears clear, focused, and in need of only a few trims and a tweak or two, can disappear during a development process if the writer does not articulate and embrace The Sentence.

Honoring The Sentence helps every artist retain a connection to the play's original intent—even when The Sentence changes drastically and the play along with it. The Sentence ensures that everyone can articulate the play's goal and the question the writer explores when sitting down to write. Even if the creative team fails to agree with the direction the play takes after identifying and satisfying The Sentence, acknowledging it serves the active writer's process and vision. The Sentence helps the active writer hold onto the play and make temporary or permanent adjustments—and discuss them clearly in terms of this objective goal. Should the process become difficult, The Sentence may help the team frame and separate emotional responses from those of storytelling requirements and from truths needed to support the vision.

> Rewriting is difficult. Many enjoy the process of building a landscape where nothing existed, but few enjoy living within the boundaries and adding colors within the lines.

Such an approach results in story changes that are precise, focused, and simple. There is little need to pad the dialogue with explanations—unless that's how the character speaks—because the reason *why* behind the change is clear. It may seem as if the additions or changes will be overly simplistic and curt. Not true. The Sentence helps the writer remain connected to the first inspiration for writing and, in turn, the sound of each character's voice. The shifts in story enhance, clarify, and even elevate language so that stiff characters sound natural and natural characters have dialogue that dances across the page and in the air.

When inexperienced artistic teams assemble, four of the most common ersatz processes are: the love fest, the intellectually engaging process, the running-in-place process, and the absent writer process.

Ersatz Process #1: The Love Fest　　Of course a genuinely successful process can also exist as a love fest; where the collaborators truly enjoy one another, laugh, and pose provocative questions, but even when they hit roadblocks, the writer emerges with a strong draft, a strong vision of the play, and an understanding of the play's Sentence. More often than not, however, artists engaged in an ersatz process masked as a love fest, experience a process effusive with false praise, comments, and discussions about the play—in other words, conversations that skirt the issues— but at no time does anyone focus on the play's critical elements in a way that the writer or the artistic team can use to sharpen the play's dramatic action. Sometimes, active conversations do occur, but the writer has difficulty using the information to evolve the play. This doesn't mean the process was fruitless or that the conversations were entirely lacking, simply that the playwright doesn't yet fully see how the play works or may not be able to execute rewrites. Many enjoy the process of building a landscape where nothing existed, but few enjoy living within those boundaries and adding color within the lines.

Ersatz Process #2: The Intellectually Engaging Process   Effective artistic teams can and do have intellectually stimulating conversations peppered with dramatic theory, philosophy and philosophical quotes, and explorations of how the audience should respond or *feel* at any given point, to glean a vibrant, active script by the workshop's end. Ineffective philosophical conversations, however, remain focused on how the group or individuals in the group feel about the idea or how an experience impacts life without any attempt to transform these observations and thoughts into active or dramatic expressions that move the story along. Using theory or philosophical ideas as a lens can help magnify an issue and (often) its root cause; active dramaturgs, however, work to identify how the root cause fuels the drama and facilitates conversations that explore this vibrant and theatrical side of the idea.

Ersatz Process #3: The Running-in-Place Process   Some processes appear on track either from the get-go or once the team establishes a language and a bond. During such workshops, the director, playwright, or dramaturg does what the project requires, but contributes little that will have a lasting impact on the creative process or the play. When the playwright adopts this stance, an active Sentence for the play may appear and evolve suggesting a deepening connection with the play and the development process. Rewrites that support The Sentence and address the creative team and actors' questions may even arrive in time for rehearsal. In this process, however, the writer makes superficial adjustments that move the play slightly closer to a stronger version, but never truly grows. Once the workshop ends, the writer deletes all adjustments and ignores or derides all questions, sometimes publicly.

Identifying the running-in-place process during the workshop may prove difficult, for the play appears to grow just enough. Active dramaturgs listen and look out for playwrights who step away from the process by over involving the dramaturg or director in the rewriting and reviewing process. Yes, creative bonds should be honored, but when these connections encourage a writer to cede control of the play, the theatrical development process ceases to exist. The active dramaturg also looks out for the factions that sometimes form leaving the play to suffer because conversations focus on personal rather than critical and objective responses among the creative team, which leads to comments and questions that fail to strengthen or clarify the work.

Another hallmark of the running-in-place process: a lot of in-workshop exploration occurs, but the team fails to commit to any discoveries. Again, identifying this behavior during the process can prove difficult. However, when the playwright repeatedly avoids building upon the discoveries made in the workshop, the active dramaturg must question whether the creative team misunderstands the writer's

vision. If, after achieving some clarity with
the vision, the playwright continues to ignore
the comments everyone seems to agree upon, the
writer either has no desire to develop the play
or has difficulty with rewrites. This situation can
often arise during a workshop for the play written
years before or has been workshopped numerous

> The active playwright
> enters the process
> with goals to achieve and
> questions to explore during
> the workshop.

times. A writer who willingly reveals the play's development status allows the rest
of the creative team to approach the work in a way that benefits everyone and uses
talents well.

All workshops include a level of exploration that provides the team with information to mull over that often manifests itself in two or three drafts later. Learning
and running in place are different. Learning suggests growth over time, and running
in place, the exact opposite. The only sure way to differentiate between the two is
to track the artists and the work over time.

Ersatz Process #4: The Absent Writer   As odd as it may sound, some
workshops do not include the writer. Granted, this rarely happens, but it can. There
is no question a process that chooses to not include a living writer is suspicious.
Sometimes, however, writers do not participate due to unforeseen work conflicts,
family emergencies, and travel delays. When the writer cannot participate in person
or via video call, the process ceases to be a developmental workshop and morphs
into a standard rehearsal of a fixed-text play. The dramaturg may write notes and
pose questions, and a line or two may be cut, but on the whole, the fixed-text
production dramaturg draws upon a different skill set. Also, because the writer isn't
present and often misses the presentation, the writer learns nothing about how the
play works.

A Common Thread

A preference for talking *about* an issue runs throughout each of these ersatz processes. To talk about an idea is to focus on an idea's results or its final impact, but
not the effect throughout. To talk *about* something is to repeatedly focus on one's
emotional response to individual points or aspects (positive or negative) and to
ignore the critical elements and how they inform the story, action, and plot. Active
explorations of ideas by probing deep into *how* an idea influences thought, the
actions it provokes, and the actions an emotional impact provokes leads to useful
conversations within a workshop and a rehearsal process.

Setting the Frame for the Play Development Process

To facilitate an active and successful process, the active dramaturg seeks to engage
the active playwright and use the active writer's expressed needs and questions to
frame the process. In addition, the active dramaturg takes any revelations following

the initial readings of the manuscript, reflects on the critical elements, and connects them to the writer's expressed vision or need. When questions stemming from the critical elements fail to connect to the writer's need, the active dramaturg sets the questions aside temporarily or until a connection may be made, or it becomes clear that the play's direction has changed and the question's relevance disappeared. The foundation of the game plan consists of three components—innovative writing, a writer's passion for innovative writing, and the writer's ability to distill the play's action into a single, active sentence. (For examples regarding how to use the sentence to shape the process and character exploration see Appendix.)

Final Thoughts

The Sentence serves as the foundation of the active dramaturg's play-development game plan. The Sentence defines the process by articulating and reflecting the play's objective and the play's vision. Using The Sentence ensures that the workshop remains under the active writer's purview, because no one other than the writer creates The Sentence. As simple as The Sentence is, it is a difficult concept to master because it morphs throughout the workshop. Also, because The Sentence can and does evolve throughout the writing and rewriting process, some erroneously believe the play shifts endlessly without direction. In fact, because a strong, active, sentence provides a full picture of the play's journey and the world the characters inhabit, the play becomes clearer rather than diffuse. As the play's ideas transform the work isn't diminished. The better The Sentence, the greater and stronger the writer's connection to the play. The Sentence facilitates a collaboration where everyone is working on and discussing the same project.

Chapter 2: Building the Game Plan

As much as Sherlock Holmes models some ideal dramaturgical behaviors—asking open, unanticipated, game-changing questions based on observing that which others take for granted or ignore—he is a loner. He works out the answers to problems in his flat or while on an excursion. Yes, Watson helps, but often without knowingly contributing to the solution. Holmes is not a great collaborator.

Active dramaturgs must be great collaborators.

Active dramaturgs must engage with others *and* remain somewhat on the sidelines, for the dramaturg does not actively write the play nor solve the play's challenges—the active playwright does. And yet, the active dramaturg must, like Holmes, lead the search for answers, and also like Holmes, the active dramaturg has a game plan or strategy guiding the process. A game plan provides focus for the collaboration and any creative or critical comments a collaborator makes.

Creating a Game Plan

The game plan does not fuel one (or a number of) collaborator's agendas; rather, the game plan serves as the frame for much of the workshop and pursues the play's agenda.

When an active playwright articulates the vision for the play's story and action, it becomes easier for collaborators to support what the writer intends through the game plan. Without grounding the workshop in the active playwright's vision, the process becomes diffuse and supports the play each collaborator *imagines*. Yes, differing points of view provoke the discussion needed to inspire creativity and discovery; however, not knowing a vision prevents the team from growing the active writer's play and often leads to discussions that confuse and alienate the writer, as well as weaken the play. Creating a game plan grounded in The Sentence gives everyone a way to approach either the collaboration or the discussion and helps each artist maintain flexibility when considering what responses to offer and how these comments best dovetail with what others have to offer. A game plan helps the active dramaturg articulate and share professional observations and find common ground between and among the comments offered by other members of the play development team. Please note that finding common ground doesn't necessarily mean universal agreement; it means recognizing what works best for the play and finding an appropriate language for those comments.

What Is a Game Plan?

A game plan exists as more than a goal or desire for a particular outcome for the workshop. A game plan identifies areas or questions to explore with an awareness of how these might impact more than one area of the play or production. A flexible and broad game plan can respond to and incorporate discoveries made during the process as well as the game plans other artists bring to the process. For example, the director may seek to better understand the play's physical world.

The Need for a Game Plan

For a dramaturg, or anyone using dramaturgical skills, to enter the development process with the assumption that the completion of ideas A, B, and C will occur in a limited number of days will produce nothing but frustration—for everyone involved. Certainly once the writer establishes the goals and priorities for the project it may be possible to anticipate that an exploration of A, B, and C ideas will occur, but it's unclear as to in what order and to what extent. A game plan allows for an organized approach to exploring and reconsidering aspects of the text in any order and, to some extent, within any time frame.

The Game Plan Defined

When building the game plan the active dramaturg does more than create a list of points for discussion. The active dramaturg works to isolate the significant elements needed to help address the creative puzzle and the possible paths to the solution. Even if the solution itself remains unknown, the idea of what the team seeks to achieve outlines the possible solution and fuels its active search. For the game plan to work well, the active dramaturg, and those using dramaturgical skills, determines the various critical elements that work well in the play and those that work less well. However, to have an effective, empowering conversation, the active dramaturg works to connect these observations to the active writer's Sentence. Because The Sentence expresses the writer's goal, passion, and inspiration for writing (and rewriting), then the more ideas, comments, and observations connected to this single idea makes the rethinking and rewriting process easier.

What might this look like?

A Game Plan in Action

Consider the following: Perhaps a writer has seen an article in the newspaper that details an unusual and particularly heinous crime. Instead of penning an episode of *Law and Order*, what grabs the writer's attention is the victim's understanding of what's happening around the incident, not the event itself. Perhaps the core of the writer's Sentence charts the victim's understanding and eventual forgiveness of the aggressor. The Sentence reveals the victim's overall progression moving from confusion to understanding to forgiveness. Certainly other emotional epiphanies present themselves throughout the play—anger, hatred, unwillingness to forgive, desire to escape or shut down entirely—but these revelations occur in the story and to what degree the character experiences them remains for the writer and character(s) to decide.

The basic nodal points to the story's progression—confusion, understanding, and forgiveness—shapes the game plan. Rather than exploring how the character responds and reacts to the legal process alone (or at all), the developmental conversations might involve the thematic idea of forgiveness—what it looks like and what propels victims toward this goal. The conflict may then lie within how the victim debates and/or considers forgiveness and who is worthy of receiving it.

The active dramaturg's resulting observations then fuel open questions and a general discussion that helps the active writer see a new way into the story and the areas to clarify or reshape. More clearly defining the twists and turns in realizing forgiveness in the world this play defines will change the play, The Sentence, and its overall impact on the game plan as the workshop evolves.

> The possible solution for a vague character may be to clarify what motivates the character. If the active dramaturg has prepared the game plan well, regardless of where or how the conversation with an active playwright starts, at some point the conversation will touch on the topics or points the active dramaturg has identified and prepared during the reflection process. What defines the solution and the path the writer takes will remain open. The fluidity of the game plan will allow the writer or creative team to establish a language and mechanism that works for this play and the story it chooses to tell.

Using the critical elements to shape the game plan helps as well. For example, time may temper or inflame the victim's passion for forgiveness and affect the imagery and metaphor used while navigating the various phases of forgiveness (or anger). Considering possible thematic through-lines will help provide boundaries for the conversation, and those defined parameters may help the conversation flow effortlessly. An example would be creating a game plan that points to how language may or may not divulge the victim's state of mind and eventually impacts how the character's journey progresses, as well as how the dialogue unfolds.

Rather than beginning by pointing to specific moments, it is possible to build a game plan that inspires a creative conversation and embraces any comments from the creative team. However, at some point the active dramaturg must focus on specific moments to develop, clarify, or strengthen.

The Game Plan and Moments of Zen

Moments of Zen are those moments in the play that work extremely well and tangibly support The Sentence or the ideas that the play advocates. The moments of Zen provide the writer an example of what works—and how it works—so that the writer can return to and use it when exploring and rewriting the script.

Moments that diverge from the moment of Zen may work for actors on a basic dramatic level, but do so without creating greater clarity in story or character, excitement or forward moment to the play's dramatic tension, action story or character development.

The Game Plan and Meditation Moments

Meditation moments are those parts of the script that stump everyone. These moments may need to be eliminated, rewritten, or the surrounding moments sculpted. Meditation moments refer to areas in the play significant enough to the story that they warrant attention. If a majority of the play constitutes meditation moments, The Sentence may be wrong or the play itself may not be ready for the development process. Too often plays come to development before they, or the writer, are ready for the necessary work, which can lead to untold workshops, great frustrations, and no productions.

Using the Moments of Zen or Meditation to Inform a Game Plan

Taking time to identify how the critical elements inform the moments of Zen and meditation moments will help establish a game plan. Isolating what causes certain moments to engage, grab, excite, or confuse will enable the active dramaturg to begin articulating what leads this play to stand out as inventive as an original story or an adaptation of one ages old.

When Sarah Ruhl's *Eurydice* first premiered, it included a character who was subsequently cut for the New York premiere. The grandmother, afflicted by both the forgetfulness Hades imposes and a tinge of Alzheimer's from her earthly life, played a significant role in the premiere production. Her presence clearly moved the play from a story about fathers and daughters to one of children parenting parents. The latter, a decidedly more universal story, allowed the play a greater resonance. What's more, the grandmother's moments of dancing slowly to music only she hears, were silent monologues voicing the joys of a corporeal youth long since past, which lives eternally within every person.

Now, she no longer appears in the play.

One reason may be that the playwright no longer wanted her in the story. Another reason may be the expense and difficulty associated with hiring an actor who appears infrequently and utters not one word of dialogue. It may be that the dramaturg did not or was not given the chance to articulate the character's significance. In truth, the active dramaturg may not have prevailed either, and, frankly, individual victory isn't the goal. However, identifying *why* elements work well and the implications removing or reshaping key elements will have on the story is the active dramaturg's responsibility. In the end, the writer chooses the path; all the active dramaturg can do—is required to do—is point out the possibilities and the possible ramifications for choosing one path over another.

Perhaps such creative conversations will result in locating additional moments that resonate with the moments of Zen. Or, such creative conversations allow the team to give homage to excellent writing before eliminating it entirely because the discussion reveals that either this scene, character, or moment does not belong in this particular play no matter how sublime.

Imagine Caryl Churchill's *Far Away* included more specific details than it does. Imagine Churchill had submitted a manuscript that clearly identified the political party Joan's uncle belonged to. Or, that Churchill had made it clear that thirteen years had passed between the opening scene and the first scene at the millinery factory. Imagine that the causes that the other side espouses were defined, articulated, and perhaps even championed by Joan. Suddenly the play becomes less of a timeless treatise on the sameness of war and more of a political tract tied to a particular era and specific skirmish. A theatre with an allegiance to a strong political agenda might receive this manuscript well, but what would the life of the play be? Also, the play would appear dated almost as soon as the first rehearsal began.

Had a draft come in with the specifics articulated, a mediation moment could lead to the following questions: How does identifying time limit or expand the story? How does identifying the political causes limit or expand the story? How does defining the war limit or expand the story?

No doubt Churchill makes the difficult decision to leave everything purposefully undefined, but note that undefined does not mean vague. In *Far Away*, Churchill grounds the moments needed to make the points about war and its consistent qualities such as the murder or slaughter of individuals. Whether presented in the opening scene referring to the people in the barn/garage or those lined up in hats, no one character can defend the activity, suggesting that the heinous acts aren't as just as everyone believes them to be. Loosening the definitions within the play gives voice to other more serious truths about war and political aggression; that the causes, opinions, and allies change as often as the definitions of right or wrong. Truth is slippery.

> When crafting questions, consider the goal. When an exploration or conversation is the goal, including *how*, *what*, *when*, or *what* transforms the question from closed to open.

In the end, a meditation moment may also signify moments that work fine but limit the play's impact and possibilities. Paying attention to The Sentence will help determine when the writer seeks to create a play as timeless as *Far Away* or as era specific as Lynn Nottage's *Ruined*.

Understanding the Time Frame for the Workshop

This rather obvious but often overlooked fact—the length of the workshop—determines the game plan in numerous ways. If the workshop lasts three days, rarely will a major rewrite of the entire play take place. Few people can stay awake for seventy-two hours straight or juggle the various comments and then set them to paper in ways that remain true to the characters, the play, and the play's story. Even fewer can rewrite or write during rehearsal while listening to actors read the words aloud sometimes for the very first time. Knowing what other collaborators must do to support the public or private presentation determines how much time the writer has for script development.

The Length of the Workshop

Workshops vary in time, but generally follow a three-day, seven-day, or two-week or longer format.

In essence, a three-day workshop leaves one night and perhaps a few hours during the second day for the writer to address issues with little time to devote to major writing or form questions/issues. The remaining time tends to belong to the director and actors as they address how to present the play to the audience. Three-day workshops tend to culminate in public presentations to either the theatre's subscribers or an invited audience.

The five- to seven-day workshop generally provides a writer with three days or evenings to devote to rewriting and the final two for preparing the presentation. These longer workshops can end with private or invitation-only readings. Of course, the option for a more public presentation exists.

The two-week or longer workshop or residency provides the writer with the greatest amount of time to devote to writing, discovery, and rewrites. For these longer workshops, the rehearsal period includes ten or more days or evenings and a number of full eight-hour rehearsals. Without careful planning, this luxurious amount of time can stymie a writer and the creative team. The active dramaturg plays a key role in managing the time, which does not mean doling out assignments, but rather the active dramaturg identifies ways to use time well by working with the writer to prioritize concerns. Many of these lengthy workshops culminate in private readings where other creative teams may attend as well as key personnel from the theatrical community.

For the active dramaturg, to aid in setting priorities means to identify whether the critical comments (identified following reflecting on the private readings) might result in major changes or minor adjustments and the length of workshop can dictate how much work will occur and which changes to explore first. For example, small tweaks may seem easy, but actually waste time because when the writer tackles the larger issues many of the small tweaks shift yet again. In helping to set priorities, the active dramaturg also prepares the group for what may not change during the workshop. Preparing the actors for the possible shift in tone or character, helps the team during the process. Addressing such tonal shifts in the pre-presentation speech to the audience, allows actors to work less hard to make connections that do not exist and the audience needn't wonder why the play shifts so severely. The active dramaturg sets parameters so that the active writer experiences a greater sense of freedom to explore and not feel compelled to come up with a solution that addresses a single need rather than satisfies the lay's needs.

Most workshops exist as opportunities for writers to deepen their relationship to the play with the help of a creative team. Only a few workshops have the goal of completing a new version of the play in time for the final reading; these tend to be pre-production workshops, and in these cases the play has often had other workshops or needs little development.

Regardless of the workshop's length, many active dramaturgs and those using dramaturgical skills often try to offer responses that will fuel the writer's creative process long after the workshop ends. However, everyone must be clear (and few are) which questions could impact, rather than overwhelm, the current workshop and which to address at a later time.

Experience writing plays or participating in development processes doesn't determine the number of rewrites or edits produced during a workshop. Quite simply, the time available, one's ability to understand the questions asked and to then imagine the answers, makes all changes possible. However, the workshop's brief duration can spur some playwrights on and result in an incredibly fruitful residency while causing others to freeze. The imagined or real pressure to create within a group and on the spot can stymie the best. The active dramaturg works to support the writer, creative team, and the workshop process by identifying the areas to explore and develop, and balancing those with a realistic vision of the time available. If the director has a clearer sense of what textual adjustments may come, the approach to actors will differ. If the producer has a clearer sense of how the story may change, the external pressure will lessen. If the writer has a clearer sense that everyone appreciates the challenge the time frame presents, more solutions will be found during the workshop even if the necessary dialogue comes weeks later.

Putting the Elements of a Game Plan in Place

The active dramaturg's game plan grounds itself in the observations made following reading the play and reflecting on the critical elements. As the active dramaturg considers how to shape the game plan, the knowledge that it will and should change as soon as the active writer articulates The Sentence can make the effort taken to create the first game plan seem like an exercise in futility. In fact, although a few specifics in the game plan may change, the information used to build it remains crucial and vital regardless of the shifts taken when responding to and realizing the game plan the active writer (and director) put forth.

Build a game plan by identifying these areas before meeting with the writer and/or the creative team. Prioritize which area or two will produce the greatest change to clarify or activate the story and begin there. Connect as many (or all) observations following the reflection period to these key ideas. Yes, assemble these ideas before hearing the writer articulate The Sentence. When meeting with the writer and learning The Sentence, the active dramaturg then adjusts the areas to develop, but the preparatory thinking helps to focus the active dramaturg's thought process during the conversation. If the writer cannot contribute ideas, articulate The Sentence, or identify a passion for the work, the active dramaturg begins by helping the writer identify answers to the following questions ensuring that the writer will move from a passive writer to active.

The principles at the core of the game plan are preparation and flexible thought.

1. Read the play.
2. Reflect on the play using the critical elements.
3. Identify strong themes.
4. Identify moments of the play that relate to and support the themes.
5. Identify moments of Zen.
6. Identify moments of meditation.
7. Prepare open questions.
8. Prepare closed questions.
9. Prepare to listen and adjust.
10. Employ flexible thought.

Perhaps Begin with a Few Closed Questions

No doubt, open questions remain the active dramaturg's single most effective tool, but a few closed questions are crucial when beginning a process or development conversation.

This is especially true when collaborating with an active writer for the first time or with a writer who may be less familiar with the development process or the organization's unique style of development. It seems ironic to suggest beginning with closed questions, but sometimes the answers establish the much-needed boundaries for a fruitful creative conversation.

Helpful Closed Question #1: Where are you in the writing/development process for this play?

To know whether this draft is fresh off the printer, draft ten, or the product of five workshops, helps the active dramaturg frame the discussion. For fresh or perhaps even incomplete work, the game plan needs to shift toward more open questions that guides a conversation toward discoveries regarding the play's facts, world, or rules. If the writer considers the work well on its way, the conversation will probably move toward honing ideas and include a more critical discussion of the play's facts and rules using the critical elements.

If this creative conversation precedes the first reading and workshop, the length of the residency will help determine the game plan.

In the end, the active dramaturg looks to understand the length of time the writer has spent engaging with the ideas. A qualitative evaluation such as finished or almost finished, serves the process less than understanding the active writer's relationship to the material. Passion for the subject matters a lot, but a strong, nuanced connection will ensure the work will grow when passion wanes, which it sometimes will.

> Listen for phrases or images the writer repeats. Probe these poetic and repeated phrases for definition or clarity. Doing so will build a creative vocabulary for the process and provide details that enrich the play's dialogue and world.

Listening well to the writer's commitment to the process of writing will reveal what questions the writer grapples with and how fully the writer explores those questions. Listening slows the active dramaturg down—which is ideal—and brings the active dramaturg more in line with the writer's creative process. To be ahead of the writer's process is akin to the audience that is ahead of the play's story. If the dramaturg and writer proceed at different speeds, the writer tends to struggle with the dramaturg or director throughout the conversation rather than focus on the play, and the collaborators risk bringing about a lopsided creative conversation.

When the dramaturg stays ahead of the writer by presenting conclusions, listening and creating doesn't occur. The dramaturg who develops tasks for the writer to execute or presents solutions that work in the abstract serves neither the play as written nor the writer. In addition, when the dramaturg and writer proceed at different paces the workshop transforms into a playwriting class. An active dramaturg does not teach a playwright how to write. In a workshop, ideas should unfold organically according to the creative conversation. The active dramaturg uses the discoveries made during the reflection process to shape the discussions or clarify questions to signal possible paths that lead to active solutions.

> What did you hear? What did you expect to hear? What do you think about or feel about what you saw or heard? What questions arise?

Helpful Closed Question #2: What is the best single sentence to describe the play's story, action, and plot? If the writer believes the play is further along than the creative team, it's important to begin where the writer is and immediately identify The Sentence for the play. Regardless of how difficult or easy the writer finds it to articulate The Sentence, the play's through-line will provide the frame for all the work to come. In this instance, the writer will fashion a sentence that tells the creative team that they misunderstood the play—as a group—or that what the writer wants to write and what's on the page does not align. Either way, the work needed for this workshop will become clear; identify which story the writer wishes to tell——the story coming across on the page or the story articulated in The Sentence.

Helpful Closed Question #3: What ignites your passion for this story each time you pick up a pen or sit down at the computer? This question usually leads directly to a conversation that defines The Sentence. Often before a writer succinctly articulates what shapes and propels the play's themes, the writer can identify what sparked the creative journey. The roots for the inspiration will inform all subsequent creative discussions and in a manner or language that the writer can relate. This conversation about passion—dominated and directed by the writer—introduces the elements that, along with The Sentence, will ground the game plan, and at some point the active dramaturg will find a way to connect most, if not all, of the comments following the reflection process to this exchange. Using the writer's language, words, or passions will make it possible for the collaboration to follow the writer's vision and avoid moving ahead of the writer.

Ideas That Sound Distinct but Are Actually One in the Same

When an active dramaturg begins to build a game plan, numerous observations, questions, and ideas may come to mind while reflecting on the play and when listening to the active writer discuss the play. The active dramaturg works to separate the received information into a set of categories noting which are similar and which herald creative challenges. This task helps avoid overwhelming the other artists with a lot of notes and fractured ideas, and makes it possible for the active dramaturg to identify when others raise similar ideas or observations even when worded differently. Inevitably, those seemingly different and disparate ideas will rise to the surface and distract the entire creative team unless the active dramaturg helps to corral them. The active dramaturg does the same with the ideas and questions that function as yet another hurdle to be cleared and those that correspond to a previously identified obstacle. Lessening the magnitude of rewriting remains the active dramaturg's chief responsibility when crafting the dramaturgical game plan.

Identifying Sacred Cows

At some point in the creative process, artists identify their sacred cows—the things they absolutely want to see make it into the project (or wish to banish forever). For example, an active writer may want to preserve a character who speaks only two lines; or, a writer may never want to divide a two-act play into two distinct one acts. The active dramaturg works to represent the play's sacred cows *and* listens for the writer's must-haves. The ability to identify and define these must-haves makes it possible to hear when other members of the creative team propose game plans or critiques that ignore or conflict with the sacred cows. This happens more than one might imagine. When the team fails to acknowledge sacred cows, the conflict that arises appears to come from nowhere and artists seem to be intractable, irrational, or difficult collaborators. Sharing sacred cows doesn't mean that no one discusses or debates these ideas or why they are so important, but acknowledging them does impact how the conversation flows. When the discussion shifts from what I want versus what you want to *what does the play need*, the collaboration improves and an emotional argument transforms into a creative argument.

Because an active dramaturg assists in shaping and articulating ideas the workshop will focus on, the dramaturg may not always believe he or she brings sacred cows to the table. The sole sacred cow should be to represent what best serves the play. Sometimes this means honoring the writer's must-haves, sometimes not. When the active dramaturg believes the writer's must-haves conflict with the play's wants, a clear and non-confrontational conversation can unfold if the writer fully shares the sacred cows and the reasons behind them.

Embracing the Game Plans of Others

Every artist will enter the conversation with a game plan—their ideas for shaping the artistic conversation. Some artists will enter the conversation with an agenda—a rigid set of expectations and tasks that must be accomplished at the expense of discovering new topics for discussion or review. Artists with agendas make for challenging collaborators. Agenda-driven artists prepare to hear problems and solutions in a particular language and look for solutions to be made in a similarly prescribed manner. Also, agenda-driven artists see time lines rather than time frames. Artists who use time lines (which are necessary at some point) believe that a task will occur at a specific time and end at a specific time. Artists who use time frames have a sense of what to accomplish, but have not determined how the group will realize the solution or by an exact line order. The caveat is that as the workshop ends or the production's premiere approaches, deadlines must be set. Keep in mind that these are production-induced deadlines.

There Is No I in Team

Because a game plan operates under the assumption of flexibility and a desire to arrive at a solution best suited to the play, the active writer or the group will find that using the game plan to organize thoughts makes it easier to embrace other's ideas. A key reason for the increased ease, is that game plans often encourage artists to articulate observations and facts of the play through objective language rooted in the critical elements rather than I-statements.

I-statements such as—I am somewhat unclear or I wonder what would happen if—begin to move the creative conversation away from the artistic team or the writer's direction and to the person making the I-statement. Of course, some 'I-statements' are needed and welcome throughout the process. Articulating what worked well for you, resonated emotionally with you, or captured your imagination strengthens the bond between and among collaborators. However, when exploring the work—to determine what themes to explore or change or which sections to build upon or de-emphasize—grounding comments with as much objective language as possible helps everyone remain engaged and motivated. Such objectivity also allows for and acknowledges the play's voice and vision.

A Crucial Element of the Game Plan: Listening

Throughout the creative conversation, the active dramaturg listens to everyone's comments—especially the writer's—in order to adjust which critical element and observation/reflection to lead with as well as what the focus of the play (or character or scene) truly wishes to be. Listening well is the foundation of flexible thinking, which is crucial for the game plan to be fluid and to serve the creative conversation well. Listening well also leads to uncovering the writer's relationship to and passion for the story.

Two Kinds of Listening: Hearing What You Want versus Hearing What Is Said

When collaborators—and this includes the writer—listen for comments or questions that only reinforce what they believe the play deals with, the play's development either stalls or proceeds quite slowly. The dramaturg who listens with this selectivity works to bring a new dramatic work in line with preexisting plays, films, and writings. What makes working with a living playwright or new play exciting, is that the artist brings a new perspective or vision to the art and the writing expresses that vision uniquely—the essence of innovative writing. The dramaturg who listens for what he or she knows or wants may unintentionally bring banality to the work rather than innovation.

The active dramaturg listens for the comments and ideas that support the play's vision and those that challenge expectation to support original and unique dramatic writing. When the playwright or active playwright begins to articulate a vision or responds to questions and comments, the active dramaturg hears what's repeated, what isn't said, the fears, and the outlandish. The active dramaturg works to support these concerns or cleave them apart in hopes of mining richer material. The active writer may struggle, but always engages fully with the rigors associated with this challenging approach but artistically rewarding process.

How to Listen Actively

Listen for ideas that repeat with the same language or new language, such repetitions reveal either great affinity for an idea, or if little else can be added to them, demonstrates the limits of the writer's vision or where the story ends. It may be possible for the active dramaturg to help expand the repeated points by posing open questions that lead the writer to new, exciting discoveries.

Listen for stumbling blocks. Repeated ideas may reveal a stumbling block as a moment in the conversation when the writer simply stops talking about a specific aspect, point, or event in the play. Brave writers will simply admit where they are stuck and whether they are ready for help or if they need to leave that area alone while other questions are explored and answered. The active dramaturg takes note and listens for clues as to how to be of most help when asked; listening for the moments of passion and deciphering ways to connect them to the bewildering moment.

Listening for ideas that do not enter the conversation requires great talent. To hear what isn't said moves well beyond preparation and research and understanding the critical elements. It's the result of using current events, cultural and ethnic experience, esoteric knowledge, NPR reports, or anything else to trigger the recognition that something critical has been overlooked. The active dramaturg who begins focusing on what isn't said and why, can help identify ways to move the already distinctive play to become even more so. The tricky point here is to not overstep and begin writing the play, but to provide an additional context or a rationale for looking into another source for insight or inspiration.

Truly taking the time to listen will do more for the creative process than hours of excellently researched notes or apt use of the critical elements. To listen and become a flexible thinker who can support the work and help the process move forward and remain moving forward is key.

Listen for the aha moment. The discovery may have come while the dramaturg or other member of the creative team offered comments or as the writer thought out loud. When the writer has a true epiphany it's crucial that the active dramaturg—or any member of the creative team—stop talking. The temptation is to continue to refine the thought for the writer.

Resist this temptation.

Why?

Because until the writer articulates the revelation it's possible someone will restate the trigger and not the realization and force the discovery to grow outside the writer's vision. Also, the idea of the creative conversation and the game plan is to help the writer make the discovery *and* identify a possible solution.

So, let the writer have the floor and run with the idea.

Then begin the connecting process all over again—unless the writer is ready to end the conversation. Just be sure to hold onto the aha moment as well. In future conversations this may serve as an excellent window to discussing other meditation moments or moments of Zen. What's more, the aha moment introduces a new language for the writer, one that the creative team should take advantage of.

Flexible Thinking

Many mistake flexible thinking as preparing to consider all options. To do so would stall the process and not demonstrate flexible thinking. Flexible thinking does consider options, but simultaneously seeks to create a path for creativity and action. In actuality, flexible thinking quite simply means to prepare to listen to what's been stated and what's been left out, and then consider ways to either expand these ideas and comments or connect these ideas to observations raised by any member of the creative team to The Sentence or another crucial critical element.

When thinking with flexibility, the active dramaturg considers the possible impact each idea or choice may have on various aspects: first, on the *current* moment, scene, or additional critical elements and character in question; second, on the *upcoming* moments, scenes, or additional critical elements and characters to be encountered; third, on *previous* moments, scenes, or additional critical elements and characters encountered. Does the new idea allow the deck to shuffle into place with greater ease or does it require additional changes? If so, where are those areas and what impact will aligning them with the new idea have on the three areas mentioned above? As with many elements of the theatre, the aforementioned thoughts represent simple ideas that remain difficult to practice. The challenge lies in two areas—thinking while listening and embracing thoughts best for the play but not any particular member of the creative team other than the writer.

The active dramaturg places the following at the fore for each process: How to think flexibly during a conversation? How to remove the desire to be correct and therefore limited to only one way to realize an answer to a question? How to emulate a practice that helps others think more openly, but still moves the project forward to take a risk and move a plan forward?

To Think While Listening

To actively listen means to do more than hear what the speaker says. Active listeners process information by considering options and the impact of what's said as well as developing questions to respond to the information. Classroom lectures demand active listening, because students not only hear new information but pose questions in response to what preceded and occurred on the day's lecture. The comment of, "Good question," often follows the rarely posed question that displays a student's attempt to take the new information forward; either knowingly or not, the student sets up the next topic and helps the class flow organically. The challenge of such thinking is to continue to listen while engaging in the task at hand without imposing a result.

The ultimate goal when listening is to ensure the active writer knows he or she has' been heard and that the comments have been heard in relation to the play's needs.

Often the thoughts needed to form the question require such multi-faceted concentration, that at times crucial information may be tuned out. When collaborating on a creative project, the challenge is magnified because the focus needed to generate and embellish new ideas leads the listener to tune out while thinking, and the active dramaturg faces an additional challenge, for without care the options considered and embraced (or appear to be embraced) may address only one artist's needs—the active dramaturg's.

Taking an idea in every possible direction equals brainstorming. At times, flooding the conversation with myriad thoughts that inspire exciting, unusual, often irrelevant, and ultimately unsuccessful ideas that distract and diffuse the story, is necessary. Brainstorming sometimes clears the cobwebs. Active dramaturgs listen throughout this creative session and focus on the strongest line (or lines) that grow or expand The Sentence and the writer's passion while connecting to and enhancing the critical element the game plan highlights. Therefore, an active dramaturg takes care when listening in order to focus one part of the mind on the conversation and the other on how to use the game plan to support paths toward solutions the active playwright seeks.

Although that idea sounds difficult, perhaps even impossible, it isn't. Everyone considers more than one idea while listening; the challenge is to not become distracted by the possibilities a good idea inspires so that the thoughts assist rather than impede progress.

Without some element of rigor to the thinking, the active dramaturg runs the risk of simply brainstorming, which at the wrong point in the process leads to confusion among the team and can cause the writer's energy for writing to flag. Using the game plan can help. The game plan's key features—reflections on themes and aspects of the critical elements that support those themes—provides safety lines or boundaries for creative thoughts. Using an observation or reflection to connect the new thoughts will always remind the active dramaturg what fueled the inspiration and how it connects to The Sentence, the writer's new idea, or any other creative team's provocative question. When an idea lives outside these boundaries, it may represent more of a new idea that redirects the creative process rather than deepens and focuses it.

Balancing Comments

The other challenge to thinking while listening comes when balancing the various comments from the creative team, especially when the ideas do not coincide with the play's needs or wants. As others offer critical comments, the active dramaturg must differentiate between those ideas that serve the individual artist's needs at the exclusion of the play's or the writer's, or those that serve a specific artist while simultaneously serving the play's needs. The active dramaturg's goal is to help identify ideas that serve the play and the active writer first.

Sometimes it is obvious when a particular artist's ideas neither align with the play's nor the writer's vision. For example, imagine a female playwright crafts a play around women only and they discuss men (favorably and not so favorably) and a male director (or producer) continues to ask why the men remain absent from the text. At first and second blush, this predicament seems an obvious case of an artist not seeing himself represented and wants and needs to have a character on stage who can help him enter and live in the world. These are not reasons to add a male character to the play or to change the dialogue. At third blush, these comments suggest another more interesting dramatic question: Whose vision of the male character can the audience trust?

The question of truth within the world impacts the vibrancy of the characters on stage and the audience's ability or inability to connect to the world on stage. The active dramaturg works to rearticulate the concern or question in a manner so that its impact on the play is clear to all. Too often creative conversations derail because personal opinions rather than critical comments influence the discussion and lead to unnecessary and unhelpful changes. In this scenario, adding a male character to the cast would violate the writer's vision, but identifying ways to include a male voice or point of view through the female characters may improve the play's balance. For example, a character may regularly share her father's wise words or find a letter that brings an unfiltered male voice into the play.

Sometimes the creative conflict emanates from the writer's decision to knowingly write a moment that is impossible to stage or design. Many active writers intentionally write an unstageable moment in hopes of pushing the play's theatrical vision. Sometimes this imaginative moment emanates from something far simpler than a difficult moment to stage, but requires a complex design. Sometimes the challenge stems from safety concerns. Safety concerns obviously take priority.

When a writer imagines an unstageable moment, the idea is to challenge the collaborators not harm them. That said, a safety concern leads to a reimagining of how to stage a moment so that everyone is safe and the play's needs served well.

When the design is difficult (safe, but difficult to build or position in the theatre) or impacts the budget, the active dramaturg faces a unique challenge when lobbying for the effect. Because the artistic director and producer and production manager often participate in this conversation, the active dramaturg's role and responsibility changes from advocate for what works in the interest of the story to one who points to comments that propose temporary changes to the play that accommodate the theatre's limitations versus permanent changes to the play. If a theatre doesn't have the funds needed to execute an effect or design element safely, everyone needs to work to make adjustments accordingly. Even when the design team has a viable and safe option that the theatre can support, the possibility of not wanting to meet the creative challenge may arise. If a more exciting design option arises, wonderful. If, however, the playwright is asked to change or rewrite the moment, the active dramaturg works to identify the root of concern, the reason or reasons for the requested change. The active dramaturg also works with the active writer to articulate these reasons and support the writer and the play.

Here the challenge of thinking while listening is that the active dramaturg considers how to serve every need and begins to function more like a mediator than a creative consultant and facilitator, for the play and the active playwright, respectively. If the design element stalls progress, it will quash any forward motion for the play and, perhaps, any goodwill the collaborators have enjoyed. It is crucial for the active dramaturg to identify what lies at the heart of the concern—safety, budget, fear of executing an effect poorly, or some other concern outside the play or playwright's purview—and then the active dramaturg must address the concerns with the appropriate people. In the end, the writer shouldn't be asked to change the artistic vision because other artists fear the challenge.

When the Idea of the Play Is Too Small

Sometimes writers identify an exciting topic or idea, but in the end it is only the idea that fascinates; the idea does not possess the breadth needed to support an entire play. Yes, a play could be as short as one second, but if that's the case, what other one-second plays combine to make a full theatrical experience?

If, while listening to the writer discuss the play's intentions and after reflecting upon the critical elements, it becomes apparent that the play's idea is too small to sustain the scope, vision, and dramatic action the writer articulates, the active dramaturg begins to look for ways to expand The Sentence by connecting it to other topics, themes or questions the writer raised when discussing the initial idea. The tendency to expand a limited idea for the sake of expanding should be avoided. If a play is short or an idea too small to sustain, it's fine to abandon the idea either permanently or until a later time. Another, larger, thematically richer idea may be present in the play or discussions. If so, the active dramaturg looks to engage the active writer to consider this larger idea's importance and the possibility of refocusing the play. It is also incumbent upon an active dramaturg to propose options such as making the piece a one-act or suggesting the playwright write a companion piece. This second piece may appear as a way to expand the initial play, but indeed it is not; it is a way to expand the time spent in the theatre. Yes, this second (or third) piece may comment on or build upon the plot, characters, or themes of the initial piece, but if the new work avoids deepening the initial work in any way, that's fine, too.

When the Idea for the Play Is Too Large

When a writer chooses to explore an expansive theme or idea, like war, a health scourge, or family feuds, the story can sometimes overwhelm the writer and lead the play to grow without limits. This untamed growth isn't the same as developing a play of unusual length (four-plus hours). Untamed growth means just that, story lines that sprawl and work to include every nuance and variation that can be successfully argued as necessary but ultimately overwhelm The Sentence, the play, and the writer's true intent.

Angels in America began as a play with an extremely large idea: AIDS and America's silence. The play was so sweeping and all-inclusive that it was initially nearly double its current length, if not longer. Aside from dividing the initial work into two plays, then dramaturg Oscar Eustis also worked to facilitate the identification of a central dramatic story: what hiding any part of our true self does to us and the people (institutions) we love. With a more focused vision it is possible to create a number of poignant and affecting scenes dealing with American institutions that were actively ignoring not AIDS per se but a community of people who contribute (positively or negatively) to the success of our nation.

When the Ideas Suggested Take the Play Far Afield

Sometimes an idea presented is as wrong as wrong can be. Take, for example, an all-female play written by a female that may include discussions of one or many male characters and a collaborator insists on adding a male character. Or, imagine the opposite: a male world written by a male writer and women are discussed throughout. The inclusion of a female character might, once again be completely wrong. And yes, a male can write an all-female play and a female an all-male play, but the idea remains the same: the world on stage focuses on one gender and adding a member of the opposite sex because it may help members of the audience (or members of the creative team) better relate to the world demonstrates a wrong idea that if employed can and will take a play far afield. The reason or need for adding the character has nothing to do with the play's needs, only the needs of a small group of artists who erroneously believe the audience must see themselves somewhere on stage to engage with the story.

Many August Wilson plays, most with successful and lucrative Broadway runs, do not include Caucasian characters (or those of other ethnicities) to put non-African

Americans in the audience at ease. And yet, many a playwright of color must field suggestions to include references that Caucasian members of the theatre-going audience might understand or provide ways for these patrons to more easily connect with the story. How often do producers, theatres, or collaborators ask Caucasian writers to add references that would help people of color enter the dramatic world with ease? The expectation is that people of color will learn to see beyond color and ethnicity, but the same does not hold true for Caucasian audiences. The active dramaturg recognizes that this inequity exists and works with the active playwright to resist this outdated rationale.

Rarely will anyone articulate the real reason for making a suggestion that takes a play off track such as the example mentioned above. Instead a rationale such as needing to hear this character's perspective because so many discuss him (or her) might be offered. In the end, however, such offerings present smoke screens for personal discomfort and needs. If the red-herring argument gains traction, and the writer appears overwhelmed, an active dramaturg can help refocus the conversation in two ways: first, to identify the flaws in the argument; and second, to identify and articulate the larger concern and lead an exploration that may address those concerns without disturbing the writer's original intent and the play's needs.

Identifying the Flaws in the Argument   No question a great deal of tact is required if one plans to identify the flaws in the aforementioned argument of demystifying characters to appeal to audiences. When teams have collaborated often or a newly assembled team has a strong rapport, less tact may be required. Either way, this choice holds many dangers. No one wants to hear that the impetus for a suggestion rests exclusively in a personal need. In fact, taking this path inevitably leads to strong arguments, feelings of ill will, and may result in the active dramaturg losing a place at the creative table. Even if the writer (and director) agrees with the dramaturg, the risks associated with this choice may outweigh the benefits making it a last (last) resort, which is not to suggest the active dramaturg should avoid the conversation.

Seeking to Identify and Articulate the Larger Concern   Taking the time, and it requires less than imagined, to explore the challenging comment not only averts an explosion around the table but may uncover ways to strengthen the play and its story. And please note, this applies to an oft-repeated comment or one that seems to have taken hold, and it clearly should not have.

For the example above, the active dramaturg looks to identify what questions adding a member of the opposite sex would answer. Posing the question simply—if a male (female) character were added, what might we learn? This question can lead to a focused discussion and expand simply to include each character or thematic idea by extending the question to, "might we learn about X?" Beginning generally and then moving toward specific explorations of various areas within the play, will allow the suggestion to be explored by the person or persons who suggested it. Either the idea will disappear as connections become extremely muddy and everyone clearly

sees that this idea distracts rather than clarifies the play, or the conversation will begin to
reveal an area of genuine concern and ways
the current cast of characters can address the
problem. The solution may remain unclear,
but a tangible, text-based reason for the
stumbling block emerges.

> KEY TO A GAME PLAN:
> 1. Discover the play's story.
> 2. Identify the play's Sentence.
> 3. Tune the play's voice so that all
> moments and characters exist in
> the same world.

For example, the answer to the question,
"What will we learn?" may reveal a desire to better understand the nature of the
relationship between the male and the female characters. If the play enriches each
female character but her perception of her interactions with a male (as described
above) remains vague, and the ability to identify a truth for performance diminished, the writer needs to clarify the woman's connection to the new, male, relationship. In the end the writer may not necessarily add an additional character but
improve the other characters' dialogue to convey deeper thinking regarding the
influence males have on the female characters within the play.

The difficult shift for most during a creative conversation when grappling with
an idea that exists well outside the play's world, is to help others see the value in
the thought that inspired the idea. It may take time to separate the insight from
the original conversation, but the active dramaturg should not shy away from this
challenge. Although identifying the root reason behind a suggestion may not take
long to discern, conveying the importance of what inspired it—if and only if those
thoughts lie outside personal taste—probably will.

Sometimes a suggestion is so right everyone stops and just knows it's the way
the piece should expand even if the idea leads the work in a wholly new direction.
This is when the active dramaturg can be most effective. Here the active dramaturg can underscore and articulate how and where the play already supports this
idea and where the new shifts may work best. Ultimately, however, the active dramaturg works to corral the ideas and the changes it requires in a way that synthe-
sizes and simplifies the effort needed so that the task of rewriting remains exciting
and avoids appearing burdensome and difficult. An effective active dramaturg can
simply and clearly identify three of the play's major thematic ideas that will make
this major shift in creative thinking appear as simple as cutting a stage direction or
changing a typo.

So then what is the game plan?

A game plan is simply an approach that allows the active dramaturg to use questions that arise after reflecting on the critical elements to attain a clear response to
the active playwright's Sentence for the play.

Final Thoughts

It's possible to misunderstand new-play dramaturgy and walk away thinking it is a
process defined by do this and then do that; pose a question and then listen to others think aloud. However, just as an actor's process is more than memorizing lines,

play development is similarly more complex and involved. The active dramaturg listens for ways to connect observations to the writer's passions or concerns and for patterns to emerge. The active dramaturg works to shine a light on possible solutions by using the writer's language to further define the world.

Because the active dramaturg and the creative team cannot craft a new written version—only the playwright can—they come to the workshop with open questions and reflections to fuel the creative process. As the writer shares a vision and responds to questions posed, the active dramaturg arranges the information in ways that support the writer's vision. The vagueries that arise (regardless of how the active dramaturg assembles observations and reflections) in light of new juxtapositions the writer's vision suggests adds to the game plan as well.

Game plans improve the active dramaturgs ability to respond to the writer's needs and vision while balancing the play's questions and needs. The game plan serves as the ever fixed mark for the dramaturg.

Ways to accomplish tasks (helping artists clear the time away and seeing the tasks as small, but having great impact on many parts) comprise the game plan that the active dramaturg develops in order to facilitate and support flexible thinking.

In the end, the game plan consists of the thoughts and the process that will frame the development process in ways that encourage the best use of time and resources (other collaborators) to explore the writer's vision and the play's needs.

PART II: Active Dramaturgy, Active Playwriting, and the Workshop

Chapter 3: Understanding the Lay of the Land or the Eight Stages of a Workshop

For Sherlock Holmes, each case provides the experience needed for the next, except when it doesn't. Like any artist looking for personal and professional challenge, Holmes often takes—or is given—cases that defy expectation. To best prepare for unknowns, Holmes conducts numerous experiments and researches seemingly esoteric topics. Each case follows a known pattern—introducing the problem, considering the problem, observing witnesses, assembling clues, identifying suspects, interviewing suspects, test suspects, use evidence to identify the offender, close the case—and the only unknown other than whodunnit is when will the case shift from element to element. Whenever Holmes and Watson find themselves stymied, they look to the form of solving cases to direct the process and realize a new path to weather the confusion. Similarly, the active dramaturg benefits from knowing and understanding the steps of a play development workshop.

Elements of a Workshop

Regardless of its duration, all workshops adhere to a basic structure that includes eight components. Understanding the eight steps will help an active dramaturg weather a workshop's hiccups and hurdles, and employ the game plan to greatest effect. Just as a director learns to break down the rehearsal process or an actor learns to break down a scene, an active dramaturg interested in play development should understand the workshop's steps. To navigate the workshop's steps means to understand the expectations that accompany each phase of the workshop and an ability to faciliate the writer's needs in order to best serve the play and game plan. The skills of listening well, posing open questions, and connecting all observations and questions to The Sentence, help an active dramaturg execute the steps well.

Whether developing a play in class, for a dedicated workshop, or in anticipation of a production, the steps of development remain rather consistent. The steps are quite simply:

1. Pre-workshop
2. The initial table reading
3. The post-table read discussion
4. The writer/dramaturg/director process and goal conversation*
5. Presenting rewrites
6. Repeating Steps 2–5 throughout the workshop
7. The presentation reading

8. Post-workshop
★This step can occur any time between 1–3.

Throughout these steps, the active dramaturg assists the creative team by identifying and adjusting the play development goals in relation to each new step and shifts the play takes. Such responsibilities may suggest that the active dramaturg bobs and weaves at great speed throughout the entire development process to keep up with the many changes and the various collaborators. That would be an exhausting process to be sure. In truth, the active dramaturg works to minimize both the appearance and the act of shifting gears while negotiating the turns that arise whenever a play grows. The active dramaturg efficiently manages the workshop flow by identifying the few thematic ideas or critical elements that drive and shape each adjustment. Isolating the key theme or idea that targets the most points minimizes the amount of unnecessary adjusting. If every shift an active dramaturg makes not only looks connected but *is* connected, the work is less overwhelming and the rewriting process more efficient. Focusing on a few large ideas allows the play's evolution to manifest itself and minimizes the sense that a thousand tweaks and changes have occurred (or are needed), reducing the possibility of overwhelming the writer or other members of the creative team.

> When offered the opportunity to develop a play, dedicate yourself to developing the play. Playwrights: leave the acting, directing, dramaturgy, stage management, design, and photocopying to others for these few days or weeks, even if you plan to act, direct, design, and stage manage your own work. Writers, allow yourself to enjoy the gift of working on the play's world and the words needed to bring that world to life. At the end of the day, it's the world and the words that matter most.

When the creative team remains ever fixed on the mark provided by these large, over-reaching ideas and elements, it is easier to chart progress by recognizing how much clearer these few ideas have become. A dramatic text works because the entire work functions; the active dramaturg serves the collaborative process by keeping that end goal—and a path toward it—in focus throughout the workshop process.

A Note about the Creative Team

The creative team for the play development process includes the playwright, dramaturg, director, and actors. Each artist plays a key role in shaping the text. At some point designers contribute ideas and even stage managers may chime in, but the key contributors for the bulk of the development process are the writer, dramaturg, director, and actor(s).

Directors and the Development Process

Although an entire book could be written to discuss the approach to directing new work from the workshop phase to opening night, it is important to note a few important differences between directing a production and a workshop. First, in a workshop, the director focuses on the play's language and guiding the actor to convey the story clearly with the proper pacing. Stage pictures and physical pacing rarely have a place in a workshop; they are, however, a primary concern when directing a full production. Second, a new-work director must help the actors negotiate changes in text and characters. Sometimes this is as easy as identifying when a character's knowledge of events or biography changes. At other times, the director must help an actor accept that when a writer eliminates a character it is done for the story and not as a reflection of the actor's ability or passion for the work.

Given the amount of discussion and exploration of character, world, and story, during the workshop every member of the creative team can influence the play's growth, especially the director. Yes, the writer drives the process and the active dramaturg facilitates the process, but the director retains the position at the helm. Because of this position and its inherent authority, a director must recognize the impact and influence any comment has on the creative conversation. Similarly, a well-placed question or comment can redirect a moribund conversation toward an exciting exchange.

In general, new-play directors take a backseat during much of the workshop process, offering comments, questions, and insights at strategic moments.

During the conversations with the writer and dramaturg, during breaks or after rehearsals, the director places many actor- and production-related comments in context. The director's role also focuses on helping a writer see how or what is needed to successfully stage a moment even though little to no staging occurs during the workshop presentation.

Actors and the Workshop

Just as a director's role alters during a workshop, physical actors have a similarly altered role. Actors who explore character through movement may find workshops challenging as there are rarely physical improvisations. Actors who enjoy and are comfortable exploring language and building character around the table, thrive. The workshop's challenge lies within building character within the context of ever-evolving dialogue. Actors who excel at understanding the entire play's journey and story as well as how characters move through the play, also do well during workshops. Most importantly, actors must build characters quickly and with relative depth to best assist the writer during what may be a brief workshop process.

The Workshop Processes

Most workshops fall into one of three time frames: a short process that includes between sixteen to thirty-six hours of rehearsal; a midrange workshop that lasts four to seven days; and a long process that includes a residency of eight days to four weeks (or longer). Each of these processes demands a different focus and use of time, and these varying foci were discussed in-depth in *The Art of Active Dramaturgy*.

The sixteen to thirty-six hour rehearsed reading remains the most common workshop. Because of the limited time, few rewrites appear and little exploration of the entire script occurs. A writer may delve into one or two scenes and address a single question that the active playwright, active dramaturg, and director discussed prior to the workshop.

The four to seven day workshop does allow for some rewrites and creative discussion, but can also present a false sense that this is a lengthy process. It isn't. For a week-long workshop, only four days exist for creative conversation and rewrites with a day and a half to prepare for the presentation. If the play is part of a festival, the sixth and seventh days include the readings. Often, everyone is expected to attend each reading, so all work ends on day five. A concentrated rewrite means that the writer focuses on a specific question or two that the active playwright, active dramaturg, and director discussed prior to the workshop. A similar set of focused rewrites may involve characters. On occasion, an entire act may be written or rewritten.

The long-term residency lasts eight days or more. These lengthy workshops are rare and most prized. Generally, the cast meets every other day allowing the writer a full day of rehearsal and a full day of writing before the next meeting. To glean the most benefit from the residency, a clear plan should be made, regularly reviewed, and changed based upon the writer's discoveries and needs.

In spite of these differing goals, the general approach and basic steps governing the process remains the same and is discussed below.

Workshop Step #1: Pre-Workshop

The Pre-workshop period includes three phases for the active dramaturg: Phase I, work prior to speaking with the playwright; Phase II, speaking with the playwright; Phase III, repeat Phases I and II until the workshop begins.

Phase I   During Phase I, the active dramaturg reads the script and uses the critical elements to engage in the reflection process. In preparing for the conversation with the playwright, the active dramaturg identifies themes to clarify, moments of Zen, meditation moments, and creates a few back pocket questions in case the creative conversation lags.

Phase II   Meeting and conversing with the playwright to discuss the play for the first time defines Phase II. Here the active dramaturg poses a few closed questions to glean the active writer's passion and hopes for the workshop. As the conversation progresses, this phase takes on a life of its own. Regardless of how well the dramaturg and writer know each other or how many plays each has worked on throughout their respective careers, each must remain open to the process for the play at hand, which means accepting that this play evolves as it will. Both the active dramaturg and the active playwright must resist the urge to skip ahead in the development process, especially if the collaborators know each other or have worked together.

The desire to look ahead or to think about a later phase in spite of the real need to begin at the beginning for each and every process, and each step or phase of that process, is a fact that will always need to be managed. Writers may become impatient and want to see the play on its feet to determine whether a moment or scene or act lacks clarity. Dramaturgs may become impatient as they work to manage the various creative and critical comments so that the play's goals and needs remain prominent and respected by all. Regardless of these temptations, the goal and purpose of the initial conversation between the active dramaturg and the playwright is to discover three things: the writer's passion for the play, the passion statement and/or story of the play and the beginnings of the Sentence, and the writer's vision for the workshop (hopes, goals, concerns). If appropriate, thoughts on casting for the workshop (dates, structure of the work day, etc.) may enter the conversation.

Following the initial conversation, the active dramaturg seeks to document the discussion. Most often a brief email to the playwright and a call to the theatre company, artistic director, or director on the project suffices. Sometimes a brief narrative helps everyone—including the playwright—clearly identify what occurred and the expressed hopes for the development process.

Phase III   Phase III during the pre-workshop (returning to Phases I and II) phase remains optional. Some workshops begin right after the second phase of the pre-workshop step; whereas, others begin months or weeks later. When theatres or companies ask writers to explore the play before the workshop, the active dramaturg and active writer have an opportunity to collaborate and focus on specific areas prior to inviting a number of creative voices into the process. Such private time allows the play to grow and the active writer to clarify ideas without a cacophony of voices. The active dramaturg must take care, however, to provide the playwright space to create rather than just refine and shape, especially if the work is unfinished or early in its evolution. Time during the pre-workshop affords the active playwright opportunities to write and receive immediate feedback based on how well the play articulates The Sentence and uses the critical elements to buoy the ideas and propel the action. Even so, writers will serve themselves and the play best by identifying ways to remain focused on the whole story so that feedback doesn't lead to miniscule rewrites or changes that address an individual's needs rather than the play's.

Workshop Step #2: The Initial Table Reading

The first table read remains one of the most exciting days for those who engage in new work—everyone involved has a chance to experience the play's birth. As actors begin to read without making choices, words on the page spring to life. The words begin—for the first time—to dance in the air, humorous moments come into the light and sad moments cast a pall. Up to this point, each person may have read the play (perhaps numerous times) alone and quite probably silently; the words resonated in the mind only. Yes, other days in a play's life hold similar appeal—first run, first complete tech, first preview and opening night—but of these, the initial table read reigns supreme for it is the first of firsts.

How to organize the time around the table differs from artist to artist. Sometimes the active playwright introduces the work to the cast with an opening statement in addition to expressing gratitude for the workshop. Other times, the director articulates a vision for the workshop and an appreciation for the play before the actors begin. No single approach emerges as best. However, a commitment to always fashion an environment where the writer avoids defending or explaining the play—before or after the initial read, or any read thereafter—will lead to a healthy and collaborative creative environment.

Regardless of what the playwright or director chooses to do to preface the read, the active dramaturg rarely opts to address the company. Of course, basic housekeeping notes may be given, such as whether a discussion will (or will not) follow the initial read and a description of the dramaturg's role during the workshop process; otherwise, the active dramaturg focuses on listening to the play and watching the cast's responses, excitements and confusions just as if this read were taking place before an invited or public audience. As the cast reads the play aloud, the active dramaturg listens for whatever the active playwright and director asks for and the questions the active dramaturg's preparation inspired.

Even though the actors perform the roles, they also listen to the play during this initial read and function like an uninitiated audience.

Area I: Listening for Clarity   Every story and every play should be clear. Now, clear doesn't mean overly simplistic and transparent. Clear means that ideas build in a way that the audience can follow, engage with, and question, while remaining connected to the story. Ambiguity for its own sake will lead audiences astray—if it doesn't infuriate. Intentionally ambiguous moments provoke questions and deepen the story and the play-going experience, but these moments should also provide clues for a roadmap so that as the story lands the audience remains connected to all or some of the characters. Listening for clarity also includes harkening for and noting moments when the audience knows more than the play or when the audience is ahead of the play.

Area II: Listening for Energetic Moments   A play's rhythm varies; quick at one moment, slow at another, the pace of normal life at another. Any combination of these cycles will place a play in energetic balance. A director might infuse a quicker pace throughout the production, but will still honor the play's meter, internal tempo, or energetic ebb and flow. The initial table read reveals the energetic shifts, and the active dramaturg notices where the play chooses to retain a heightened intensity and how this helps or hinders the play's journey, the character's journey, or the audience's ability to remain connected to the world and story.

Area III: Listening for Enervating Moments   Because a play's rhythm fluctuates, it may appear that any moment following an energetic or quick exchange should be labeled as an enervating moment. In truth, a moment that lags is simply when the story fails to move ahead with energy or pace, which is not the same as a scene that follows a slow tempo or rhythm. During an initial table read, the actors have little time to consciously make choices and shape the play's energy through their unique characterizations, which means that the actors follow the roadmap drawn by the dialogue. For example, a line concerned more with conveying an intellectual idea or plot point rather than a character's vision, energy, want, or need, will disrupt the play's rhythm and result in an enervating moment. Active dramaturgs listen for these moments or for the moments when actors struggle with lines (differentiating from reading difficulties and tongue-tied moments). Enervating moments indicate something—a line, a scene, a character relationship—needs further examination and exploration.

Area IV: Listening for Time   Time, how it passes and is chronicled in a play, reveals a lot about form and the evolution of plot, story, and character. In many ways, time exists as one of, if not the single most important element influencing the organization of dramatic storytelling. Most television and film writing emphasizes plot—what happens next—rather than how the story builds or why, both of which time influences. Questions that inform or shape time's evolution provoke answers that dictate sequencing—before, during, and after—or, when an idea is discussed, the logical flow of that idea framed by if-then statements, all of which suggest how time passes. Yes, logic statements do parallel plot, especially in police procedurals, a television staple. The actual difference manifests itself in charting character growth and change—a by-product of time and event—rather than just working or factual knowledge—a by-product of experiencing or responding to an event. When used well, time shapes the growth of the play's world.

That said, active writers may choose to chronicle time in obvious ways like David Ives in his brilliant collection of dramatic shorts organized around the concept of suspending or quickening the passage of time, *All in the Timing*. Or, time passes somewhat imperceptibly as in Shakespeare's *Hamlet*. In part, *Hamlet* shows both how quickly and slowly time passes while grief envelops a world or a character. When Franco Zeffirelli opted to chart the play's story by acknowledging the many months *Hamlet* encompasses, Zeffirelli illustrates the intense grief the young people experience following the murders of their respective fathers. Showing how slowly time can pass while mourning keeps these youths out of joint and harshly juxtaposed against the adults' quick and steady sense of the world moving on. Exploring how time works to keep characters in conflict with the world as in Zeffirelli's *Hamlet* or to regulate how events unfold and influence emotional responses as in *All in the Timing*, provides the active dramaturg a way to expand how the active playwright and the rest of the creative team regulates time and action in the drama.

Area V: Metaphor   Metaphor exists as a sophisticated storytelling device largely because it allows a writer to express sometimes dangerous thoughts and sentiments as innocuous comments. When pushed to its limit, metaphor transforms to allegory and sometimes satire, but to successfully push a metaphor to its limits without tasking an audience's patience takes care. The active dramaturg listens for the moments when metaphors confuse the story, character journey, or simply lose their effectiveness. The challenge when discussing metaphors comes when giving notes. A simple note acknowledges the metaphor fails in some moments. A more advanced note points out where the metaphor lags or confuses and the impact those confusions or inconsistencies have on the story as a whole or a specific moment or character. To point out a murky moment does not suggest judgment. Active writers embrace this truth and use the comments as fuel for the creative journey. An active dramaturg's note goes even further. It begins to articulate questions that pinpoint specifics, but also presents options as to how the metaphor might be adjusted and how those adjustments impact the play's future (and preceding) moments without out dictating the playwright's choice or dictating a step-by-step approach to execute a change. The active dramaturg seeks to strike this delicate balance even in the face of directives from producers, directors, or even the writer, who may ask for notes or examples that dictate solutions rather than open the door to discovery.

> Listen to the room's changing dynamics.
> Listen for the joy.
> (*The Art of Active Dramaturgy*, p.103)

Workshop Step #3: The Discussion

Once the initial table reading ends, the creative team—cast, director, playwright, dramaturg, and stage manager—often engage in a rich, wide-ranging conversation regarding the material and the personal and professional responses it evokes. Sometimes the discussion organizes itself around a number of questions the actors pose, sometimes around a conversation of personal histories the play's story and events connect to. The goal of this first discussion is to allow the team to come together and share each other's insights and connections to the material. As the conversation unfolds, actors begin to shift and explore how characters relate to and interact with one another. When this begins to occur, many questions about the play and its world emerge.

These questions mark the beginning of a truly fruitful developmental conversation. Yes, responses of what resonates with the creative team buoy the writer and, more importantly, demonstrate where the power of the play lies even if some of those points exist well outside the writer's intention. But the questions pinpoint where the story grabs the actors and poses challenges—either because they stretch the actor or director in a good way, or they lack some important facts needed to ground or frame the world or acting choices.

The active dramaturg listens throughout much of this conversation largely because following the first read—the cast's first encounter with the play—this discussion helps the cast gain the same level of comfort with the play that the active writer, director, and active dramaturg have. In addition, the active dramaturg listens for new insights regarding the play's moments of Zen and meditation moments to help the active playwright throughout the process. Most importantly, the active dramaturg listens to and notes everyone's comments and questions (either mentally or on paper/electronically) not just those that support one artist's perspective.

For an active dramaturg to truly serve the play and the writer, one's loyalty must remain with the play *and* the active playwright—but sometimes just the play. No question this allegiance presents many challenges. Rarely does the writer hire the dramaturg, and as a result, the theatre sometimes asks the dramaturg to develop the play a particular way; perhaps turn a two-act play into a trilogy or two distinct one-acts. Sometimes producers feel compelled to direct the dramaturg to strongly suggest cutting (or to simply push to cut) a character or to discourage adding a character even when it is clear the play needs an additional character. The active dramaturg must decide early on how to articulate and then demonstrate where his or her loyalties lie. To have someone who believes in and works for the play helps everyone focus, but can sometimes make the active dramaturg a controversial figure, because the active dramaturg's job—to advocate for the play and the playwright— may be at odds with the wants of others involved in the workshop, thereby transforming the active dramaturg's role from one of creative facilitator to manager of a political minefield. Most theatres and organizations dedicated to new work make that easy: their loyalty and the active dramaturg's loyalty lie with the active playwright and the play and most often with the person rather than the work, which speaks well for long-term creative relationships.

At times during the discussion around the table, actors pose questions that sometimes come across as veiled (or not so veiled) attempts to lobby for character adjustments that serve that individual artist not the play. Actors who are new to the new-play process haven't always yet learned to distinguish between important actor homework questions and character development questions. Actor homework questions focus on information an actor needs to build the character and a strong performance. The play provides details to help shape character and at times the details are specific (an actual birth date) and at other times more general (a birth month or season). Inexperienced workshop actors often ask for specifics largely because the writer is present, and the more specifics suggest a more successful performance because an actor merely needs to connect the dots. An experienced new-play actor asks questions that explore a character's contextual relationship with the story and its world or areas for tension between the character and story, its world, and other characters. This conflict needn't result in adversarial encounters on stage. Rather, the opposition intensifies dramatic moments that propel the play forward. Sometimes these tense moments need to be written into the script, and the active dramaturg assists by listening for which moments to recommend the active playwright enhance.

Usually during this initial post-reading conversation, the playwright opts to address the cast and sometimes answers questions less to declare one impression correct and another incorrect, but to tease out more specifics so as to better understand where the actor's question comes from and how it impacts the play's story or world or both.

Should the conversation lag, the active dramaturg may have a series of back pocket questions at the ready. These questions involve the areas shaping the active dramaturg's listening—clarity, energetic moments, enervating moments, time, and metaphors—as well as general impressions regarding moments or lines that stood out or resonated. In many ways, this post-festival discussion could begin to resemble a post-presentation talkback held with an audience (private or public). As with any discussion, the active dramaturg listens for questions or comments that direct the playwright on how to address a concern either directly or indirectly and reframes them so that no one may be accused of telling the writer what or how to write.

Workshop Step #4: The Active Writer/Active Dramaturg/Director Conversation

Once the conversation around the table ends, the writer, dramaturg, and director often choose to gather and debrief. If the team hasn't had a discussion prior, this conversation can become quite long and unwieldy. Most often, however, the three lead artists will have met, if only briefly, before the reading so that the post-discussion conversation can focus on connecting, exploring, and prioritizing the observations made around the table. Each comment and question raised often influences the overall rewrites even if the present workshop chooses to focus on select concerns. For this reason, the active dramaturg, active writer, and director discuss as many concerns as possible, for a goal of the workshop is to leverage the rare opportunity of having the team read and develop the play so that the active playwright has enough feedback to fuel the creative process during the many weeks and months at home before the next workshop or premiere production.

Initially, the need to debrief and share all emotional responses to the reading and the subsequent discussion dominates the conversation. For the active dramaturg, this debriefing reveals whether the post-reading comments overwhelmed or inspired the active playwright. Identifying which responses land (or somewhere in between) helps direct how the active dramaturg navigates the conversation so that the workshop remains energizing and fruitful for all. To avoid an enervating conversation and development process, the active dramaturg works to focus the questions raised so that they organize themselves around two or three previously identified critical elements. Once everyone has offered their initial gut responses, the individual creative roles begin to direct how the comments based in the critical elements fuel the collaboration progresses. By utilizing the language the active writer uses when discussing the play, these questions are easier to address and connect to The Sentence. Sounds simple. Remember, the simple things are usually the most difficult to achieve.

The challenge of when to corral points and comments and when to let the conversation roam always lies before the active dramaturg. Connecting observations too quickly or early may lead to the erroneous assumption that the dramaturg sets forth a series of tasks and homework assignments as a teacher might.

An active dramaturg is not a teacher.

An active playwright is neither a student nor a secretary executing changes at the behest of the creative team.

An active dramaturg, and those using dramaturgical skills, works to frame the questions so that the creative process unfolds for the writer with greater clarity and, in many cases, speed. The goal is to leave the workshop with a greater understanding of the play's story and the elements that shape it.

Grouping ideas and comments goes only so far, and if done poorly can leave a writer with a sense of a huge (if not never ending) list of issues to address. Notes articulated in the abstract—even if grounded in the play's present or missing facts—do not always promote a sense of security or an ability to organize the rewrite process. To help simplify the magnitude of the playwright's task, the active dramaturg connects the comments to The Sentence. If and when the comments connect to the writer's articulated vision of the play's action, key themes, and images, the steps needed to fashion ideas into dramatic dialogue, plot, or story points appear fewer. No matter how disparate, the ideas will work in concert because they serve a central idea at the core. Rewrites become more difficult to conceive and realize on paper when they exist as many unrelated points and tasks. An unorganized creative process can often discourage a writer and enervate rather than energize. To rewrite anything requires a great deal of energy and focus. The active dramaturg understands this and works to simplify the process by aligning the comments with the writer's vision and then connecting each comment to that vision.

> Think of the play's Sentence as a clothesline and each comment as an article of clothing to hang on that line. It doesn't matter whether the clothes were washed separately or are pants, skirts, oxford shirts, or women's sweaters—everything needs to dry on the line, everything needs a different amount of space and drying time, but once sorted and addressed or washed correctly, everything that belongs on the line will be placed on the line.

When charting the group's observations, the active dramaturg and the director engage in the simple task of pairing like comments and then connecting them with the play's themes. Without judgment, the creative team may begin to identify which points resonate and connect to both the playwright's concerns and the team's concerns raised prior to the read-through. As the group runs through the comments, the conversation will range far and wide. The active dramaturg works to encourage the brainstorming aspect of the conversation until ideas begin to repeat or before the playwright becomes overloaded with information.

Managing Expectations Within the Workshop's Time Frame

To explore and discuss the comments means, near the end of the discussion, to prioritize the comments. This usually occurs right before or exactly when exhaustion or repetition begins. To prioritize comments means to help the active playwright order the comments into at minimum three basic categories: those that may be worked on in the amount of time available, the writer's passion for an idea, and the idea's connection to critical elements and The Sentence.

Prioritize in Relation to Relevance   For all decisions, the active drama-turg has two guides: the playwright and the play. The active dramaturg works to ensure that both the active writer and the play have a voice throughout the process. If the theatre or director or actors present ideas that fail to land with the writer or ring true with either the play's story or voice or both, the idea may not have relevance. If many raise a similar point or repeat the comment often, the active dramaturg considers the ideas and looks for relevance even when at first or second glance the comments seem outside the mark. When prioritizing, the active drama-turg articulates why some comments lack relevance to help achieve a transparent and open process. The active dramaturg seeks to validate and honor all voices in the same way he or she lobbies for the play and the writer, and an open dialogue should others disagree. The active dramaturg facilitates the process, but when done without care, facilitation can appear as dictatorial leadership. Transparency mitigates some of that misperception.

Prioritize in Relation to Time Available   No human can rewrite two acts or an entire play in eight hours. It may be possible to rewrite half the play, but the entire play requires super-human ability. Certainly no one should squelch a writer's *desire* to attack the entire play, but presenting realistic boundaries given the time available demonstrates true support. For example, when a writer participating in a three-day workshop presents a rewriting schedule for day one, two, and three, the active dramaturg can gently inform or remind the writer that on day three the director and actor will be in the space preparing for the reading and working with the person reading the stage directions. The playwright may choose to write, but should not expect the presentation to feature the day-three rewrites. The informa-tion regarding time may lead the writer to request that the entire workshop plan change or choose to skip day three in the hall in favor of a writing day at home. The goal of setting priorities in relation to time is to identify what areas need focus and what concepts will add (or detract) from the play's story and set all others aside. The active dramaturg helps the writer manage and maximize the time in the rehearsal hall and input from others to fuel the next few weeks or months of writing at home.

Prioritize in Relation to Passion   Passion for the story or play is neces-sary. If the playwright doesn't feel excited by the play or understand why passion is important rewrites won't happen. Rewrites. Won't. Happen.

Similarly, if most of the creative team understands a comment and sees how that comment could shift the play close to or exactly where the writer wants the play to be, but the writer can't understand or embrace the comment, the active dramaturg may choose to back away and consider options for a later time and date that may help the playwright at least hear the comment—perhaps a mere eight hours later. Stepping aside allows for some creative space and reflection. A different challenge arises if the active writer lacks a connection to the work because considerable time has passed between drafts; in this case, the reading plus a post-reading discussion may reignite the fire. If, however, the writer chose the topic to satisfy a grant, commission, or assignment—and nothing else—nothing will infuse the process with passion, and no matter how focused the active dramaturg may be, the process is prone to self-destruct. However, if the team chooses to address the workshop as a time to explore, the group may find that prioritizing refers to identifying what topics recur or which generate the most passion from the writer or the creative team.

The active writer leads the discussion about which elements to work on first. In a true collaboration, the decisions will manifest themselves organically and appear to come from no single individual; however, it can take awhile for the team leaders to get in sync. Understanding who takes the lead (and when) can help when the collaboration stumbles or is in its earliest stages.

Workshop Step #5: Presenting or Introducing Rewrites

When first submitting a play or presenting the draft to the actors, introductions or prefatory remarks rarely accompany the work in an effort to reduce bias during the reading. However, when bringing these changes to a group familiar with the work and invested in its growth, rewrites should be introduced with some care.

To introduce rewrites "with care" does not mean that the writer defends choices or presents the work in ways that suggest the new material be treated with kid gloves. Instead care means to introduce the new material so that the creative team experiences it with an open mind and avoids judging a change as a validation or rejection of a particular person's comment or insight. Similarly, those who work in new-play development often understand that pages created overnight may not offer the ultimate solution but the beginnings of a new path, and reading a fresh set of pages allows everyone to gain a sense of that new path. Active dramaturgs work to remind the creative team of the creative process. Sometimes, of course, the new work strikes gold.

When the changes or new material involves a large section of the play or a number of scenes, directors assist with the introduction by asking the cast to simply read the pages aloud so that the writer can hear what was written. The active writer may ask that no one discusses the material following the read or may request feedback from a select few—the director, dramaturg, and another artist—outside the presence of the cast.

When the changes involve various lines and minor tweaks that individuals can enter by hand, writers often deliver these edits to the cast orally before reading the new pages. Sometimes the active dramaturg presents these minor changes, especially if the active writer chooses to continue working on scenes outside the rehearsal hall. Who presents these changes matters less than *how*. Although it seems basic, the confusion surrounding the process of adding changes to the script occurs at almost every workshop for one reason: when giving changes people forget that the cast cannot see where to place the changes on the page. The process outlined below may appear lengthy and repetitive, but it leads to clarity and success.

A Suggestion for Introducing Changes

1. Identify the page number.
2. Identify the character delivering the line.
3. Identify how far down the page the line appears (e.g., second speech; middle of the page).
4. If the line of dialogue is brief—one to four sentences—identify within which sentence the change occurs.
5. Begin to read the line by saying, "It begins. . . ."
6. Introduce the change by saying, "Character X currently says '. . . .' Please, replace those words/lines with the following: '. . . .'"
7. Repeat Step 6 and the new language to insert slowly.
8. State the new line as it should read.
9. State the entire speech or set of lines, as it should read.
10. Read everything without inflection or emotion to avoid offering an unintended line reading.
11. If the line of dialogue is more than five sentences or a monologue, identify where the change occurs: near the beginning, middle, or end of the speech. Perhaps count the number of lines down (then follow Steps 7–10).
12. Move to the next change.

Sometimes writers print out sheets with the cuts and additions for the cast. These pages help because everyone can see the changes, but having someone guide the cast through the edits ensures that everyone inserts the new lines correctly. Printing out new pages remains an option, and works extremely well except when the changes are minor and the choice appears to waste paper. Also, as the workshop progresses, actors have notes in their script and they prefer to avoid transcribing notes to new pages for a few word changes or a tweaked sentence.

Sometimes, the new pages may not align with the old script. When new pages must be inserted, it's best to use a new numbering system. The tried and true method of using the alphabet to order pages—11, 11A, 11B, 11C—works well. The active dramaturg assists the active playwright in managing this process and pages to minimize confusion so that the excitement generated by new material continues to infuse the room in spite of the complicated regimen.

Because the material is new and additional adjustments will come, some moments may fail to flow. The active dramaturg listens and begins to prioritize comments as before. The discussion that follows the reading of new pages outlined earlier allows actors to articulate how the cuts or additions change, help, or confuse the character's journey.

When the Changes Are Not Well Received or the Read-Through Does Not Go Well
Sometimes active writers bring in changes that do not address anyone's questions—even their own. These are the easy conversations. If everyone knows the new work hasn't hit the mark, either move to a different section for the day or find ways to explore the moment so that the writer's process moves forward. The director may create an improvisation, the writer may shift some

Introducing Dialogue Changes

Usually the writer introduces changes; however, sometimes the dramaturg has this task because the writer is writing or prefers to listen to the changes. For quick cuts or fixes (the wrong character was indicated for a certain line, etc.) please make those in the moment in case a second read takes place.

Just call out the page number and identify the character and/or the line's relative placement on the page—top of 20; middle of 20; bottom of 20—to make life easier.

Now, here is where it can get tricky.

Some people like to simply say, "Change Max's line at the top of 20 to read: 'I like cake.'" The challenge here is that Max has two lines at the top of page 20.

It helps when the writers say things like, "I'd like to change Max's line at the top of 20" (once the cast has found page 20). To help the cast find the line, inform everyone that the current line reads: "These are a few of my favorite things."

"Please change this line to 'I like cake.' So it will read: Becky says, 'Raindrops on roses . . .' and Max says, 'I like cake.'"

The same approach is taken for cuts.

"I'd like to cut three speeches or lines beginning at the top of page 20."

"The section currently begins with Max's line, 'I'm sad, really sad without you' followed by Rose's line, 'Raindrops on roses' and Max's line, 'These are a few of my favorite things' followed by Rose's line 'Yes, we are in sync. We should get married right now.'"

"Please cut those three lines. The section will now begin with Max's line 'I'm sad, really sad without you' followed by Gerry's line, 'Dude, take a chill pill.'"

Repeat these directions until everyone has the changes.

lines, there may be more discussion, or everyone may discard the new pages and move on with rehearsal.

Sometimes the director, dramaturg, and writer like the direction of the changes, but an actor struggles with the new character shift and this discomfort or confusion comes across as disliking the changes. The active dramaturg collaborates with the director to manage the initial moments of pushback from an actor so that everyone can determine whether the actor's challenge is based in confusion or genuine dislike (that is, the changes seem well outside the character's journey) for the changes. The active dramaturg helps manage this situation by identifying how the changes work within the existing world or the world the writer wants to develop. If not handled well, a supportive actor who has to shift choices quickly may come across as difficult and unhelpful. Not only can the group begin to resent the actor but

Introducing New Pages

A few interesting hurdles may occur when writers bring in new pages, especially if the playwright uses a traditional writing software rather than a playwriting program where the pages can be locked. A few things help manage the order for the new pages:

1. Date each new page in the header or footer.

2. If possible add a draft number (make up your own system, for example: Workshop Draft #4).

3. If you are essentially replacing a page—page 20 for page 20—things are easy.

4. If the new page 20 extends a few lines, the next page should become 20A, and so on, through the alphabet. When you hit the dialogue on page 21, just pick up with 21 even if the new page, 20A, includes a few lines only.

5. To help create the pages, INSERT A PAGE BREAK just before the section that is to change. Sometimes writing in a new color helps identify where the changes are so that you can make the page changes at the very end.

6. If the changes are huge and somewhat confusing, always pass out new pages.

Remember, the theatre needs time to organize and copy the pages; be sure to find out when the playwright should submit pages to the stage manager.

any insights that hold value may be ignored or quite difficult to hear. Through a series of character and theme-based questions, the active dramaturg can help frame the discussion with the actor so that everyone—writer, director, cast—can explore where the character may go and *why* as well as *what* the story gains and loses by this shift. During that conversation, the active dramaturg listens to identify whether the actor's frustration lies within the play development process, the actual rewrites, or personal frustration or confusion. After consulting with the director, the dramaturg can then manage the situation while preserving the writer's passion for the project and, hopefully, the entire cast.

Workshop Step #6: Repeating Steps 2–5 or, the Workshop

The nature of a workshop is to repeat each of these steps until the writer completes the work or the workshop ends—whichever comes first.

Workshop Step #7: The Presentation or Reading

No question, presenting work to an audience, be it invited or the general public, generates a great deal of nervousness and tension (if not apprehension) for the writer and the entire creative team. Everyone wants the reading to go well. During good readings, actors perform within established boundaries and provide the playwright with a clear sense of the play's strength and life; sometimes teams ignore this simple rule. I have witnessed readings where actors chose to move well outside the agreed upon choices and emotional map at lights up. I have witnessed rehearsal processes where directors approached the reading with a level of complex staging appropriate for a production. In these cases, the artists were either not in control of their craft or they were so eager to demonstrate and exercise their talent they extended themselves beyond what was necessary. Most often, the simple choices work best when presenting new work. For a successful reading, as with anything, the successful group works to arrive at a simple solution; a complex set of choices must be explored and winnowed to its best for the group and the situation.

The Active Dramaturg During the Reading   Usually the presentation involves work the entire creative team has seen, heard, read, and come to understand. Rarely do writers introduce large amounts of new, never before seen nor read aloud writing to the cast for the presentation; however, it does happen and often proves quite exhilarating for everyone, but this is a rare event. Because the reading contains little or nothing new, the active dramaturg knows the script, knows the actor's choices, and has a sense of where the writer has achieved the goal and where the search continues. So why watch the reading? Indeed. The active dramaturg's responsibility during the presentation is to watch the audience.

Watching the Audience   Choosing to watch the audience allows the active dramaturg to track responses—what grabs the audience, what evokes laughter, what propels them to lean forward in their seats or stop shifting, what provokes them to shift, when do they flip through their program, search their phone, or doze off. Watching the audience allows the active dramaturg to identify the possible next steps for the active writer.

Incorporating Observations   If a conversation about the play follows the reading, the active dramaturg who watches the audience has information to use during the talkback. For example, "A lot of laughter followed these moments (name them), what grabbed you most?" Finding out that the audience loved the verbal word play reveals just as much as learning they responded to a character's struggle. The writing for the scene may be right on, but it's worth tracking the movements actors make to ensure that the laughter works for the story *and* the writer.

> The Quincy Long Rule:
> when a problem in the story arises, look to a moment or two before the problem to identify the cause; address that concern, and a number of unclear moments including the one in question will become clear.
> (*The Art of Active Dramaturgy*, p.132)

Noting when audiences stop shifting and begin to listen with greater interest reinforces moments where the story lands. If these moments correspond to newly rewritten pages, these successes can help carry a writer through to the next set of rewrites by confirming the choices and the amount of hard work exhibited during the workshop. Shifts in unexpected areas (moments everyone thought were clear) helps identify places to examine and employ the Quincy Long rule.

Active dramaturgs learn a lot by watching the audience and should consider it a wonderful opportunity to sit to the side or behind the audience to watch and listen to the people the creative team works to connect with.

Preparing for the Reading   In addition to watching the audience during the reading, active dramaturgs have an opportunity to help shape the script for the reading itself. Active dramaturgs can play a role in deciding which stage directions to include in the reading. Sometimes an active writer includes a number of stage directions and physical actions that actors can communicate, even during a reading at music stands. At other times, stage directions prepare us for events revealed during the scene and audiences do not need to hear the same information twice—for example, an actor can wave—no one needs to read that action. On occasion, certain gestures or facts do not come across through the dialogue. In these instances, adding stage directions helps clarify possible confusion, but does not alter the play's story. The active dramaturg can help craft reading-only stage directions, thereby relieving the active playwright of this task so that the script's development continues as planned.

The active dramaturg may also help by editing the stage directions for the reading only. Removing details that the actors can convey or that a sound effect provides helps reduce the amount of narrative voice present throughout the reading. This is especially important for plays that include a lot of direct address that can often come across as narration. The active dramaturg plays a crucial role in balancing the voice of the play with stage directions so that the audience and the writer can experience the truest version of the play.

When the Play Includes Ghosts or a Secret   Ghosts and characters with a secret always add a level of difficulty to a reading. The active dramaturg must apply a vigilant eye when considering what to reveal and when through the stage directions. At times these choices will benefit the play beyond the reading, especially if the active writer wants the person or persons encountering the play to feel as off balanced as a primary character or the world the characters inhabit. In short, never underestimate the level of dramaturgical analysis an active dramaturg can render to supposedly minor storytelling elements.

During an early version of Karen Zacarías' *Mariela and the Desert*, it became clear that a character was both an older version of a child character and that character's ghost. Learning these facts about the character through the stage direction placed the audience ahead of the play. When an audience knows more than the characters or the play intends, audiences follow the story less closely, shift in their seats, and become distracted. Had the reading omitted the language describing the character and simply said, "A figure appears and then disappears," the air of mystery would have remained and, quite possibly, the audience would have remained in step if not a little behind the play and its characters.

Workshop Step #8: Post-Presentation

After the reading, a number of events may occur: the company may have the artistic leadership meet with the director, playwright, and dramaturg; the literary manager or director of new-play development may meet with the playwright; there may be no formal post-reading meeting, but a phone or conference call a short time later.

A number of workshops begin and end with no guarantee that the organization will continue a relationship with the play or the artists. The workshop may have gone well, and the artists been well liked, but the goal was to encourage work and artistic growth and not a promise of more development time or a production. Regardless of the organization's response, the active dramaturg looks for ways to support the writer to the next phase of either the play or a writing career.

The active dramaturg must strike a balance with the end of workshop notes. Too many notes or too much detail can overwhelm a writer or suggest a level of collaborative relationship that does not exist, especially if the theatre created the arrangement for the workshop. Follow-up notes also assume the writer will continue to develop the script. Sometimes a writer will; sometimes not, for the workshop may reveal that the play's story lacks what's necessary to move to the next level. Taking the time to craft notes that encompass the workshop, reading, and evaluative conversation with the audience or the company's artistic leadership (or both), may not resonate with anyone or win the dramaturg friends. Then why do it?

Consider the final set of notes the equivalent of a thank you note following a party (be it good or bad); good manners may not be understood by all, but they should be followed because it is the least one can do to remain humane and decent.

The note can take any direction the active dramaturg wants, but identifying a way to have the note assist the active writer's next steps will help the process move forward. This does not mean the note includes a list of unfinished tasks or items the writer tabled until after the workshop. Rather, the note seeks to signal paths of creative possibility.

Final Thoughts

Workshops take on many forms, but at the core function similarly: they exist so that those interested in the work can better identify and connect with the play, and provide playwrights the rare opportunity to create one day, and have actors well acquainted with the new work and its quickly changing process read it the next day. The active dramaturg cultivates a process that inspires the writer to create rather than write what others want or dictate, reducing the writer's role to one of a secretary. Throughout, the active dramaturg works to balance the play's articulated needs and goals with the active writer's passions and goals, along with the many creative voices offering feedback, especially when these do not align through regular conversations and, when helpful and at the end, written notes.

Chapter 4: Developing a Flexible Eye: When to Work the Game Play and When to Let Go

The great detective Sherlock Holmes rarely faces true opposition to his methods. At times, those unfamiliar with his ways appear shocked by his methods and emotional distance, but these reactions do not impede his ability to find success in the face of opposition. Yes, Watson sometimes serves as a buffer when Holmes asks the simplest of questions that unintentionally ruffles feathers because the insights triggering the questions remind the others that he, Holmes, is thinking ahead of everyone else. The active dramaturg does not have the luxury of finding a congenial sidekick who helps with damage or perception control. Dramaturgs—active or not—must collaborate and engage in ways that help them facilitate *a process* of discovery *for* others. Holmes seeks to discover and then reveal insights *to* others. To create a welcoming process for discovery, the active dramaturg does not seek to avoid presenting challenge to the other artists, but to invite artists to consider a few perspectives or options. Sometimes these viewpoints cause artists to struggle, a response some creative individuals transform into a personal dislike of the dramaturg—active or not. The result of an unwillingness to look at a variety of solutions can lead a collaborator to be unnecessarily sidelined or removed from a project. At the same time, the play's meditation moments and challenges are not addressed and the play's promise often goes unrealized. Insight into and appreciation for how difficult it is to develop a flexible eye and thought process, helps the active dramaturg collaborate well and retain a place at the table.

The Foundation of Flexible Thought

When an active dramaturg reflects on the play after reading the manuscript and later speaks with the playwright to identify the play's themes or major questions, the possible paths to guide the play's exploration emerge. Beyond using the critical elements and analytical tools to investigate the play and strengthen the artistic team's relationship with the play, the active dramaturg looks to open these foundational and structurally significant ideas so that the active writer and the creative team can explore the impact any changes to key moments have on the action that follows and precedes the changes. Most dramaturgs, and those using dramaturgical skills, have difficulty at this point. Many dramaturgs and writers can point to a moment that doesn't work well or even identify a cut that fixes the immediate problem and perhaps the entire scene and the scene that follows. Few, however, remember to consider the subsequent scenes after or the many before the altered moment and the subsequent domino effect when one seemingly insignificant word or line changes.

To better understand this concept, consider what happens when cutting a Shakespearean text such as *Hamlet*. When looking at the character of Laertes, many choose to trim his early appearances to focus his initial scenes on Polonius and the wisdom the father dispenses. Narrowing the play's focus even more allows Laertes to come across as highly protective of his sister, somewhat shifting his rationale for returning to Elsinor to protect his sister and avenge her honor first and avenge his father's death second. When Laertes returns in act 4, many also choose to cut a key line identifying the new role Laertes plays within the kingdom: "[. . .] The rabble call him "lord,"/ . . . (They) cry, 'Choose we, Laertes shall be king!'"(4.5. 112, 116). The lines clearly indicate the people's support for Laertes and introduces the possibility that the people have abandoned Hamlet's entire royal family. In one brief line, Shakespeare tells us how much the commoners support change, revolt, and a more proletariat successor to the royal family. Such a shift in politics makes Fortinbras' eventual appearance and assertion for the throne as either credible, likely to be embraced, or reviled, but not because he comes from Norway, but because he is a royal. Laertes' often-cut line also makes it clear that, from a royalist's perspective, Laertes must die, for if he doesn't, the people could choose to rise up and support him rather than quietly accept the noble Fortinbras' ascension. Cutting this seemingly small line throws much of the play's power structure and resolution out of balance. The same can happen when developing new work—one line change can reverberate throughout the whole.

Understanding how the aforementioned line and the general character of Laertes actively relates to the play's form, themes, and evolution of ideas increases the likelihood of an active dramaturg understanding how to help the creative team to make cuts that maintain the play's integrity while reshaping it.

When working with a new play, an active dramaturg and active playwright have less time to consider the options and impact when lines are cut than when dealing with a 400-year-old masterpiece. If the active dramaturg listens to the discussions while simultaneously considering the impact of each shift on every character and the play's overall form, the likelihood of identifying whether a shift challenges or benefits the text increases greatly. Sometimes pinpointing a possible cut or addition as something to embrace temporarily alerts enough of the team, including the active writer, to pay careful attention to how the suggested cuts impacts the play's characters and story. Such attention may mean that only a few additional changes will occur within the actual development process leaving the playwright to solidify changes that greatly impact the play later. Only when everyone on the creative team erroneously believes that a cut or addition presents the complete solution does the active dramaturg need to assume an extremely vigilant eye. Rarely can a single cut or addition require no additional changes be made to balance it within the story.

What to Do When Cuts Are Proposed During a Workshop

Often when considering cuts to manuscripts during workshops, the creative team asks the actors to read a scene or section first with the cut and then without it.

As everyone listens for flow, the active dramaturg also listens for three things: first, the information the story loses; second, the hiccups in the narrative its omission inspires, or new possibilities it creates, as well as an air of mystery the cut could encourage; and third, the moments when the actors use information (or could use in future scenes) that no longer exists to justify choices.

Listening for the Information the Story Loses

In a perfect world, any cut the writer makes removes information and facts that repeat without negative effect. These eliminated moments or scenes are cut because they stop the flow of action or reinforce character and story details without deepening the character or shedding new light on the play's world. These moments are easily removed because they make the play longer or prevent us—audience and characters—from arriving at and experiencing a crucial or more fully dramatic moment. Sometimes cut lines or scenes do not appear as superfluous because they are beautifully crafted, hysterically funny, or richly poignant. Active dramaturgs and playwrights know that scenes that fail to move either the action forward or create an artistic lull in action—for a dramatic or emotional purpose—need to be eliminated or trimmed. Each repeated event or word reveals a lot about the character—what is important or serves as a guide star or as an anchor to the character— and losing those references and moments means that the character has changed and everyone on the team and in the cast needs to be aware and possibly to adjust. Suddenly, major and minor choices must change; subtle subtextual moments may dissolve and with these losses the roadmap the cast relies on blurs if it doesn't disappear entirely.

Cuts that occur early during a full rehearsal period allow the cast and artistic team time to maneuver the changes with relative ease. When changes to story and character occur during a new-play workshop, when every rehearsal minute counts, the active dramaturg serves an important role by sharing with the director where and how the shifts change the story. Through one or two brief, but pointed conversations, the active dramaturg and the director can collaborate to ease the actor's sense of pressure to realize the writer's story accurately and facilitate the writer's need, which is to hear the play as written.

Hiccups in Narratives or New Possibilities and Mystery

Sometimes a storytelling point doesn't materialize or land as it should now that a line or an entire scene no longer exists. Everyone on the creative team will acknowledge the obvious holes in the story, but the active dramaturg looks for when the cut creates an unclear moment much later in the play and continues to track that idea even as it becomes difficult to separate this change from the others that accompany it. The active dramaturg watches and listens for these hiccups identifying where the action zigs instead of zags and how that deviation impacts what follows (and perhaps what precedes) the scene. The active writer can then use this information when listening to the actors or when reading the script alone, to find additional distracting moments and begin shaping a solution. The active dramaturg may also opt to identify key storytelling points or lines that clarify the hiccup. One must be certain, however, to clarify whether those lines or facts would serve the play best in that moment—in the gap created by the cut—or somewhere else. The active dramaturg also notes at what point in the play when it may be too late to learn the information that clarifies the question.

Throughout the workshop, the active dramaturg works to identify the moment or moments that need new focus or attention so that even if the active writer cannot address the concern during the workshop, the active dramaturg has helped the playwright forge a plan for the days following the retreat. A workshop provides an opportunity to hear the play, clarify moments, and discover what work, if any, remains. An active dramaturg works to help the playwright identify a game plan both during and after the workshop.

The Difference Between Mysterious and Vague

At its best, a cut cinches the play together to shed new light and injects an air of mystery that entices the audience or deepens interest in the play. When the cuts introduce an air of mystery, openings for multiple character interpretations and directorial choices are also introduced, and the play truly begins to take on its own life; its own personality. An active dramaturg works to acknowledge the difference between an air of mystery and vague or unclear character or storytelling moments.

> Vague moments often fail to connect to the play's world or follow the play's rules, which leads to confusion. Vague moments lack the specifics needed to ground the story and free the performer's imagination. If a character had an illness in the play, it's possible to never specify the disease in the writing (lymphatic cancer or hemophilia), but the illness's progression must be as clear as the limitations it imposes. Failure to create specifics governing these moments leads to inconsistent character actions and behaviors, and vague moments throughout.

To distinguish between a play that embraces mystery and one best described as vague, an active dramaturg isolates a clear throughline and rationale shaping the clear moments versus those unclear moments that cannot add depth to either the character or story or plot. At first glance, mysterious and vague moments can appear as the same. One often begins the exploration (the first or even fifth time) with, "I don't know what's going on here." Vague moments unravel with each pass and the discussion of a vague passage includes a lot of justification rather than an ever-clearer articulation of what fuels the moment and how it connects to the larger whole. Vague moments may work on a small level and clarify a portion of the question, but they do not satisfy the broader analytical questions or the audience's search for a satisfying set of possibilities. Vague moments compound a sense of confusion and draw out moments often increasing a sense of boredom. Mysterious moments, however, heighten the play's dramatic tension. Active dramaturgs encourage fixing vague moments rather than cut them; however, if nothing transforms them into grounded or mysterious moments, it may be best to cut them.

The Ladder of Evidence

Whenever engaging in a conversation of possibility, the active dramaturg works to identify the play's needs and goals, the active writer's wants and needs, and helps to keep track of how events and facts combine and connect to support the afore-mentioned needs. These storytelling facts build along a ladder of evidence. Each plot point within the story or significant moment of action around which the story evolves, serves as a nodal resting point or ladder rung. Visualizing where items hang or rest on the ladder often helps people to see the rewritten moment as something easily managed and that it is working along a continuum.

As the play moves from workshop to production, the ladder helps when discussing cuts should the play run too long. Because any cut alters the play and some significantly change the work in ways that the characters and story no longer resemble the original draft, the ladder concept helps to identify the story and its key elements (characters and plot points) and where to begin pulling specific rungs or moments that will disrupt the story the least. First, using the ladder image to identify the less crucial moments and then the more significant ones can help with obvious cuts. Second, use the ladder to pinpoint major moments that could be reshaped or cut entirely with adjustments elsewhere in the play.

The Challenge of Relying on Information that No Longer Exists in the Play

Directors of new work often hire actors who are able to analyze and connect with characters quickly, especially for developmental workshops. As a cast works closely with a text, each actor begins to understand his or her characters quickly to establish intimacy; in addition, the actors take great care to note key character and storytelling points. Sometimes, however, actors and members of the creative team hold onto information that impacts the character and story differently because of a moment that no longer exists in the play. The active dramaturg serves the active writer, the play, and the creative team well by identifying and focusing on moments when actors execute choices or make arguments based on information that once existed, but no longer does. At times, this comes across as nitpicky and bothersome, but imagine what happens during the next rehearsal when the actors look to the writer (if the writer is still involved) and wonder how to move the story from scene A to scene B? The active dramaturg works to ensure that even the smallest cut only enhances the story so that future casts can concentrate on questions of character and vision, and not those of basic form and storytelling.

When cuts or new scenes arrive and the entire team evaluates them together, the tendency to discuss consistency within the narrative can prove equally challenging.

Active dramaturgs must weigh whether to bring up issues of consistency to the group or privately with the active writer and director. Identifying new information and how it connects to what precedes and follows the scene helps the cast move forward with the changes and eliminates the need for certain amounts of homework between rehearsals—time that rarely exists during play development workshops. When information is lost, however, the decision of when and with whom to discuss the challenges these absences cause remains tricky.

> A key way to identify the difference between information that's needed to tell the story rather than to shape a character is to note its influence on an overarching critical element. The impact may appear ridiculously insignificant, but if it helps connect the beginning action to the ending action, then no doubt exists—include the discovery. The active dramaturg's role in shining a light on those newly discovered moments remains primary during any phase of development work. The challenge lies in identifying the moment to include and when to raise it and how; sometimes the question of where to place the insight exists as well.

On the one hand, the omissions must be acknowledged and quickly. On the other hand, if the entire creative team (cast, director, active writer, and active dramaturg) becomes involved in the decision or discussion, forward progress may be stalled as actors lobby for information to remain in or insist they can act it. It may be possible to convey the information through acting; however, if it no longer exists in the text, such a choice works against the play and the writer's vision.

In most instances, the director, active playwright, and active dramaturg confer following the first few readings of the new material. This allows the active dramaturg to identify possible narrative shifts caused by eliminating some facts. If possible, a quick conversation regarding what the story gains (or loses) if specific information appears before or after the new scene can help the writer begin to make decisions that will inform the cast by announcing what is lost and where so that actors can shift choices and biographies if needed. When such a private conversation cannot take place, the active dramaturg must consider sharing the value of the missing information to the story with the larger group. The active dramaturg works to discuss information that impacts the time line and rationale for major actions with the group. The preferred scenario for other changes would include robust dramaturgical conversations with the writer and director prior to changes so that at least these artists have a sense of what to expect and areas of concern, and possible repercussions may be discussed in advance reducing the number of hiccups when the new pages arrive.

What Works and Why

The temptation to solve each individual question and challenge as it arises often distracts active dramaturgs. Identifying the moment when confusion begins helps address multiple questions; however, this only assists in articulating where to insert adjustments. Addressing many areas simultaneously requires exploring the common questions raised by each moment or character. Following thematic threads roots the story and will, when assembled, point to what factual storytelling information remains ambiguous or conspicuously absent. After which, a conversation regarding the benefits or drawbacks of those ambiguous or absent moments can begin. This conversation will always prove extremely enlightening to the creative team and inspiring to the writer, because the team articulates most clearly what each can do to support the story without needing the story to explicitly articulate an idea and which points must enter the story.

Areas of Concern Arise at Different Times

That everyone collaborating on the play sees the same areas of concern simultaneously remains the greatest assumption and misconception surrounding new-play development. Certainly, the creative team may recognize the same few tweaks, but each collaborator will identify different problems and solutions to those areas and different solutions to a problem everyone sees. The reasons why the creative team identifies different moments at different times often preoccupies scholarly articles and post-rehearsal conversations. One reason stems from the various disciplines' ability to work around the problem. Sometimes every artist sees the same obstacle, but describes it differently because of their discipline's demands, and the team struggles for a bit to recognize that they are all trying to address the same concern. The active dramaturg, however, uses the Quincy Long rule to inform and guide the critical process—ideally before an impasse arises—to arrive at the true moment of concern in ways that each discipline can appreciate. Once identified, the active dramaturg connects the root of the current obstacle to the active writer's passions and inspirations to articulate how a single solution can assist in solving a challenge in multiple areas.

Final Thoughts

Just as a ladder begins to lose its usefulness as rungs disappear or weaken, the same remains true for a play that loses facts and scenes that influence thematic development or the play's storytelling basics. Without clear connections, the potency of the play's story lessens and the audience becomes confused or disinterested. The moral isn't to write an obvious play that telegraphs every conflict and twist from the first moment and leads an audience by its collective nose; the goal is to support the audience's journey of discovery. An active dramaturg works to articulate and identify the essential ladder rungs and may even suggest ways to mask or pad the rung so that an audience remains unaware of the support, but any creative team can find it when needed in building a strong, theatrical event.

Chapter 5: Back Pocket Questions

When Sherlock Holmes looks to accept a case, he often waits for a mystery that presents perplexing questions he has never encountered or a typical puzzle with clues that unfold in unique or unusually clever ways. He also opts to aid people, especially women of a certain ilk. Regardless of case or personage, Holmes begins each conversation similarly. He asks his potential clients to relate the tale and then, before confirming his interest, he asks a few key questions. Dramaturgs—active or otherwise—rarely have the option of deciding to participate in a project this way. Even so, before entering any creative conversation, active dramaturgs and artists prepare by reading the material—akin to listening to Holmes' potential client's tale—analyzing it using the critical elements as a frame, and crafting a few back pocket questions to have at the ready for that initial face-to-face conversation.

These predetermined back pocket questions provide the active dramaturg with material should the initial conversation with the playwright or director lag, or later in the development process, the talkback with the audience stalls or veers into unproductive territory. Sometimes, the active dramaturg will never utter the question during the conversation; at other times, the prepared question will take a different form than originally intended. In either scenario, back pocket questions shape the active dramaturg's process and, when executed well, come across as spontaneous thoughts or a solid question emanating organically from the conversation. Rarely will back pocket questions sound like previously constructed aspects of the game plan—if the active dramaturg listens and connects them to the discussion.

Back Pocket Question #1: What Is the Story? What Story Does the Play Tell or Want to Tell?

This crucial question often causes confusion for two reasons. The first involves the tendency to confuse plot with story. Simply defined, plot is the elements of the story or the who, what, why, where, when. Think: Hamlet on the battlements at midnight. The basic facts of the play rarely convey the emotional tenor or qualitative aspects of narrative that separate a plot-driven scenario from a gripping dramatic or comic tale. Story, simply defined, is how the plot elements come together to weave a dynamic drama or comedy. Story also includes an active exploration of why events (plot points) unfold as they do. Story does not exist without plot, but plot can exist without story.

Often, members of the creative team (actors, director, playwright, dramaturg) can confuse plot and story, which makes a critical discussion of the play and its evolution difficult. When the creative team confuses plot for story, plot points or events in the play become the focus of the conversation. A creative team discussing the story explores why or how characters behave as they do, or why events unfold a particular way resulting in a vision for the play. For example, Shakespeare may have thought of the *Hamlet* story as an examination of how grief or the quest for power skews actions and deed regardless of one's station in life. Once the team begins to define these elements (plot and summary) similarly, the second point of confusion regarding the first back pocket question emerges and is easily clarified.

The second point of confusion with the play's story is which story to tell.

In *The Art of Active Dramaturgy*, I recounted a moment in my dramaturgical evolution when I asked a director what story would we tell and the response was simply, "The play's story." A deceptively simple truth. What other story would a creative team tell, could a creative team tell? Unfortunately, many a new-play experiences a hiccup in its progression because the creative team chooses to tell different stories—or cannot find a way to unite the many narratives within the dramatic text.

To tell a dramatic story is to either highlight one or two of the play's themes at the exclusion or serious limitation of other themes, or to follow the journey or evolution a character or group of characters takes. In truth, a strong work weaves the themes to the character journeys; in a less strong work, the story focuses on a single theme or journey at the exclusion of all else. A creative team, led by the director, might elect to realize the play through a philosophical or analytical lens—think feminism or multiculturalism or post-post modernism—and connect the play's themes to these philosophies. Such an approach is fine in its own right and often provokes interesting commentary on the play and fascinating discussions, but—and this is a big but—such an approach rarely serves a new play's development.

The purpose of developing a play is, at its core, to clarify the play's story. This may mean either the plot needs focus or one—or many—of the critical elements needs clarification. To confuse the issue and compound the work to complete during a workshop or process for a premiere production with a thematic overlay, does not serve the play or writer.

Development processes exist to provide the play and the active playwright an opportunity to realize the play's full potential through a clearly told and strongly realized story. When any member of the creative team encourages the exploration of a critical element and/or plot in the absence of the play's story, that member neither serves the play nor the development process. Of course, a development process may focus on a key critical element or two, which also serves the play's story or the active writer's search to clarify the story.

Back Pocket Question #2: What Do You Want to Write?

This may come across as both an obvious and insulting question. What writer would conjure worlds that are personally insignificant or not know what to say? And yet, too often workshops begin with the producing or creative teams voicing their objectives, wants, and desires in ways that ignore or supersede the playwright's. A writer might craft a politically or radically charged play and be encouraged to shift the narrative or lead character, which diminishes its political charge to provide a traditional theatre-going audience an easier entrée into the material. Or, a play may follow a two-act structure with one act playing like an outrageous comedy and the second act as a heart wrenching tragedy, only to have the theatre suggest it be transformed into two separate one-acts or a two-act comedy (or tragedy). Yes, a writer needs to enter the workshop with a desire to explore the work, but the outer boundaries or foundation of the work should be clear to the writer and all those collaborating on the project. Asking the question helps ensure the team is on the same page and allows the writer to function as an active writer.

Sometimes the workshop's constraints—rehearsal time, quality of cast, the expectation of a reading versus staged reading—impacts what the writer will rewrite or write during the residency, but the play's foundational story should not change if the active playwright comes to the development process with a clear vision of the story. (Production and staging limitations may influence storytelling as well.) The goal of the workshop remains, however, to identify solutions that support the play's story and the active writer's goals and vision. When these expressed limits reduce and hinder the writer's solutions, the active writer—with the active dramaturg's support—should mark the section and continue to search for the ideal solution or craft a temporary solution for the workshop's reading. If the active writer and active dramaturg communicate clearly about the play's goals and needs and the writer's vision, they can successfully collaborate and ensure the play's evolution.

Throughout the development process, the active dramaturg helps to identify and differentiate when the process shifts the writer away from desired goals that emanate from workshop-based discoveries and those that grow out of externally imposed ideas. No question this responsibility can cause tension between the dramaturg and the producing entity or director and even the writer when he is unaware of how others fail to truly serve the play. When the tensions arise due to the aforementioned situations, the active dramaturg works to help the active writer retain a clear vision of the play.

Yes, during the creative process tensions will inevitably arise. The question is are these tensions good, bad, manageable, or hindering the creative experience?

Good Tension   Creative teams want good tension. Good tension comes about via questions that encourage the team of artists to look beyond the expected, predictable solution. Many argue that good tension fuels creativity and drama and that without it innovative thought and solutions do not occur. When artists lobby for their preferences respectfully and hear the opposing viewpoints and move them forward to continue a true collaboration, good tension exists. In short, good tension equals the push and pull of opposing ideas that serve the same vision or desired outcome.

Bad Tension   When members of the artistic team begin lobbying for personal choices at the exclusion of other's suggestions, bad tension has infiltrated the process, which means that the team no longer agrees on the project's goals, vision, or needs, or that the agreed upon goals were never well defined; instead, the team agreed to ideas as a concession so that the process would move forward. When the team begins working at cross-purposes, bad tensions arise.

The active dramaturg works to ensure clarity of purpose by shaping a process that welcomes or invites artists to change their intentions and needs in ways that the process can support.

To transform the process, the active dramaturg works to ground all comments within the play's facts and the critical elements. Although the active dramaturg always works to ground comments in the critical elements, when a process encounters bad tensions, the active dramaturg works to make these efforts even more transparent.

Often the audience will help underscore the dramaturgical comments, but this vote of confidence comes late in the process. So to mitigate bad tensions early on, the active dramaturg looks to strike a balance when providing feedback and comments that the team can use during the workshop or later. To remain in strong collaboration with the producing entity and the creative team, the active dramaturg looks for ways to bring each party's wants, needs, and desires in line with one another or opening a dialogue so that the true points of confusion may be identified and, hopefully, solved. In the end, the active dramaturg's allegiance lies with the work.

Sometimes, however, the play works well and the director's vision fails to complement the writer's. It can prove difficult when the director has a different view from the active writer and dramaturg. When this happens, the active dramaturg works to bring the play into the discussion even more while constantly working to support the writer's vision. The most challenging situation, however, is when the writer and the active dramaturg are not on the same page.

When the active dramaturg and writer (active or not) are not aligned, the project suffers most because the playwright, the creator of the play, lies at the center of the process. Whenever possible, the active dramaturg works to empower and support a writer's focus during the development process. The active dramaturg understands that to serve the play and the writer means to place the project's needs before all else. The dramaturg may be sidelined during the process, but the active dramaturg works to articulate—through written notes or oral comments—what works and why it works, how those sections move the play and its story forward well, and relate these moments to those that stumble somewhat, or the project's goals even when the dramaturgical role is in question. Also, the active dramaturg continues to look for ways to encourage the writer to remain connected to the passion for the project and articulates how the choices relate to it. Such an approach allows the active dramaturg to give voice to critical comments that cannot be misconstrued. Yes, the challenge remains how to fairly represent the choices that fail to support the play's actual or professed journey. However, through an approach of always connecting points to what works, the active dramaturg maintains the possibility of helping the work grow, salvaging the relationship with the writer, and continuing the workshop's collaboration process.

Back Pocket Question #3: How Does This Moment or Scene Support the Writer's Stated Story?

Whenever suggestions are made or rewrites submitted, the first litmus test is: How does this support the writer's stated story?

When changes arrive, the temptation is to stop, celebrate the submitted rewrites, and merely tweak the lines or scene when, in fact, the entire rewrite fails to serve the play's story and the writer's intent. The active dramaturg responds to the new material using the writer's needs as the frame for the critical questions. Taking care to delay celebrating the rewrites may help diminish the possible tension that could arise after calling into question the impact/import these specific rewrites have on the larger work. Carefully connecting the new material to the stated goals and identifying how some moments succeed and where others may need to shift or be reconsidered will also help mitigate possible tensions.

Firstly, the active dramaturg acknowledges many moments within a scene and has the ability to see both the parts and the whole and can distinguish between what works and what works well. Secondly, the active dramaturg acknowledges where success lives, and thereby indicates which tweaks may better serve the work and when a new start would best serve the project. In short, the more specific the comments can be, the more successful the creative critique will be. First, the active dramaturg clearly separates the parts from the whole to help make the monumental task of rewriting appear considerably less gargantuan. Second, the active dramaturg works to shape the rewriting process so that the process is clear and its goals easy to achieve. Third, the active dramaturg acknowledges the road map the rewrites establish even if the entire draft needs to be set aside. This step opens the possibility for a conversation to consider how the play's story and the writer's needs have evolved during the process. Fourth, the active dramaturg acknowledges the possible ways to discuss the work at every interval so that the writer hears a balanced response.

A Few Back Pocket Questions to Avoid

What Does the Title Mean?   Many early dramaturgs will pose this question in hopes that it jump starts a conversation that focuses on the play's theme or themes. A well-intentioned thought, but this question will not elicit the wanted results. Titles change and a conversation about the title may direct the conversation away from the play's story. Yes, the title could be significant but what's more important: the title or the characters and the story? Ask questions about the more important enduring elements of the play—character and story.

Who Is the Protagonist?   Does it really matter? What if the play focuses on an ensemble of characters? And what do we gain when we learn that one character is more important than the others? What happens when the protagonist is off stage forever as in *Waiting for Godot*? Godot triggers all action—waiting—but never appears. Finding out which characters propel the story and why and how, is more important. The better question is: Who or what drives the action and why? This helps identify who is a catalyst and who can be cut.

Why Is This Character in the Play?   This question exemplifies one of the most closed questions anyone could ask, and the response will be a dismissive, "Because he/she is." Yes, collaborators who are on good terms with one another will often ask this question at some point in the process in order to better understand how to connect actions to this character, and this will provoke a pointed and creative conversation. When, however, this question initiates a creative relationship, it fails to engender a respect for the play or the writer. A better question explores the relationship between the character in question and the others in the story. This approach will clarify whether the character should, with some tweaking, remain in the play or look for another story to call home.

Final Thoughts

Active dramaturgs always enter into the creative process with a plan and set of questions to help realize that plan. Although the planned or back pocket question may never be posed during the conversation, the thoughts that inspired the questions will shape the creative conversation and eventually fuel a question that inspires creative results. These results are the product of hard work wrought through methodical thinking and sustained effort.

Chapter 6: Preparing for and Running the Post-Presentation Discussion

When solving cases, Sherlock Holmes rarely opts for the public recitation of facts and revelations of whodunit as Hercule Poirot, Miss Marple, or a host of other sleuths do. Holmes crafts letters, informs the police, and sometimes reveals the truth privately to Dr. Watson well after the guilty have been punished outside the law. For Holmes, the inciting question and the process of unraveling the evidence proves more exhilarating than unveiling the solution. Similarly, for those involved in new-play development, the process of discovery is as important as the solution, if not more. The public or private reading serves as an opportunity to uncover how the analytical discoveries and subsequent rewrites hold together outside the rehearsal hall. In some ways, readings mirror the explanation of facts and unmasking of the murderer in an Agatha Christie mystery. The greatest difference is that no one quibbles when the detective reveals the solution to the puzzle. In contrast, often when a dramaturg, active or not, presents what prevents the play from succeeding, the notes and comments are often deflected or ignored. Sometimes playwrights and creative teams defer important developmental work with the comment, "Let's wait and see how the audience responds."

Such a comment suggests a great misunderstanding of a workshop and the audience's input.

The goal of soliciting responses from an audience or panel of artistic peers, isn't to use the comments to write a play that bends to the audience's whims or to validate a writer's vision, but to find out how the questions explored land and how audiences react to the scripted story. An audience may dislike a play and its characters because the work pushes an audience to wrestle with uncomfortable questions but they can still find it a rewarding drama. Many consider plays that challenge successful, but those that equate an audience's full enjoyment with validation will consider tough and polarizing theatrical work failures. Just as Holmes, et al., would never think to reframe the evidence to ensure that the least liked character, rather than the truly guilty, should be arrested, a playwright should not rewrite to appease one audience or one artistic collaborator.

Sometimes, however, artistic teams opt to hold decisions or certain textual changes until the audience weighs in, with the simple phrase, "Let's see how it plays before an audience." This approach can help the playwright who responds to notes to simply appease collaborators rather than to pursue an artistic vision. As sound as this strategy may be, waiting to explore and implement textual changes presents a host of challenges, except in rare cases. What if the intended or ideal audience—let's say, an audience of mature women—and the audience that shows up are not of this demographic—let's say, adolescent boys? Jokes will fall flat and certain references will not land. If the play best serves a youthful audience of say, seven-year-olds, but teenagers populate the audience, the presentation will crash and burn quickly. If the intended audience needs a wealth of cultural knowledge that the attending audience does not have, much of the play may fall flat and also present a skewed response. Of course, a play should present ideas specifically and clearly enough that the universal elements connect with all, but if the writer hopes to capture a particular audience first and another second, and the attending audience does not support the initial artistic vision, waiting to "see how it plays before an audience" will work against the development process.

Similarly, what happens if the presentation or reading takes place just once? Whether or not the ideal audience attends the reading, should one audience serve as the barometer of excellence, especially if it fails to represent the writer's ideal audience?

Using the presentation or reading to simply hear how the story comes across—which is more than discovering how specific story points resonate with the audience—and to identify how the new approaches clarify or confuse the intended story, will better serve the artistic team and the process. The active dramaturg often has the unenviable task of encouraging all audiences and organizational leadership to avoid considering the attending audience the chief predictor of success. No question audience response matters, but one audience should not determine a play's success or failure. Audience response—especially during a development process—exists as just one element to help gauge how the play's story connects with people. If an audience helps select the next season's offerings from the play development series, their opinion does matter more, but it should still register as just one vote among many. Even with this collective response, the active dramaturg works to protect the play's integrity and the writer's process by advocating for the play's needs and the story's demands rather than tabling decisions regarding clarity in favor of audience ratification.

That said, solicited responses from audiences can embolden a writer's creative vision and increase a theatre's resolve to produce (or not produce) a play. An active dramaturg, and those who use dramaturgical skills, must work diligently to shape a post-presentation conversation so that it serves the development process. To shape a post-reading conversation well, a commitment to addressing the following points remains critical:

- Identify areas the writer wants to avoid discussing as well as those the writer wishes to explore in-depth.
- Identify questions that lead the audience toward or away from the key areas to discuss or avoid.
- Identify how to present the work in ways that does not defend the work or makes the creative team appear defensive.

These key points govern all talkbacks regardless of whether the creative team seeks feedback through a questionnaire inserted in the program or passed out after the presentation, by collaborating to generate questions for a post-play discussion, or preparing for a private conversation with the leadership team.

The Pros and Cons of Surveys or Questionnaires

Survey Con #1   I first encountered questionnaires when working at a regional new-play festival held in the south. Here artists were asked to create three to five questions on the third day of rehearsal of a week-long process. The survey encouraged audiences to respond with one or two sentence answers. Requesting the questions from the creative artists so early in the process engendered some backlash. On the morning of day three, ideas regarding what to work on and how were still bandied about. In addition, the team had yet to decide what to present (one act or just songs) and how. The morning of day four better suited the team and, the teams thought, still allowed the literary office time to print the surveys. However, what suits the teams doesn't always work for the institutions. Over the years, the deadline at this theatre shifted, but the guidelines for the questions and initial request were still delivered on day three. Regardless, the request always provoked tension because the request rushed the creative team to decide what they wanted the audience to focus on.

Survey Con #2   The other challenge often associated with surveys manifests itself on the day of the reading. When entering the theatre for the presentation, audiences receive the surveys in their program. Such early exposure to the questionnaire provides the audience an opportunity to read the questions before the presentation. Some might think such access benefits both the reading and the audience. In truth, reading the questions before the actors take the stage often means that the audience experiences the reading with the questions in mind, using them (consciously or unconsciously) to filter and shape all responses. The goal of a presentation, however, is to share the play with an audience who experiences the work with fresh ears and eyes. Distributing surveys before curtain, places the play and cast at a disadvantage and lessens the readings effectiveness.

Survey Con #3   Sometimes audiences leave their manners at home and share inappropriate thoughts or express well-intended responses in less than elegant or tactful ways. Active dramaturgs or producing institutions serve the playwright and process best by distilling and transcribing the written comments and weeding out the thoroughly inappropriate comments. The dramaturg and theatre should not spare a writer the negative comments, but deleting those comments that defy all rules of manner and thought does serve the process. If these opinions had been delivered in front of a live audience the moderator, often the active dramaturg, or other members of the audience would have spoken up to reshape or rebuke the most offensive comments. Or, we can hope this would have happened.

The Survey Pros   The greatest benefit of the survey is that it provides a tangible record of what excites that audience or specific audience members. A writer can take the surveys or summarized responses home and refer to them for encouragement when the future of the play remains murky or the rewriting (or writing) process has no end in sight. Some comments may even contain hints as to how to redirect a character or moment in the play.

Suggestions for Transforming a Few Challenging Survey Questions into Winners

If a theatre chooses to use surveys in spite of these challenges, it's best to inform the dramaturg well before the workshop begins. The active dramaturg works to navigate the pitfalls a survey presents by tracking the questions the artistic team considers from the earliest conversation to the first few days of the actual workshop. These artistic questions reflect the collaborators' concerns and more accurately inform and shape the active dramaturg's questionnaire so that the survey serves the play, the playwright, and the producing theatre's time line. In other words, the work to craft questions begins well before the theatre makes its request. Throughout the workshop and creative process, the active dramaturg finesses questions so that audiences, rather than only peer collaborators, understand them. Yes, the audience plays an active role and may be considered an additional collaborator because the audience has a fresh perspective and may represent a variety of backgrounds and experiences, but the audience usually has only one limited opportunity to actively participate in shaping the play. The active dramaturg takes care when forming questions to enhance the audience's experience and the creative team's access to unique perspectives; the reasons why appear below. Please know, the questions and the accompanying analysis that appears below is in no way exhaustive.

The questions that follow either most often appear on surveys, are most often heard during talkbacks, or they lie at the heart of many questions artists have and audiences ask.

These experiences may differ greatly from the creative teams, providing ample material to help deepen and enrich the work.

Common Question #1: Which Character Did You Identify with or Follow?

At some point in the history of dramatic storytelling, someone introduced the idea that audiences must follow one character and one character only. This belief, and blatant disregard for ensemble casts and plays, leads many a post-presentation survey astray. First, the question assumes that audiences connect with a single character and such an assumption diminishes the play-going experience, especially if the audience enjoys a host of characters and story lines. The question's second problem, it ignores the possibility that audiences respond to an actor's performance and not the writer's depiction of character and character journey. Although audiences who choose to attend presentations of new work have an unusual and amazing passion for theatre and the arts, and many of these individuals have a discerning eye and ability to articulate their responses, do not assume that the audience (or its individual members) can distinguish between a written character, an actor's performance, or a director's approach. Many seasoned professionals cannot distinguish between these ideas. Asking an audience to parse performance and written language, rarely serves the writer well or produces the desired feedback.

What Lies at the Heart of the Question: Which character did you identify with or follow?

The first approach when adjusting this or any question remains the most difficult: identifying what the writer wants to learn from this question. In this case, a play-wright may wonder if, in a dark and humorless play, any character displays redemptive qualities or if the audience likes a certain character. To focus on whether a character displays redemptive qualities can serve the process and the writer, but in this context the ambiguous and generally uninteresting characteristic of likability informs the question. Do audiences like Richard III from *Richard III*, Michal from Martin McDonagh's *Pillowman*, Walter White from *Breaking Bad* or Tony Soprano from *The Sopranos*? Would you want any of these men at your dinner table? Or, is it fairer to suggest and say that these characters fascinate us and captivate our sense of curiosity (and ire) because although we understand what they do and why, their world and rationale for their behavior exist well outside our own. Audiences watch and engage with these characters because the dramas allow audiences to silently and safely root for the character without stepping outside known and honored boundaries governing good behavior. Audiences enjoy these and other reprehensible characters because the actors portraying them do so excellently and the writing for each excels largely because no writer cares whether an audience likes the character. No writer comments on the character or provides them with a level of insight that excuses or justifies the behavior according to society's more common moral and ethical code. (If anything, insight creates internal tension for the characters, which interests and attracts audiences even more.) These characters follow the beat of their own drum without hesitation or questioning. The question most dramaturgs pose does not lead to a response about the qualities just discussed, but it should.

> A question asking audiences to connect character to events within the story ensures a response focused on the play, rather than the audience's psychology, general feelings, or an actor's performance.

How to Adjust the Question: Which character did you identify with or follow?

If the writer wants confirmation that the dialogue leads an actor to create a captivating character, the active dramaturg watches the rehearsal and the reading as well as listens to the actor's questions, which can indicate clarity or points of confusion. If the active writer wonders whether the character's journey makes sense and the audience can follow it, explore questions that focus on story and the revelation of certain ideas or plot points. For example, what does [character name] search for throughout the play? Did anything prevent him/her during the search? Did any part of [character name]'s search confuse you? Did you care if [character name] succeeded or failed in the search?

If the active writer wants to know if a certain character grabs our attention and leads us to reconsider our personal ethics or limits, craft a question that wrestles with that large idea. As tempting as it is to ask, "Which character's world view or personal ethics differs from yours?" the question reads like an essay question and encourages audiences to talk about themselves, their very personal viewpoints rather than the character(s) and the play. The goal of a post-presentation discussion is to hear responses to the material presented rather than provide a forum for audiences to explore their personal psychologies, which is a wholly differ-

> The goal of a post-presentation discussion is to hear responses to the material presented rather than provide a forum for audiences to explore their personal psychologies, which is a wholly different goal from a post-play discussion following a set-text production.

ent goal from a post-play discussion following a set-text production. Few dramaturgs and talkback moderators recognize the differences between the discussions for new and set text plays, hence the proliferation of questions that fail to serve the writer during a development process. In brief, set-text discussions resemble literary discussions because the writer is often absent and the material somewhat distant from all involved (cast and audience) simply because the text will not change. New work involves a living author and with that a sense that the text can and will evolve. As such, many (rightly or wrongly) have a sense of ownership for the work. Ignoring these differences can lead a post-presentation discussion for a new work down a terribly destructive path.

For a Possible Rewrite of the Question *Which character did you identify with or follow?* Consider: Which character's responses to the play's events surprised you and why?

This revised question encourages audiences to discuss a particular character, point to a few key moments, and then describe the innovative moments. Each answer will reveal which moments land with the audience and how audiences react to, perhaps even ethically wrestle with, particular situations. If the play tells a cheery story, the creative team still learns which key events land with the audience and whether the story or character's trajectory follows a predictable path or introduces innovative storytelling. Either way, a question asking audiences to connect a character to events within the story ensures a response focused on the play rather than the audience's psychology, general feelings, or an actor's performance.

Common Question #2: Was the Story Clear in Act 2?

When developing new work, the balance between acts 1 and 2 (or the first and second halves of a play) often preoccupies the creative team because most workshops begin at the beginning, which means most work takes place on the first scenes or act. The reason for a sometimes-lopsided approach, is that readings begin at the beginning and character discussions often start when characters first appear, which for most, occurs early in the story. Another reason most play development begins at the beginning: clarifying most of the unclear points or moments later in the story depends upon getting the early setup right. At some point, however, the play's second act or half must receive its due. The presentation in front of the audience sometimes offers the first opportunity to explore whether clarifying key moments early successfully transforms the murky points so that the playwright can focus on other moments after the workshop.

The challenge with this question and all others phrased similarly, is that it assumes too much. For example, which story? A strong play tells more than one story simultaneously. Yes, one story looms over all others, but the general phrase—which story?—might confuse the responder. The question also assumes the audience knows what the playwright intends with the story—specifically intends—as if a pre-presentation dramaturgical conversation took place and the playwright shared The Sentence with the audience. If a writer did address an audience this way, the audience experiences everything through a filter and every response either contradicts or confirms the writer's statement. Also, the question may solicit a simple 'yes or no' answer, which stops the conversation or the written response, and the writer learns nothing about how the story impacts the audience or which elements resonated with the audience. Remember, the goal of a reading is to determine what lands with the audience. That said, professional theatre artists can use The Sentence as a frame and filter or ignore it, making the question okay to ask in a professional setting, but inappropriate with general audiences because they aren't trained filter and frame.

How to Adjust the Question: Was the story clear in Act 2?

As with the first common question, the active dramaturg works to pinpoint what the playwright truly wishes to know. Often when seeking to learn what makes a story clear, effective, interesting, and engaging, asking what lies at the heart of what everyone wants to learn is easiest. Quite simply, focus the question on the actual area of interest. Sadly, nothing is quite that simple.

By watching the audience, the active dramaturg, or any member of the creative team, can see when people shift in their seats too much, doze off, or stop leaning forward to better engage with the story. These physical signs will reveal that something fails to resonate. But what falls short? Where does the hiccup occur? The answers to these questions are what the team seeks. How to get the audience to recall, analyze, and then articulate their experience for a written questionnaire?

For a Possible Rewrite of the Question *Was the story clear in Act 2?* Consider: When telling your friends about this play, what will you say happens in this play? Or, what are your thoughts regarding how the characters respond to the play's events?

If this question appears in a survey, certain story points or comments will repeat and everyone on the creative team will know what lands. If this question comes up during a talkback, as a single audience member recounts the play's big points and conflicts, others will chime in with nods or verbal agreements. Some responses will fall within the range of what the creative team expects, others will not. If the responder writes honest feedback, everything will be of use even if it may need to be filtered before sharing it with the writer. The positive and negative reasons regarding the play's impact will help the writer and the creative team. The active dramaturg may have suggestions for framing the negative responses if they relate to lack of clarity or predictability within the story. Remember, every story is not for every person.

Common Question #3: Was It Clear that [Character Name A] Is in Love with [Character Name B]?

This question has a lot in common with the questions, "With which character do you identify?" and "Is act 2 clear?" Essentially, Question #3 asks audiences to validate a storytelling style. Once again, this question leads audiences to respond to the survey with a simple 'yes or no' answer and move on without providing the playwright with more crucial information. For the sake of ease, let's name Character A, Alex and Character B, Jim. The writer may want to know when, in the story, Alex's love for Jim first became apparent. Or, the writer wants to toy with the idea that only Alex has feelings for Jim. True, the performances will help a lot here, but some may understand this question to ask, "Is it clear that Alex and Jim are in love?" Again, if this question appears in a survey inserted into a program, the audience will watch for signs of romance between Alex and Jim and pay less attention to other forms of platonic love between these characters. All other characters, relationships, or stories will receive little or no attention during the reading.

How to Adjust the Question: Was it clear that [character name A] is in love with [character name B]?

As worded, this question invites a critique of the actors and their performance rather than or in addition to the play and the playwright's vision. What lies at the heart of a question focused on particular relationships? Does the writer want to present a nuanced love interest or fairy tale romance? Certainly the play's overall story and themes will shape the reasoning and rationale for the question. Also, love may not capture the truth of what the audience witnesses. If, for example, the play explores the perverse aspect of relationships, it may not be clear that a character loves someone and that that informs the acts depicted. In such a case, it may benefit the play to explore the differences between genuine emotional connections or feelings confused with interpersonal connections built on common interests, superficial attractions, or addictions. Identifying whether the script's scenarios guide the actor to convey a more genuine emotional connection would help the writer and provide the play with nuance.

For a Possible Rewrite of the Question *Was it clear that [character name A] is in love with [character name B]?* **Consider: Which characters in the play express a genuine romantic connection or desire for another? Are those feelings reciprocated?** *Do these feelings matter to the evolution and impact of the play?*

With this question, audiences know that relationships in their various forms lies at the heart of the play and their development, at the heart of the workshop. Knowing that unrequited feelings rank as highly as those that are reciprocated, will ensure that audiences evaluate all levels of relationship. Asking audiences which character exhibits genuine romantic interest in another character through the dialogue may direct attention to language and not just the acting choices made. Remember, no one knows how Lady Anne comes to choose Richard III and on some level it doesn't matter; she simply does. The actor has the joy of discovering and presenting a rationale for why.

Common Question #4: Could You Follow the Flashbacks and How Time Shifts between Scenes?

At its heart, this question explores how time flows within the play. During a reading, an actor reads the stage directions, which often document shifts in time and place in addition to specific movements. In other words, the stage directions may herald the flashbacks thus rendering a question focused on flashbacks or how time flows superfluous. If the writer wants to understand how time impacts the storytelling, the director may choose to omit those time-oriented stage directions to help the active playwright identify when the shifts in time and place occur seamlessly; in some rare cases, the question has merit. Rare because, if the setting helps to indicate a different era along with language, the option of losing the stage direction that establishes the set's look—a crucial storytelling element—does not exist. For example, the director may cut the stage direction, "The next morning," but may not cut, "In the kitchen. Dark. NPR's *Morning Edition* theme song plays and we hear the announcer say, 'Good Morning.'" It will be clear through the stage direction or sound cue that it is morning thus establishing the scene's time frame.

Some plays or aspects of plays do not translate well in a reading. Pinter's *Betrayal* may have read well because as much as it moves backwards in time it provides a forward look into human relationships. Charlotte Keatley's *My Mother Said I Never Should* presents a different obstacle. To shift from World War II to 1970 to 1960 to 1980 without stage directions would place an undo burden on an audience's imagination while in the reading. Similarly, presenting a reading of Lynn Nottage's *Las Meninas* proves quite difficult given its flashbacks to the court of Louis XIV and a convent some fourteen years in the future. Sometimes, however, in spite of these difficulties writers need to use a reading to identify whether the challenge of tracking time works.

How to Adjust the Question: Could you follow the flashbacks and how time shifts between scenes?

Time almost always shifts between scenes; rarely does a play take place in a variety of locales over the course of the same five minutes. Such a question makes the survey feel a bit like a multiple-choice test, but at least the writer no longer takes the defensive position. Removing the assumption that no one could follow the flashback helps take the play off the defensive and lessens the audience's ability to respond with a simple yes or no.

Because the question focuses on time as a structural device, exploring ways to pinpoint how time passes and how audiences follow time may help. Establishing the eras or notion that scenes shift forward and backward in time during the initial set of stage directions may help create context for the question. The focus can be on whether the shifts in story occur in a manner that allows audiences to identify which storyline to expect to follow and how to assemble and connect plot points or clues to the main story.

For a Possible Rewrite of the Question *Could you follow the flashbacks and how time shifts between scenes?* **Consider: How do the time shifts enhance the sense of discovering the characters and the mystery surrounding the overall story?**

Crafting a rewrite for this question presents numerous challenges: one, how to avoid a simple 'yes or no' question; two, how to encourage audiences to identify a variety of stories or plots (or both); and three, how to connect the stories in a way that doesn't lead the audience down a path so that they are ahead of the story. When audiences know more than the characters in the play—and the story doesn't want to support that advanced knowledge—audiences will rustle in their seats a lot. The rewritten question assumes the audience notices the shift in time through language. Yes, the initial stage directions establishing various times or eras and, perhaps, a reference to the play's many eras and places, may render this distinction mute. Asking audiences if they have a sense of whether all the action takes place during the same time frame (day, month, year) and if there were shifts (how did you know time and place changed?) may prove more successful. For this to be successful, the program can't reference time and place or refer to characters as older or younger (or having the same name). Regardless, the question begins to resemble an essay question, and does that help an audience enter a play's world. In the end, survey questions about time may best be left unasked and reserved for talkbacks only.

The Pros and Cons of Talkbacks

Few theatrical events strike more fear into the hearts of professional dramaturgs, playwrights, and those training to be theatre professionals than the twenty minutes following the reading of a new play: the talkback. Who knows when the post-play discussion became the ubiquitous capstone of the workshop process and emerged as a key event during play development. During these post-reading conversations, audience members share responses and—whether requested or not—often offer ideas for improving the story or play's form. When the talkback avoids unwelcome comments and unsolicited advice, they can prove quite exciting, supportive, and energizing for everyone involved, including the playwright. Should the talkback dissolve into a group rewriting session, the level of resentment and distrust a playwright may develop for the theatre and the creative team is not only unfortunate but understandable. The active dramaturg works to prepare for the talkback in hopes of avoiding a calamity and then collaborates with the writer to identify any concerns or fears as well as topics that are off limits.

The talkback provides audiences an opportunity to share their thoughts by responding to and interacting with the writer and members of the creative team. Unlike the survey, the talkback provides a chance to exchange ideas and learn more about the why or how an audience came to think or respond a certain way. A colleague once offered that the creative team's job during a talkback was to remain largely silent because the team has spoken to the audience for at least sixty minutes, and now it is the audience's turn. This advice helps a lot when working to avoid the need to enter the conversation and defend the play or the writer's choices. The audience has a right to its opinion and to share it. Woe to the active dramaturg and creative team who opt to change an opinion through a discussion disguised as an exchange to better understand the comment. Such a conversation will never end well and will always appear to place the creative team on the defensive. As uncomfortable as it may be, allow the challenging comment to exist. Ask if others in the audience feel similarly and remain silent. If audiences engage in the discussion and try to change each other's minds, the play looks to be controversial, thought-provoking and debate-generating (all good things). Also, the creative team may learn something about the play's power to address or provoke divisiveness and result in rewrites that underscore or eliminate this quality.

In short, talkbacks have many benefits, chief among them the opportunity for the playwright and creative team to hear directly from the audience and obtain a general feel for the group's connection to the play and shared responses.

The risks associated with talkbacks revolve around audience comments that may lack tact and grace and—without strong moderation—can cause the conversation to spiral out of control quickly. Similarly, responding to certain comments can lead the writer and creative team to appear defensive, which leaves no one with a positive impression of the reading, the talkback, the theatre, or the artists.

To navigate the talkback well requires practice.

A Common Talkback Format: Liz Lerman's Critical Response Process

Nothing quite prepares a talkback moderator to transform—on the fly—a vague, insulting, or possibly damaging question except practice. One must go through the gauntlet. Adopting the mindset that *experiencing* the talkback rather than *controlling* it will result in a better, more genuine event for all—especially the moderator. Given the ease with which a talkback can move from wonderful to contentious, a few structures for shaping the talkback do exist. Liz Lerman crafted the most common feedback format. Her Critical Response Process has six steps (originally) and most talkbacks at theatres use the first three or four because public forums seem to be inappropriate places for writers to share their next steps in the play's life. Lerman's Critical Response Process began as a way for collaborating artists to discuss their dance pieces while in development. During the early to mid 1990s theatre artists began to use Lerman's approach first among colleagues and then with their subscribers or audiences who attended the presentation or reading.

> Liz Lerman's Critical Response Process
> THE CORE STEPS
> 1. Statements of meaning
> 2. Artist as questioner changes
> 3. Neutral questions
> 4. Opinion time
> 5. Subject matter discussion
> 6. Working on the work or next steps
> http://danceexchange.org/projects/critical-response-process/

Lerman's process grew out of a need to help the collaborators, those familiar with the creation of the work, have a way to enter the critical conversation with some level of neutrality. Because Lerman's company, the Dance Exchange, works with people of all ages and dancers of all levels, be they amateur or professional, her Critical Response Process exists as a model available to all. However, to facilitate and even participate in it well actually requires considerable training. It can take weeks to learn how to craft an opinion-free or unbiased question and even longer to comprehend what constitutes a neutral question. Remember, most audiences engage in critical conversations following play development workshops once a year during a theatre's festival of new plays. Most audiences have little time to perfect their role in the Critical Response Process.

It should come as no surprise then that when applying Lerman's approach to a talkback for a production or a play in development with a general audience, most find Lerman's process challenging. And yet, many dramaturgs and talkback moderators continuously try to direct audiences to follow Lerman's opinion-free question model and are stunned to discover that most audience participants do not know, or do not care to know, how to adhere to the introduced format or honor the discussion's parameters. Accepting that someone will always try to diverge from Lerman's prescribed path and that the talkback will take on a life of its own, may help reduce the inevitable sense of panic when someone poses the most inappropriate of questions or the writer abruptly leaves the stage or an argument erupts.

Rest assured, these are examples of extreme and rare behaviors. Usually, people ask simple, straightforward questions and want to support the writer and the creative process so the talkback proceeds, if not effortlessly, certainly without incident.

A Different Approach to the Talkback: The Active Talkback

Many dramaturgs design their talkback format around Liz Lerman's well-respected and quite effective Critical Response Process. Identifying ways to and practicing how one might transition from various discussion topics will help reduce the sense of rigidity and help the active dramaturg maneuver through the process with confidence or discover a more personal presentation style. Inserting personal touches enables the active dramaturg to remain present throughout the conversation and moderate without overwhelming or commandeering the conversation.

The active dramaturg approaches the post-play or post-workshop discussion differently. Of course a plan exists, but at the heart of this game plan, the active dramaturg works to meet the audience—amateur or professional—where it is immediately following their first experience with the play. It often takes time for an audience to separate itself from the play's emotional journey (this is true for a tragedy or a comedy) and articulate clear, cogent thoughts and insightful questions. The process outlined below allows audiences to respond honestly and provides playwrights a chance to leave the conversation with clear indications of what audiences liked about the script, answers to specific writer questions, and insight into the audience's concerns or expectations.

The Active Talkback

The Active Talkback has eight steps, seven of which take place with an audience. The final or eighth step occurs when the active dramaturg writes up the event for the active playwright after the talkback. The Active Talkback requires that the active dramaturg or moderator shifts among three states: involved participant; represenative for all voices; and silent, but engaged, observer. Tempering one's desire to control the event so that everything flows in an ordered manner allows the audience to truly feel that this discussion belongs to them. To ensure the conversation moves in the direction that will best serve the active playwright requires the active dramaturg or moderator to listen to every comment, observe each rustle, and construct alternative game plans on the fly, just in case.

The Basic Steps of the Active Talkback

1. Preparing for the Active Talkback
2. The opening statement
3. Positive comments or images

4. Fielding questions
5. Questions to the audience from the playwright or creative team
6. A second round of positive comments or images
7. The closing statement
8. The final note

Step #1: Preparing for the Active Talkback

In many ways the talkback and the survey resemble each other. The questions asked through a survey do not differ from those the active dramaturg works to craft in conjunction with the writer or creative team as the five back pocket questions for the talkback. These back pocket questions—five is an arbitrary but good number—are held in reserve for the talkback in the event the audience asks nothing or focuses on issues of little importance to the writer or may be used to reframe general or inappropriate questions the audience asks. (For an in-depth discussion of back pocket questions, see Chapter 5.)

> The back pocket questions can include the standard questions that appear in Chapter 5. These questions may have been created or shared with the playwright and creative team or not.

Prior to crafting the back pocket questions, the active dramaturg and the writer discuss the goals of the talkback—what the writer would like to learn—and the writer's level of comfort with public discussions. Also, determine if any areas should not be discussed. For example, if the second act was not touched during the workshop, but will be presented in the reading, the writer may want to discourage questions and comments that focus on act 2. The active dramaturg may reduce any of the playwright's tensions or concerns by reviewing the talkback format and the plan to divert the conversation should the conversation go awry.

Step #2: The Opening Statement

For some reason whenever people write about talkbacks, the opening statement receives no attention. These few words set the stage for the conversation, establish any areas or topics to avoid, and offer the active dramaturg an opportunity to provide the audience with a behind-the-scenes look at the workshop/play-development process. The nuggets of information included in the opening statement may also serve as reference points throughout the discussion.

A Common Opening Statement

Hi. Thanks for coming and staying for the discussion with the playwright. While we set the stage, let me introduce myself. I am [NAME] and worked with the

playwright J. Doe. In a few minutes, we will talk about the play and get your
thoughts on the story. This is also a time to ask questions. So we will start in a few.
(Time passes.) Great, we are ready to go. Let's start with the first question: What did
you think of the story/play?

This opening statement succeeds in welcoming the audience and introducing a few
key individuals as well as the talkback's purpose to the audience. The statement falls
short in articulating how the moderator will accomplish anything beyond these
important pleasantries. The silence that descends on the stage as time passes and the
abrupt question that opens the talkback offer two key examples of moments where
the dramaturg loses any connection with the audience.

Adjusting the Opening Statement

Hi. Thanks for coming and staying for the discussion with the playwright. While we
set the stage, let me introduce myself. I am [NAME] and worked with the play-
wright J. Doe.

No question, the decision to begin by welcoming and thanking the audience
works well and begins to establish a welcoming environment conducive to a positive discussion. The same holds true for introducing the key participants. Adding
some information regarding the roles each person plays during the development
process as well as background on this particular workshop process would improve
this overture. Audiences may (or may not) know anything about development
processes, so some descriptions regarding the people participating in the talkback
or how the workshop evolved will help. Also, the purpose and goals of each workshop differ; taking the time to fill audiences in on how the creative team used
its time can help the audience shape questions and responses. A possible revision
could be:

Hi. My name is [NAME] and I worked as the dramaturg for J. Doe's wonderful
play [TITLE]. Thank you for attending this reading and for staying to share your
thoughts and impressions with the playwright. We have spent the following [XX]
days working on clarifying what some of the main characters do in the play. As the
dramaturg, I facilitated the developmental conversations and tracked questions or ideas
throughout the discussions and as the script changed.

In a few minutes, we will talk about the play and get your thoughts on the story.
This is also a time to ask questions.

Although the audience may quickly understand that the dramaturg's brief speech
works to cover the scene change from the reading setup to the talkback, the active
dramaturg works to acknowledge the on-stage activity rather than ignore it, doing
so lessens seeing the movement as a distraction and provides the audience with more
insight into the theatrical process. Whenever possible, take the time to signal the
unique opportunity the audience has when choosing to attend a reading. Talkbacks

often provide an opportunity for the creative team to engage with the audience if the moderator creates an avenue for such an exchange of ideas. A possible revision could be:

> *While the crew takes a few minutes to set the stage for the talkback and the writer, who will join us for this conversation, please take a few moments to think about any images, language or word choices, thematic ideas, or moments in the play that made an impression. We would also like to hear any questions you might have regarding this workshop process or ideas raised in the play—in particular act 1. J. spent most of the workshop working on and exploring act 1. You are the first audience to experience this version of the play, so we are eager to hear your thoughts and impressions.*
>
> *So we will start in a few. (Time Passes.) Great, we are ready to go.*

If the dramaturg takes the stage right as the applause ends, some individuals may feel uncomfortable leaving the theatre, even if they must. To foster a welcoming environment, the active dramaturg provides opportunities for individuals to leave without rousing feelings of embarrassment. Similarly, the playwright may come to think the choice to leave reflects negatively on the play. Any statements that help frame the decision to depart from the theatre as simply that, a decision to move on to one's next activity, improves atmosphere for those staying for the discussion. Once the stage is set, any last minute directions such as waiting for the microphone or walking to the microphone will help put the audience at ease. Rather than beginning with a neutral question that will invite polarizing opinions and, most likely, comments that lead the audience to tell the writer what to write and how to fix the story, the decision to return to positive comments that point to images, language, or moments the writer wrote (possibly moments the actors created) will start the discussion off well. A possible revision could be:

> *For those of you who must leave, thank you again for coming and please travel safe. For those who are able to remain, feel free to move closer to the stage. (Pause) We have a few ushers in the audience with microphones. Please raise your hand so that they can come to you and everyone can hear your comment or question clearly. It looks like we are ready to begin. Does anyone have an image, a phrase or bit of language from the play, or a moment that struck them or stayed with them? I have to say that one of my favorite phrases or images in the play has always been: "Her haunting eyes danced." Does anyone have a phrase or image that struck them?*

The Revised Opening Statement

> *Hi. My name is [NAME] and I worked as the dramaturg for J. Doe's wonderful play [TITLE]. Thank you for attending this reading and for staying to share your thoughts and impressions with the playwright. We have spent the following [XX] days working on clarifying what some of the main characters do in the play. As the dramaturg, I facilitated the developmental conversations and tracked questions or ideas throughout the discussions and as the script changed.*

While the crew takes a few minutes to set the stage for the talkback and the writer, who will join us for this conversation, please take a few moments to think about any images, language or word choices, thematic ideas, or moments in the play that made an impression. We would also like to hear any questions you might have regarding this workshop process or ideas raised in the play—in particular act 1. J. spent most of the workshop working on and exploring act 1. You are the first audience to experience this version of the play, so we are eager to hear your thoughts and impressions.

For those of you who must leave, thank you again for coming and please travel safe. For those who are able to remain, feel free to move closer to the stage. (Pause) We have a few ushers in the audience with microphones. Please raise your hand so that they can come to you and everyone can hear your comment or question clearly. It looks like we are ready to begin. Does anyone have an image, a phrase or bit of language from the play, or a moment that struck them or stayed with them? I have to say that one of my favorite phrases or images in the play has always been: "Her haunting eyes danced." Does anyone else have a phrase or image that struck them?

Step #3: Positive Comments from the Audience

Even though those who remain for the talkback often enjoy post-play conversations, nothing says they enjoy participating. Asking the audience to share a word, an image, or idea from the play that resonates with them, invites everyone to participate without the fear of needing to sound intelligent. What's more, there are no right or wrong answers. Everyone in the audience can succeed and contribute, even the extremely shy. Opening the conversation in this way also allows people to share their emotional response to the piece and therefore process the experience.

The active dramaturg starts the process by modeling the comments, "I liked the line (insert line); or, I like the image of two suns; or, I like the concept of exploring what it feels like to lose language, but replace words with sound." Soon additional comments will follow. Some will shout them, others will raise their hands. However audiences choose to enter the conversation, the active dramaturg takes time to acknowledge the comments by repeating them for the group, especially if there are no microphones. Even if only a few people attend the discussion, remember to repeat the comments. As the moderator, the active dramaturg faces the audience and can hear most comments, but others often miss the questions or comments; the active dramaturg repeats all questions or summarizes the comments. Also, as the number of comments slows, the active dramaturg can begin to expand a comment into a question to transition into the next step, fielding questions.

Step #4: Fielding Questions

Most who remain for the talkback either want to ask the writer questions—because they enjoyed the play—or want to learn more about the development process. Few people who choose to remain do so to share negative comments. Transitioning to these questions is easily done by taking a comment, either the last heard or one shared earlier, and inviting people to share their thoughts. If a comment points to a sad or humorous moment, the active dramaturg may ask if others responded similarly and what led to that response. Yes, the active dramaturg has asked the audience a question, but this question tells the audience they can do two things: one, engage in a dialogue with other audience members; and two, shift from simple comments to asking questions.

A dramaturg may choose to orchestrate a rough transition and invite people to ask questions, but an active dramaturg prefers a more subtle transition because people participate more fully and without an uncomfortable pause when the conversation shifts imperceptibly.

The transition might happen like this: *Someone over here mentioned they liked the proposal scene and a number nodded in agreement. What about that scene grabbed so many of you?* As people offer comments—and agree with one another—someone will invariably ask a question related to the scene in question or something similar. The conversation might progress this way with an audience member saying: *I thought it was just flat out funny. How does someone write that? Did that happen to you?* With the first question from the audience, the playwright can respond with insight into process, a personal take on wedding proposals, or divulging a personal secret. Either way, the discussion now appears to be in the audience's hands. The active dramaturg can let the playwright choose to answer the question or refocus the question to guarantee the conversation progresses toward specific concerns the writer and creative team have. The active dramaturg could rephrase the question for the group by reframing the question while repeating it. *The questioner is curious about how you go about crafting humorous dialogue or situations. Do you prefer to write these scenes alone or use improvisations with actors or another process?* Now, even if the playwright has a short response the active dramaturg can open the conversation to include scenes created through improvisations during the workshop and, possibly, the scene the writer was unsure of. Or, if this was the scene, the active dramaturg or playwright can continue to ask what made this scene so enjoyable with our without revealing their predetermined interest.

Although most people are curious about the creative process and rather reluctant to prescribe how the story should unfold, quite a number may have suggestions regarding how to change or improve the play. When fielding questions, the active dramaturg works to ensure that the question that makes the writer uncomfortable or verges on rude, is quickly rephrased as less offensive to the writer. These moments can rattle the most seasoned active dramaturg or moderator. Planning how to diffuse the situation makes confronting them less unnerving.

Fielding Challenging Audience Questions

When the audience begins to pose questions, the active dramaturg listens for three things. First, does the question stray outside the parameters established in the opening statement? If yes, the active dramaturg considers ways to move the question within the established boundaries without admonishing or reminding the audience that the question concerns an area the writer does not wish to discuss. Second, does the question resemble a back pocket question? If so, a transition that brings the question close to a back pocket question will keep the discussion moving in a direction that makes the writer comfortable. Third, does the question place the writer (or the theatre) on the defensive? Each of these challenging audience questions can stymie and fluster an unprepared dramaturg or disrupt the conversation's easy flow. Taking time to identify ways to prepare for these uncomfortable moments will minimize the writer's discomfort and allow the creative team to stay on task and learn how the majority responds to the play.

Fielding Challenging Audience Questions: Those That Stray Outside the Discussion's Parameters

If none of the prepared questions relates to the challenging question asked, and no option to bring the question into the range of appropriate topics emerges, a gentle reminder regarding the conversation's parameters can serve as an invitation to have the audience member reconsider and rephrase the question. This holds true if the question involves, for example, the inconsistencies between act 1 and act 2. If the opening statement shares that act 2 saw no revisions during the workshop and some plot points may not connect smoothly in a way that does not defend the play, then the active dramaturg may repeat this information should questions about misaligned facts in act 2 arises. If such a warning was not given, and the question strays outside the topics the playwright feels comfortable discussing, the active dramaturg considers whether it's possible to respond well without defending the play (or perhaps the director). Otherwise, shift the question to the general audience and ask for their responses.

A possible question from the audience: *What does it mean that the main character doesn't do anything in act 2? I was confused because the character seemed to be on a mission, and then after intermission the character didn't do anything let alone what I expected him to do. What did I miss?*

Many dramaturgs who have moderated talkbacks field a challenging question like this quite often. Even if the opening statement gently reminds the audience that the second act saw little to no revisions, audiences often use the talkback to seek clarity even if the creative team suggests they themselves do not yet know the answers. The first question refers to a main character's inaction and draws attention to the stark difference between acts 1 and 2. In all likelihood, when the reading began, someone prefaced the work by noting the possibility for stark differences between the acts because the workshop focused on act 1. Even a room full of professionals will ignore these reminders, so the active dramaturg prepares to field this question prior to the talkback. Reminding the audience that we expected inconsistencies will not foster an atmosphere of welcome, and the talkback will end before it has even begun.

If questions continue to focus on the second act's inconsistencies, the active dramaturg reconsiders why the audience remains fixed on this idea. Such fixation reveals that the audience followed the story closely and perhaps found it engaging or gripping. The audience's comments mean that the work done to connect the dots in the first act was extremely successful and that the work paid off.

But how does the active dramaturg deal with the question the first time? The active dramaturg may choose to poll the audience while rephrasing or creating a new context for the question. A quick gauge of whether others feel similarly accomplishes two goals: the audience expresses their confusion (perhaps frustration), and the audience knows there is no need to dwell on this point because everyone has acknowledged it.

> Prior to the talkback, the active dramaturg asks the playwright whether certain topics should be avoided, or which areas the writer has no desire to address. The writer might invite or welcome the active dramaturg to address those areas or concerns. The writer may want to avoid certain discussions altogether, in which case the active dramaturg needs to decide—in advance—how to steer the conversation in a different direction, assure the writer that all will go well, and then make good on that promise.

On its own, such a spontaneous poll may backfire and lead to comments that push the dramaturg and writer to adopt a defensive posture as they field questions or comments focused on when each person lost track of or connection to the story. In conjunction with an audience question, the poll responds to and engages with the audience.

The first possible approach to rephrasing the question could be: *Others seem to be agreeing with the gentleman asking the question. By a show of hands, who else found it easy to understand and follow the character's mission or paths of action, but early in act 2 found themselves confused? Did the confusion stem from the fact that the character didn't seem to be focused on the same set of tasks or goal or purpose? Or, were people confused because the character didn't seem to do anything? Did you expect the character to do something specific?*

In all probability whoever posed the question will no longer feel lost because others are similarly confused. Now, audiences may expect the playwright or the dramaturg to clarify or place the confusion into context. At this point, a discussion, if the playwright agrees, focuses on some possible insights into what the next steps are for the character and play may arise naturally. The impromptu poll may also inspire some specific questions from other audience members grounded in context. Because the active dramaturg's question relates directly to the audience's concern, a genuine rapport between artist and audience emerges. This simple approach may open the floor to a true conversation where the audiences share what worked for them and why, and what they expected, rather than what they think the writer should write; everyone will enjoy the exchange and learn a lot about which plot points landed.

Fielding Challenging Audience Questions: Those that Relate to a Back Pocket Question or Workshop Question

The second concept an active dramaturg listens for in a question: Does the question relate to either a prepared question or a question the creative team explored during the workshop? If the challenging question refers to a back pocket question, crafting a transition that brings the audience into what the creative team also wondered can significantly help the conversation. The audience and the creative team truly appear to work together and have synchronized thoughts. The same holds true for audience questions or comments that relate to those discussed during the workshop. Again, the active dramaturg (or others participating in the discussion) can respond by sharing how the workshop process grappled with or explored similar ideas or questions. Sharing how a scene or line changed in light of the exploration helps the audience better understand the workshop process and reminds the creative team how well the collaboration benefitted the play.

A possible question from the audience: *Why does this event [insert event] happen?*

When an audience member raises a question the writer has heard from actors, one of two things will happen. One, a sense of fatigue will overcome the writer because yet another person has asked about this issue, or a sense of resignation from the entire team if they felt they had addressed it sufficiently in the latest draft but the question suggests additional work may be needed. Another response is also possible. An air of vindication may float through the air, especially if someone (or a number of people) tried to champion this idea, but others shut it down or summarily ignored it. Regardless of which response comes from the team, the active dramaturg must assess each scenario similarly—has the writer decided to avoid discussing this topic at this time or does the writer want to address it. The active dramaturg steers the conversation in the appropriate direction without defending the play or writer's process.

When everyone in the room agrees with the questions surrounding the particular event, the active dramaturg's response writes itself. A possible response could be: *Throughout this workshop we discussed this very issue. Our goal quickly became to assemble a series of questions the writer could take home and consider while we spent the workshop addressing other areas because we realized that to address this particular event properly requires additional information/research, more time than the workshop allowed.*

At this point, move to the next question quickly. If the writer opts to put a question out and poll the audience, roll with it. Most likely, however, the writer will want to move on.

It is tempting to engage the questioner and ask for more specifics: What was confusing, what was clear, why did you question the event? Remember, framing the additional questions within the context that the team discussed this very issue in rehearsal and wondered if others would feel similarly, will always help. This follow up comment could elicit a few heads nodding in agreement and others in disagreement. An impromptu poll could help a lot, especially if the audience member can't offer any answers to the active dramaturg's clarification questions. The possible question could also be: *There was some discussion around this event during the workshop and led us to wonder if others would feel similarly?*

But, if the writer wants to move on even before someone agrees with the question, that wish should be honored as quickly as possible. One way to do that is to simply and politely acknowledge that the team wants to move on from the question without answering (no need to say who on the team). A way to phrase this is:

The team discussed this very question a lot this week. We're still exploring and developing approaches and would like to move on without addressing it now, as we have focused so heavily on it and continue to consider various options.

Another approach, especially if the relationship with the audience is strong, is to add a lot of humor: *The team discussed this issue a lot this week. I think it is safe to say we have exhausted ourselves. We are continuing to explore it. I think we've discussed it as much as we can at this time, and the creative team has a few other questions we'd like to explore with you. [Insert a back pocket question to move the talkback forward.]*

Either way, pay attention to the writer's energy level.

If only one person voices confusion, albeit repeatedly, but the question generates a lot of support from the audience (nodding and verbal agreements), reshaping the aforementioned question or moving on could prove more difficult. Especially if the writer does not agree that the event needs clarification or support. Even so, the active dramaturg pushes the conversation forward by connecting the current conversation with a back pocket question.

Fielding Challenging Audience Questions: Questions that Place the Writer on the Defensive

The talkback works best when it serves its primary purpose: to provide audiences an opportunity to share their immediate responses to the play's world and story. Sometimes audiences innocently seek insights into characters and the creative process, but these often comes across with little tact and place the playwright or creative artists on the defensive. The active dramaturg listens for the questions that reveal a genuine interest, and differentiates the poorly posed question from those that knowingly seek a defensive response from the writer.

Sometimes, however, the question calls a writer's capabilities into question. When this occurs, the active dramaturg works to address the issue and avoid the red flags—if others in the audience do not jump in and question the questioner's appropriateness first. Initially, an argument crafted around artistic freedom and understanding difference through art may prove successful if the question focuses on why a writer created such a character or wrote such a story. For the question that serves no purpose except to inflame—no response will serve this discussion well—the active dramaturg moves forward with the discussion as politely as possible, perhaps thanking the questioner for participating even if the sentiment is reprehensible.

Possible question from the audience: *Why does this character behave so despicably?*

This question could provoke combative comments with audience members picking sides because it reveals a lot about the questioner's ethics, morals, and point of view. To move beyond this narrow focus, the active dramaturg acknowledges that this question seeks to address character behavior—why characters act as they do—and what the writer wishes to explore in relation to the human experience. As such, the active dramaturg steps into the conversation and reframes the question by providing a bit of theatrical context and shifting the question to a topic the question addresses, but in a less opaque manner.

Although the creative team may have discussed how and why each character makes certain choices, most theatre practitioners will avoid posing the question or observation as judgments (negative or positive). Most artists opt to explore the choices, the reasons for the choices, and acknowledge the result as just that—a result or reaction. The active dramaturg who has participated in the workshop will know whether the question will strike a nerve and lead to a defensive response from the writer (or the actor). Even if the writer (or actor) has full faith in the characters and accepts their acts as behavior to observe and respond to—in whatever way—the active dramaturg recognizes that the question can provoke responses that lead to an antagonistic, rather than a productive, conversation.

It is tempting to revise the question with a lesson so that it is changed to: *In theatre we often confront characters who many of us think behave badly. Our training and our discussions around the table during the workshop led us not to judge the character's behavior, but to explore the choices and actions and to identify a story that works for the production. When writing such challenging characters, J. Doe, how do you avoid judging your characters and let them do what they want, how they want, regardless of how you, or we in the audience, may respond to them?*

The reframing above, though full of truths, will probably stop many from contributing to the conversation because the audience will feel chastised or belittled. The dramaturg's desire to help create context—to provide a glimpse into the creative and the workshop process—should be applauded, but the general tone (intentional or not) veers toward condescension. In addition, the question has a strong journalistic tone. The moderator asks the writer to explain the creative process, a past activity. Talkbacks serve a great purpose when they focus on the recent past—the workshop period—and the play's future direction and action.

An alternative revision for the question could be: *Much of the work during this workshop focused on act 1. If it isn't too early to discuss, where is the character heading? What actions might he pursue?*

If the active dramaturg knows that the writer has no desire to discuss the next steps or act 2 in any way, the question might be revised this way: *When exploring and then writing this character, what ideas or questions shaped this character?*

Phrased this way the active dramaturg avoids asking the playwright what informs the writing process or creative process for this particular character. In addition, the writer does not need to defend a process or character actions, but simply describe how the character evolved. The rephrased question focuses on the general creative process and takes the conversation away from the play and the writer. Asking what ideas and questions shape or motivate the character opens the discussion to the character and his (or her) vision of the world or the questions or societal ills as he sees them. The conversation or answer can then bring in information about focusing on character actions rather than judging them—or not—but the revelation unfolds in a context of character development and not audience education.

Another common inflamed question that relates to cultural competency be it gender, ethnicity, age, or sexual preference: *How are you able to write this story?*

This question often comes up when people write about status or eras, generations, ethnic groups outside their own, and situations the writer could not have lived through, but members in the audience did. Sometimes the pushback comes from the actors, thus alerting the active dramaturg that the talkback could be even more contentious. At its heart, the question addresses the ideas of ownership of experience or history. Can someone who wasn't there present the situations well? And, if the writer appears to capture the era or situation well, what does doing so say about the sanctity and respect for the memories or facts presented by those who lived through the time or experience?

We know that theatre and any creative art rarely purports to present the cold, hard facts. Theatre, film, television, and any visual art—even documentary photography and film—present a story and a unique vision of that story. Some artists take great pains to minimize the veil of personal perspective, but in the end such a question reminds us all that nothing exists as entirely objective and impartial.

The inflammatory question shines a light on the regular (and frankly necessary) assumption all art responds to—the assumption of universal human truths: you either believe these exist and embrace them or rail against the assumption and work to poke holes in the truth and devastate the people who believe and perpetuate them. The question often comes out as accusatory even when the intent is to compliment the writer. Always, however, the question strikes at the heart of literary ownership and creative freedom.

It is tempting to respond with: *A joy of creating art is to enter a world via research and imagination. Although we all have to take care when creating any character as each is different from us, writers take on the challenge to breathe life into imagined or historical characters by looking for the truth in how they respond to situations.*

Most artists want to believe that everyone has the right to tell whatever story calls them. Artistic freedom and license exists as a sort of corollary to freedom of speech, where one has the right to say anything. Just as most acknowledge that the right and freedom to say what one wishes comes with the responsibility to exercise caution and reason—especially when the words reveal disrespect for others resulting in more harm to the right than good—most artists acknowledge the need to accept that certain experiential or cultural limitations may require an approach that embraces one's shortcomings and, perhaps, transforms them into an advantage. This approach informs many stories exploring ethnic and cultural differences.

In the United States, this question of cultural ownership comes often when Caucasians seek to represent people of color. Sometimes people of color encounter difficulties when representing communities different from theirs, but less often and less publicly. Obvious offenses like blackface, profane references, or depictions that purport to fully represent individuals or events, but fail to avoid stereotypes, do not evoke surprise when they raise the ire of audiences, critics, and artistic colleagues of any background. The challenge comes when the offenses appear obvious to one (or many) groups, but not to the writer and those who share the writer's culture or ethnicity.

These not so subtle storytelling points may truly go unnoticed until the creative team is ethnically and culturally diverse (or diverse in terms of sexual preference or gender) or audiences address the topic in the talkback. The difficulty artists may have may not center on representation, but rather the predictable depiction of a character or the continuation of silencing voices in the guise of providing opportunity. For example, a play or musical may center on African Americans, but instead of writing a story with an entirely African-American cast assuming the lead in all issues, the one or two minor Caucasian characters serve as the narrator to both frame the story's point of view (for example, without their curiosity or discovery the trip back in time would not occur) and drive the play's action. In short, a secondary or minor character functions like a central character simply because they are not African American. The same could happen in a play featuring Latino, Asian, East Indian, or Native American/First Nations characters.

To assume that a Latino/a dramaturg will be able to validate the choices a non-Latino/a writer and creative team makes to avoid any hiccups or vitriolic critical response, is as wrong-headed as expecting that a female dramaturg working with an all-male team will be able to ensure the one or two female characters in the largely male cast function well and make the play controversy proof. Such an approach is unfair, happens often, and never produces positive results.

In addition, placing a person in the position—intentionally or unintentionally—of representing an ethnicity, culture, gender, or sexual orientation dilutes their importance as a creative contributor, and most importantly, as a person. In this situation, nothing this artist contributes will carry creative weight, it will come across attached to the "other," and that will invariably have no impact because too few of the "other" will be present.

No easy answers lie within these situations rooted in a lack of true cultural competency and accountability among the artists and a lack of diversity within theatres. To counter the challenges presented when expanding one's creative world one has to do more than hire an individual from that group. One must commit to listen and be ready to confront one's tiny and not so tiny biases that, when placed on stage, loom larger than anyone might imagine. Recognize, too, that simply because the pitfalls and unintended hurdles surrounding writing about difference may not enter rehearsal room conversations should not imply that the depictions offered are fine or that the cast (or other artists) aren't discussing or critiquing the depictions behind closed doors. Know that the conversations aren't necessarily derisive, but the necessary process people go through to identify how to discuss what fails to work well and why. Identifying ways to address the question of cultural competency and depiction before talkbacks will serve an active dramaturg well.

One possible way to address this question could be to respond with a question. To ask, "What leads you to ask this question?" will allow the questioner to clarify the intent. It may be a veiled compliment. If so, this will allow everyone to exhale and proceed easily through the discussion. The audience member may respond by pointing to the surprise and concern surrounding an individual for many of the reasons stated above. In which case, consider asking the audience to respond to the original question. Before doing so, quickly evaluate the audience's temperature. If the audience seemed to enjoy the play and responded well to the writer, proceed. Drawing them in prevents the discussion from excluding them and involving only the writer and the lone questioner. In part, the person posing the question wants to divert the discussion and the active dramaturg needs to honor everyone, but avoid fueling disruptions whenever possible. If, however, the audience seems as confused and concerned as the person asking the question, adopt a different tack. A possible approach could be: *We asked something similar when we started the process. We asked what inspired this story? What fuels you each day you sit down to write? And the answer inspired and shaped each day of rehearsal. J. Doe shared the following. . . .* Then the active dramaturg shares what the playwright said and moves on with an eye to address this concern in notes to the playwright.

Step #5: Questions from the Writer or the Creative Team

Some playwrights enjoy talkbacks. Nothing says only dramaturgs or whoever moderates the discussion should hold exclusive rights to asking the audience questions. Also, the discussion may go so well that a reluctant playwright wants to ask a few unplanned questions. Welcome it. Embrace it. Should any questions appear to confuse the audience, rephrase them slightly while looking to the playwright to ensure you haven't changed the question. Only if the audience seems stumped by the writer's question or the responses, should the active dramaturg consider rephrasing the question.

If the writer doesn't join in, the active dramaturg connects one of the back pocket questions to a positive comment or earlier question and subtly transitions the discussion from general feedback to seeking specific responses to artistic questions, or use a comment to transition into the questions the writer and creative team want to ask the audience.

Step #6: A Second Round of Positive Comments

By now the audience feels more comfortable sharing ideas and responses. Asking once again for images, ideas, scenes, or language that resonates with the audience allows the talkback to end on a positive note that focuses exclusively on the play the writer has written. Playwright José Cruz González introduced this step during his development discussions, for it allows the talkback to end on a joyous note.

> For the final note, active dramaturgs ask someone from the creative team to jot down comments and questions from the entire talkback that can be used when writing the final note to the playwright.

This transition is easiest to orchestrate. Simply alert the audience that the talkback will be ending soon. Time for one final question remains. Take the question. Then ask the audience if they have any additional images or lines or moments from the play that they didn't share earlier. It's fine if some of the ideas repeat; hearing them again reminds the writer how powerful that moment or line is.

Step #7: The Closing Statement

Take time to craft a closing statement. The final remarks are not only to thank the audience for participating in the talkback and, if appropriate, invite them to continue the conversation in the lobby if a reception follows (or with the theatre via surveys or email). The closing statement can reinforce the idea that discussing plays is something everyone can do at any time. And though it sounds obvious, do not forget to lead the audience in applause for the discussion and their participation in it—*especially* if the talkback did not go well. Applause, like a positive comment, helps the talkback end on a positive note.

> *Thank you so much for taking the time to share your thoughts and questions with us. The feedback you provided will surely help the creative team and the writer and the play continue to evolve. Please travel safe and hopefully we will see you at our next reading (or at the theatre for our next production). Good night and on behalf of J. Doe, the creative team, and the theatre, thank you.*

Avoid the temptation to end by suggesting the theatre should produce the play. If an audience member says that, encourage them to share their thoughts via email or to call the theatre, but the active dramaturg does not make any promises regardless of his or her relationship with the theatre.

Step #8: A Final Note

For the active dramaturg to engage and to participate fully in the talkback, some-one associated with the creative team—who will not participate in the talkback—is needed to transcribe or record the conversation so that the notes following the talkback accurately reflect the conversation. When drafting the final written notes for the workshop, the active dramaturg incorporates or refutes, whenever pos-sible, comments or questions from the talkback. The active dramaturg takes care to avoid reminding the writer of statements made in ways that restrict creativity or schools the playwright. Positive comments will fuel the writer throughout the next phase, and some of the questions or points may shape the writing process as well.

Possible Final Note: For Well-Received Reading

> *What a great reading! The audience was following along. Few people fidgeted, and when they did it was during the sections we hadn't worked on. I think many of the changes you mentioned will address the concerns well. The audience was also quite responsive during the discussion. They really liked your language and your proposal scene rocked! You did awesome work. The play is almost there!*

What Works and Doesn't Work in a Possible Final Note: For Well-Received Reading   The length of a note has no bearing on its success in assisting a writer through the rewrite process. However, comments that point to specific discoveries, solutions, or remaining questions do inform a note's usefulness. The note (above) that the dramaturg sent following the reading fails to provide the writer any insights or material that will help reconnect the writer and play to the workshop's discoveries or, for lack of a better word, vibe.

What a great reading! No question, beginning with an assessment of the reading truly helps, especially if the audience responded positively. *The audience was following along. Few people fidgeted, and when they did it was during the sections we hadn't worked on.* To assume why the audience did or did not fidget fails to support the play's forward trajectory. An active dramaturg would have posed a question to gauge the audience's interest. Here, that question (or the information gleaned) will help the writer days, weeks, or months after the workshop. But instead the dramaturg wrote: *I think many of the changes you mentioned will address the concerns well. The audience was also quite responsive during the discussion. They really liked your language and your proposal scene rocked!* The active dramaturg might write:

> *What a great reading! The audience laughed when we wanted—during the proposal and that awkward first handshake/kiss—you really did write a great scene there. As I watched the audience, I saw them focus only on the actors and the reading as that scene took off. The rewrites that focused on how to push this friendship just one step beyond two people just hanging out increased the tension and kept the audience interested. The talkback comments of "they kept doing and saying things I didn't expect" or "I liked how they were never on the same page" drew a lot of nods. The consensus seems to be that you built the tension you were looking for: characters who like each other, but not for the typical reasons. It was clear that this direction will inform the play's second half that we did not address. In act 2, the characters fall into the typical romance dialogue and behavior patterns we came into the workshop to explore and, if possible, transform. You managed to tap into that in the handshake/kiss and the proposal scene. Hopefully, these will help when working on the play's second half.*

Most importantly, the active dramaturg resists the urge to suggest no more difficult work remains. The note could go on to include a few questions they had hoped to explore but did not as long as they simply remind the playwright of previous conversations. If the reading brought to mind new questions (for example, is it clear that a character does something or knows something), the active dramaturg clearly signals that the reading led to a new discovery. For example: *With all the changes to the initial stages of their courtship clarified, I suddenly began to wonder how or why X happens.* And then discuss X briefly. And of course, always end with a genuine expression: *Great work! Awesome job! Below is a list of the audience comments. (The intern did a great job taking notes during the talkback. I hope they are helpful.)*

The Revised Final Note: For Well-Received Reading

> *What a great reading! The audience laughed when we wanted—during the proposal and that awkward first handshake/kiss—you really did write a great scene there. As I watched the audience, I saw them focus only on the actors and the reading as that scene took off. The rewrites that focused on how to push this friendship just one step beyond two people just hanging out increased the tension and kept the audience interested. The talkback comments of "they kept doing and saying things I didn't expect" or "I liked how they were never on the same page" drew a lot of nods. The*

consensus seems to be that you built the tension you were looking for: characters who like each other, but not for the typical reasons. It was clear that this direction will inform the play's second half that we did not address. In act 2, the characters fall into the typical romance dialogue and behavior patterns we came into the workshop to explore and, if possible, transform. You managed to tap into that in the handshake/ kiss and the proposal scene. Hopefully these will help when working on the play's second half. With all the changes to the initial stages of their courtship clarified, I suddenly began to wonder how or why X happens. Great work! Awesome job! Below is a list of the audience comments. (The intern did a great job taking notes during the talkback.) I hope they are helpful.

A Possible Final Note: For a Poorly Received Reading

Wow. That was a surprise. Honestly, you did such amazing work. I think those people who were upset were reliving their own personal drama. The reading itself went well. It was a bit long, but we weren't sure of the running time in rehearsal. All you need to do is trim a bit to get the running time down and all will be fine. The play takes a real life event and adds a bit of magic to help us enter its world well. Some events are simply too difficult or too fresh for some audiences. Your play is awesome—it made it to this workshop! I'm sure it will have a great life. I would love to work with you further. But if you opt to change gears and dramaturgs, I understand.

Some readings do not go well. Some talkbacks do not go well. Sometimes both the reading and the talkback do not go well. Whether the writer acknowledges the underwhelming reception or seems oblivious to it, the active dramaturg has the dubious distinction of having to acknowledge it and find a way to lift the writer's spirit and renew the writer's connection and faith in the play. Only the writer can and should decide that the project's life should end with the unsuccessful reading. No one else.

What Works and Doesn't Work in a Possible Final Note: For a Poorly Received Reading   *Wow. That was a surprise. Honestly, you did such amazing work. I think those people who were upset were reliving their own personal drama.* No question honesty is always the best policy, but here the dramaturg does nothing to change the conversation and help the playwright reclaim a passion for the material. An active dramaturg might write: *Congratulations on the amazing amount of work you did this week. We identified a clear story to connect with, and with the help of a few improvisations, began to uncover how characters interact when under pressure. The audience responded deeply and passionately to the story. Some elements of the story, however, led the audience outside the play's magical world and caused some to connect personal moments to the play's; so much so they could not experience the story you wrote.* The active dramaturg acknowledged the strong reactions, but in a way that avoids reliving or reviving the emotion that shaped the conversation. Also, the active dramaturg prepares the writer that a few moments may need to be reexamined rather than the entire play with "some elements." This can help make the process of rewriting less onerous

because following a reading as bad as this, mustering the strength and desire to weather the rewrite process will be extremely difficult.

All you need to do is trim a bit to get the running time down and all will be fine. If the reading seemed long, perhaps interminable, and the audience displayed little to no connection to the play's world, more than a few tweaks are needed. In this instance, the dramaturg does the writer and the play a huge disservice by suggesting the play needs little work. It may be unclear what needs to change to make this play success-ful, but misleading the writer through such misguided cheerleading is not helping anyone. An active dramaturg might write: *The challenge is to establish a balance and the boundaries within the play's world so that audiences find it easier to focus on your story. No question we lost track of how much this true event still lives in people's memory. It may help to consider ways to make the play's world hyperfictional, perhaps not satirical, but a bit more larger than life. The fantastical moments come across as too realistic or as if we, the creative team, think that these solutions are plausible.*

The play takes a real life event and adds a bit of magic to help us enter its world well. Some events are simply too difficult or too fresh for some audiences. Sometimes an audi-ence fails to connect with a play because of who they are—generally, seven-year-olds will not connect with a play for teens—but to summarily discount an audi-ence's response ignores a fundamental theatrical truth. If theatre speaks to universal human truths or experiences, artists must look for ways to ensure that their message comes across clearly. Everyone needn't agree with the premise or like it, but the argument should be accessible. To bridge this gap, the active dramaturg might write: *No character needs to discover magical powers, but what could elevate this journey to discovery a bit? I think that the questions we used to guide the process still have merit, but adding this question of elevating the journey may help reframe the play's world so that audiences do not respond to the events with the logic needed to survive in the real world.*

Your play is awesome—it made it to this workshop! I'm sure it will have a great life. I would love to work with you further. But if you opt to change gears and dramaturgs, I under-stand. This dramaturg attempts to cheer the writer up, but given what's been writ-ten the enthusiasm seems forced. Although "'to change gears'" remains unclear—does this mean shelve the play or choose a different creative team—the dramaturg assumes too much. If writer and dramaturg have worked together for a while, this statement has merit and a level of appropriateness; if they have only just met, the comments lack awareness and sensitivity. The active dramaturg might write: *The intern did a great job noting what moments or images struck the audience; they are below. Take a deep breath. I'm happy to talk whenever you want. The story has grown, good work.*

The Revised Final Note: For a Poorly Received Reading

Congratulations on the amazing amount of work you did this week. We identified a clear story to connect with and with the help of a few improvisations, began to uncover how characters interact when under pressure. The audience responded deeply and passionately to the story. Some elements of the story, however, led the audience outside the play's magical world and caused some to connect personal moments to the play's, so much so they could not experience the story you wrote. The challenge is to establish a balance and the boundaries within the play's world so that audiences find it easier to focus on your story. No question we lost track of how much this true event still lives in people's memory. It may help to consider ways to make the play's world hyper fictional, perhaps not satirical, but a bit more larger than life. The fantastical moments come across as too realistic or as if we, the creative team, think that these solutions are plausible. No character needs to discover magical powers, but what could elevate this journey to discovery a bit? I think that the questions we used to guide the process still have merit, but adding this question of elevating the journey may help reframe the play's world so that audiences do not respond to the events with the logic needed to survive in the real world. The intern did a great job noting what moments or images struck the audience; they are below. Take a deep breath. I'm happy to talk whenever you want. The story has grown, good work.

The Danger of Readings and Talkbacks

When audiences laugh, cry, and erupt into applause or give a standing ovation at the end of a reading or presentation, most will say the reading went well. And regardless of the play's state of development, the reading did go well—the team presented a new work to the world. However, the danger of such a positive reaction is the implied suggestion that the play needs no additional work—be it polishing of scenes, developing character, clarifying story, cutting for length, etc. The likelihood of the writer misreading the event's success increases if the dramaturg neglects to write a final note or fails to articulate possible next steps. Even if audience members pose questions concerning story or character clarity, an exuberant audience response can often eclipse these well-founded observations and lead some writers to ignore the comments and questions from the audience or creative team wholesale. This can carry over into subsequent new-play workshops resulting in a frustrating process for all involved and a play's quick death or indefinite sentence in workshop hell—because the writer believes little to no additional work is needed.

The confusion that results when professional colleagues appear to contradict the positive audience response rarely surfaces immediately. When the writer has an opportunity to receive a full production or another workshop, months later (sometimes a year or two), the disconnection between work and response begins to emerge. First, the new creative team's comments may suggest lengthy rewrites rather than what the playwright thinks the play needs—a tweak here or there. Second, the time frame for such changes may be quicker as the creative team expects the writer to understand the play more fully because of the previous workshop, and yet the writer has a skewed vision of the play.

Directors and dramaturgs can also succumb to the danger of talkbacks. They can help the play move forward well or craft a successful reading and assume that they will continue to move with the play, especially if the theatre supporting the workshop will produce the play. No one on the creative team is immune from the workshop or talkback's ability to mislead, except actors. Actors do tend to understand they will rarely if ever move on with a play through its development.

Crafting a final note that captures the audience's excitement, but points to the work that remains—based on the questions the writer initiated or wrestled with—presents one way to mitigate the possible confusion for the writer. Without a note geared toward moving the play forward, the play will likely remain in its current state and subsequent creative teams will hear of the reading's wild reception in lieu of rewrites.

The Pros and Cons of Conversations with Artistic Leadership or Professional Respondents

Many of the play development workshops that last two weeks or more, conclude with a roundtable discussion between the theatre's artistic leadership and the creative team. These closed-door discussions occur between professionals without the formal structure of the more public talkbacks. Usually, the artistic team has remained abreast of the play's development throughout the workshop so the conversation often delves deeply into how well the process served the writer and the play, discoveries made during the presentation or reading, and finally how this experience may help the writer's next draft of the play and future writings.

These conversations are just that, conversations. The form can be as formal or as free-form as any discussion following the first read of a play. The active dramaturg's role in these conversations remains, as always, to help prepare the writer. No one looks for predetermined answers. The artistic advisors want honest ideas expressed as clearly as possible. If the active playwright or creative team wants feedback on particular ideas or scenes, they should come prepared with those questions. If the playwright or creative team has concerns about particular processes, take time to identify how to best phrase those concerns and to identify who should broach the subject. These sessions also help the organization improve their workshop so all feedback serves a positive purpose, simply consider the most constructive or celebratory way to address a challenge or success.

Just as the director or dramaturgy intern should take notes during the audience talkback, either the active dramaturg or director should take notes during the artistic conversation.

These conversations focus on moving the process forward for the writer. At times—rarely—the discussions become contentious. Sometimes this occurs because of tensions between the creative team, sometimes because of cultural differences between the artists and the artistic leadership. The active dramaturg works with both groups before the discussion to identify if such tensions exist and ways to address them. Many of the questions above address these areas of contention and the possible approaches will work with a small group of professionals as easily as a large theatre-loving audience. Even so, the dramaturg on the project responds as an artist and the artistic leadership leads.

Final Thoughts

Surveys, talkbacks, and artistic conversations can benefit the active writer's process post-workshop. To ensure that these critical conversations aid the writer and the play's growth, the active dramaturg works to identify questions that provoke direct responses to what the writer wrote. Carefully crafted questions and well-moderated discussions stand a better chance of achieving this goal. Closed and general questions lead audiences to respond with what they want to see rather than identify what they saw or responded to and what action those events suggest will follow.

Remembering to avoid defending the play will allow the active dramaturg and playwright, and anyone else participating, to best enjoy the unpredictable nature of talkbacks and the joy of discovering what excites audiences about the play, its world, story, and characters.

Chapter 7: Moving from the New-Play Workshop to Rehearsal for Production

To keep his mind active and sharp, Sherlock Holmes conducted numerous experiments. Sometimes, the experiments came in handy when solving a case and, at other times, Holmes simply learned what substances he should not pair or how a chemical reacts or smells when altered in some way. His experiments often sharpened his eye so that while in the field he noticed things others overlooked, thereby hastening a crime's solution or at least the winnowing of suspects.

Readings and workshops somewhat resemble experiments. In addition to providing the active playwright an opportunity to expand on ideas and have actors read rewrites immediately or improvise scenes, workshops allow the creative team to put forth ideas for presenting the play and test the play's mettle. Many find it difficult to remember that as a play moves from the workshop or experimental phase to rehearsal and then production, the process differs greatly. The more the writer, dramaturg, director, and theatre believe what works in the reading will work in the production, the bumpier the transition will be.

Just as Sherlock Holmes sometimes uses lessons or information from his experiments in the field, so too, should active theatre artists use the lessons from the reading. However, artists who build upon the lessons learned from the workshop presentation run the risk of stunting the play's growth and minimizing its theatricality. At some point Holmes either marvels at or pockets his experimental observations; active artists, especially active dramaturgs remain similarly open when collaborating on a premiere production of a previously workshopped play.

The Active Dramaturg and the Premiere Production

When a play moves from workshop to production, an exciting set of challenges for the active dramaturg and active playwright arise. First and foremost, managing and navigating the excitement of working on a world premiere production. A world premiere production presents a unique opportunity to place a mark on theatre history—either for posterity, around the globe, across the nation, or within your state and region. True, only a handful of productions chart a new course in theatrical history, but a few more manage to shape a theatre's production history. The active dramaturg who is given the opportunity to facilitate a process that may aid in launching or bolstering a playwright's career, is honored indeed.

The active dramaturg's initial challenge is to manage the excitement for the production. Just as writers and artists can enter a workshop process with a level of enthusiasm that can lead to writer's block or other negative responses resulting from unrealistic and unfulfilled expectations, the same can happen with productions. No company or artist enters a production expecting the rehearsal process to be rife with negative tension, to have the theatre market the play to the wrong audience, or to read that the critics expect the story to be told according to their biases only to have it told in a sometimes more realistic, but wholly unexpected way (especially true with plays by writers of color). Similarly, no playwright plans to enter a production process and discover that the play accepted isn't the play the theatre expects to produce; that the collaborators believe the play needs extensive rewrites while the writer imagined only a few were needed, or that the writer's expectations do not square with the artistic collaborators. For example, the collaborators may believe the play needs extensive rewrites and the writer thinks the play needs only a few tweaks. The active dramaturg often has to manage these chasms of differing opinions, as well as the mistaken perception that everyone knows of (and how to meet) the other party's expectations.

> Most theatres develop and produce new work because they believe that doing so keeps theatre alive and vital, and that stories befitting the current era or that era's point of view must be written and shared. These theatres understand that the honor and risk of pursuing and presenting world premieres brings possible reward.

Regardless of why a theatre chooses to produce a play—and the reasons are many and not always altruistic—the active dramaturg works to strengthen the play's story so that it may be realized well on the stage, no matter what the theatre's operating budget.

Most theatres develop and produce new work because they believe that doing so keeps theatre alive and vital, and that stories befitting the current era or that era's point of view must be written and shared. These theatres understand that the honor and risk of pursuing and presenting world premieres brings possible reward. First, the theatre may become associated with a particular artist or work and second, the originating theatre shares in the play's royalties for a limited time. In these instances, the theatre works with the artists throughout to ensure a successful premiere and often try to help the writer secure additional productions.

Sometimes theatres produce a play to meet a particular social obligation or fulfill a grant requirement. These reasons rarely lead to genuine interest and support from the theatre. Such institutions see the limit of their obligation—produce the work for our audience only—rather than push the work to grow so that it has a life beyond the slated run. This scenario can often accompany productions of plays by writers of color or adaptations with a limited copyright license. The active dramaturg works to honor these agreements, but also looks for ways to support and encourage the writer to move beyond these imposed limitations. A writer may see limits (the license for a first-run production only), but the active writer will always have the play and the production's reviews as a calling card; for these reasons the active dramaturg pushes for the active writer's best work when the theatre may simply want a work that fulfills their obligation.

Writers seek a production to see their work for many reasons, one of which is to see the play live as it should: alive on stage with actors, lights, set, costume, and sound. Also, when a play moves from workshop to production, this particular artist has an opportunity to shape the American (or world) theatre. Regardless of whether the play premieres at a LORT A or a community theatre, someone will see the play and the work will impact the theatre-goer's life, one's view of society, and/or the perception of this artistic discipline. What's more, no one knows whether the writer who submits and develops a ten-minute play for the community theatre new-play festival one year will later rework the play so that it morphs into an active, award-winning theatre artist within the professional American theatre. These are the factors that make working with new work exciting.

> Remember, as often (or few times) as the play has been read and workshopped, this play has never been mounted. No one knows whether the play's story and dialogue can support the rigors of the stage. A play may work with actors sitting at music stands, but can movements, silence, set changes, and other physical realities the world demands be sustained?

For active dramaturgs who focus on new work, world premieres provide an opportunity to use every dramaturgical and critical thinking skill—posing open questions, providing critical insights to aid the marketing and education departments, assisting development with grant writing or crafting arguments for foundations and donors, and, of course, assisting the artistic team as it works—to support the work on the page, and its textual evolution to the stage. If the active dramaturg proceeds without caution, the development focus may shift away from two key ideas: the play and the story the writer and director want to tell.

No doubt these dramaturgical obligations and responsibilities appear par for the course and exist as challenges to meet. The myth that most early career active dramaturgs (and early career active playwrights) believe is that because the play has been workshopped it will not need revisions. The truth is, the rehearsal process for a new play *will* include a number of script changes. Sometimes the changes involve major thematic ideas and character journeys; sometimes only strategic cuts and tweaks that impact the play's emotional through-line, but appear to leave the story largely intact. Other times, the play changes to accommodate production elements and other technical demands, which extend beyond stage directions. Whatever route the play takes as it grows, the active dramaturg has a crucial role in shaping the environment that fosters these critical examinations and informs all impacted parties (the entire theatre staff) in ways that ease anxiety as the work evolves.

Managing these various creative efforts while working on world premieres often leads the active dramaturg, and those who use dramaturgical skills, to see the rehearsal hall as a sanctuary that welcomes limited experimentation given the production time line. Remember, as often (or few times) as the play has been read and workshopped, this play has never been mounted. No one knows whether the play's story and dialogue can support the rigors of the stage. A play may work with actors sitting at music stands, but can movements, silence, set changes, and other physical realities the world demands be sustained?

The challenge of the world premiere is also its joy: everything exists as a new problem to solve. Some problems are relatively easy and others incredibly difficult. Frankly, no one knows if the problems the play presents have solutions. Problems are not negative, they are questions ranging from costume choices to the type of set and number of set pieces, to clarity of story and character journey. The play may present staging arrangements no one has attempted before or effects that artists involved with the production have never wrestled with. Either way, the challenges of a world premiere are akin to experiments. Some artists enjoy working on experiments, and others find the unknown a bit too unsettling and prefer working on plays with known solutions and innovative interpretations.

Find the Middle Ground

Two schools of thought persist regarding the approach to producing new work: first, to consider the work as strong and stable and proven as a set text; second, to consider the work malleable. To subscribe to the set-text point of view leaves the creative team—especially the playwright—open to heartache and undo stress as actors and designers question the viability of certain ideas, and rewrites or adjustments offer the only solutions. Approaching the rehearsal as a final workshop, can create an untenable situation as creative teams and writers spend too much time exploring and honing in the search for perfection preventing the cast and design staff from committing to choices and fashioning a solid theatrical world.

The active dramaturg and creative team strike a balance somewhere between these two opposing views; they find the middle ground.

Often when a theatre commits to producing a new work (the vision of the story and its presentation is clear even if its mode of delivery is not), the organization supports the writer and the writer's vision, but accepts that additional work may need to occur to bring both the story and action into equilibrium. This does not mean the groups agree on what needs to change, merely that they accept what vision the premiere production can support and what the writing can and will look like for that inaugural production.

The challenge comes when the playwright fails to hear the producing organization's questions either as genuine concerns or expectations for change, or merely pretends to agree in order to secure a production. In either case, the dramaturg—active or not—has to work doubly hard to support the writer, the play, and the theatre. Once the collaborators begin to communicate clearly, the active dramaturg can begin to pursue the work to identify the few key areas that will align the script quickly within the preexisting framework and expectations. Remember, a play set for production includes a number of designers and theatre staff whose work depends on certain aspects of the play's dramatic action remaining constant. For example, cast size dictates a costume designer's budget, as does the need to build a special costume or two. If the playwright adds a *Star Trek* fantasy scene, the costume designer may not have time to support that vision well. Similarly, a writer who suddenly discovers the cast must include an additional character that no one in the current cast can play, many budgets from operational to design to housing will increase. The active dramaturg should be prepared to lead a process where the discoveries that were not addressed or inadequately addressed will be finalized.

Why?

A playwright may have a busy schedule and little time available for this particular work. Or, the playwright may believe the current draft works better than it does. Perhaps the actors presenting the script in the workshop were "all wrong" and everything that went less well will be addressed with proper casting. Or, the audience gave the reading a standing ovation suggesting the play is, even if a tragedy, a crowd-pleasing success.

When a Reading Appears to Go Well

Sometimes a public reading makes the active dramaturg's job more difficult. Why? When a writer assumes a reading went well, meaning no additional work remains—no rewrites or tweaks needed—because people responded to the play as the writer wished by laughing uncontrollably, sobbing at the end, or gave a standing ovation, the writer tends to challenge every

> The active dramaturg often sees the questions that exist in spite of the play's successful reading—whether part of the workshop team or not—and must lead the exploration toward change so that the play remains true to the writer's vision and can stand up to the rigors of production.

question and suggestion from the director, producer, or active dramaturg. What's more, any critical comments that counter the audience's enthusiastic response highlight the writer's greatest fear—that altering anything will disrupt the play's delicate balance. Leading writers beyond this fear of destroying their own work so that they can see how the play's critical elements currently combine and, with a few rewrites, may combine more effectively, requires considerable patience and that the active dramaturg forges clear connections between the writer's vision, the play's story, and the critical elements that can heighten the play's successes. Engaging in a discussion to address the work that remains has nothing to do with censorship but ensures the play achieves a level of richness and logic that makes the play less impeachable.

Note that this is for readings that *appear* to go well.

When the Reading Goes Well and the Play Moves Forward

Some readings do go well and deserve the audience's adulation be it tears or laughter or a standing ovation. These readings give voice to a work that tells a clear story, manages the flow of time well, offer mysteries for the audience to solve, and pays close attention as the story and plot combine. When the producing organization approaches the writer, little or nothing is said about developing or sharpening the story or plot. Instead, the professional creative team may leave the workshop with questions surrounding production and minor storytelling issues.

When the active dramaturg joins this creative team, the active writer can clearly articulate the play's story, a vision for the piece, and hopes for the production's ability to underscore certain elements. If, however, the questions of story and vision remain unanswerable or the responses are vague or dependent upon factors that will change from production to production, the play and playwright still have work to do. The active dramaturg often sees the questions that exist in spite of the play's successful reading—whether part of the workshop team or not—and must lead the exploration toward change so that the play remains true to the writer's vision and can stand up to the rigors of production. In these instances, the active dramaturg adopts a pre-workshop mindset while managing the middle ground.

The Rigors of Production

When preparing for a premiere production, the theatre and artistic staff must see where the play will stand up to the rigors of production and where some shoring up needs to occur.

Rigors of production?

During a reading, the stage directions indicate what can't be shown or performed at music stands. When the play is staged, some physical actions render certain dialogue unnecessary. For example, a play may include a dream sequence and the writer intends for the audience to watch the character's reverie via staging or video. Eventually, the character awakes and begins to recount the dream. In a reading, the redundancy of hearing the dream described and then having a character recount the dream may not warrant a second thought because the stage direction is read and in a full production the event will be heard only once—no one saw the dream so hearing the character's accounting satisfies, and it was in a stage direction after all. When staging or preparing to stage the play, however, the active dramaturg and creative team may notice that these two experiences—to see the dream and then hear the dream described—risk overwhelming the audience and stops the play's forward momentum. The question the active dramaturg asks is which scene impacts the play more—watching the dream or hearing it recounted? Should elements of both remain? Should the team discuss the merits of cutting one scene entirely? The rigors of production involve questions of balancing what's seen and discerning what's performed and which serves the story more.

Other Rigors of Production that Readings Do Not Clarify

Readings rarely clarify how time passes in plays that shift between decades or depend upon flashbacks. In a reading, indicating a shift between eras causes no one difficulty because the person reading stage directions heralds the decade in question. However, when staging a scene, challenges arise. Can the actors get from point A to point B in ample time? Can the crew (or actors) transition the set? When performed does the shift from one decade to the next actually resonate?

When Charlotte Keatley's play *My Mother Said I Never Should* premiered in 1989, a number of set designers tried and failed (the production went through many during the pre-production phase) to solve the question of indicating the 1940s, '60s, '70s and early '80s while keeping a piano on stage, a piece used only during the 1940s scenes. How could the set designer indicate time? A similar question arose when premiering Lynn Nottage's *Las Meninas*. The narrating character Marie Thérèse had to travel between the near past, the distant past, and the play's present. Nottage wondered if these shifts flowed logically, but could not tell during a reading because the stage directions always pointed the audience in the correct directions.

Sometimes the only opportunity to truly test these questions comes during the stumble-throughs, run-throughs, and technical rehearsals. Granted, waiting until tech week may not be wise, but it may present the only option for some productions. If the team discusses the problem throughout rehearsal and considers various solutions up to and including tech, the team lessens the opportunity for surprises. The active dramaturg, and those who rely on dramaturgical skills, remain acutely attuned to these challenges and those that arise alongside.

Moving Forward

Commissioned plays, as well as those discovered at readings or new-play development festivals, often move toward production before a solid, production-ready script exists. Some of the excitement of producing new work lies within the need to make it work for the stage within a tight time schedule. Note that the excitement does not include working under pressure, which is often associated with working in a negative environment. When artists fail to fully acknowledge their creative process—the time it takes them to create and what's needed to produce the desired results—working under time constraints morphs into working under pressure.

Often, producing organizations request that work on the script occurs before rehearsals, which encourages the director and active dramaturg to meet prior to engaging with the writer and before the actors begin. If the theatre expresses no preference either way, the active dramaturg, active playwright, and director should try to have a conversation where each identifies what each would like to see or thinks will serve the rehearsal process best. In short, this list will identify the areas to develop within the script prior to rehearsal and the challenges the script presents to the producing theatre (for example, special effects or quick costume changes). Often, the dramaturg has this priority-setting discussion with the writer alone, reinforcing a division rather than a collaboration. The active dramaturg looks to identify ways to have each party represent their wants and needs, especially when the vision conflicts greatly with the creative team's and, most specifically, the writer's.

Entering rehearsal with a more solid, firm text, allows designers and actors to approach their responsibilities with ease, but the nature of new-play development is that aspects of story and action shift as the play moves from page to stage. Even so, every attempt to solidify the major storytelling elements should be made prior to beginning the design process and the first day of rehearsal.

To assist the active playwright, the active dramaturg works to prioritize and identify the areas of concern among the various partners: the writer, the director, and the producer or theatre. In an ideal world everyone agrees on the same areas of concern and the general look of those changes. In formulating a balance between each artists' set of questions, the active dramaturg works to place the writer's vision at the center while articulating how similar or dissimilar the other artist's critical comments are to the active writer's vision or the play's story.

> When the active dramaturg can identify the specific moments in question and articulate how they impact design and production, a shift in the rewrite process often occurs. A writer's reluctance to execute changes quickly lessens when storytelling elements such as the flow of time and place impact the set, sound, and light design.

Because rehearsals for new work rarely include additional rehearsal time to develop the script, active writers and active dramaturgs collaborate to assemble a time line that feels comfortable in spite of the demanding rehearsal schedule. The rehearsal process for new work is considerably more challenging for a set-text play, because actors are building character, committing lines to memory, and learning new blocking, all while the script changes daily. Knowing and sharing which ideas, themes, and moments must exist within the script ensure a strong production. These touchstones will help lessen the frustrations that arise when new changes or drafts arrive late or fail to realize everyone's wish list. The active dramaturg serves everyone well by identifying these must-haves and shaping the rewrite process so that these ideas remain at the forefront or are addressed early.

In addition, the active dramaturg can help identify when the script makes demands on the design that the writer need not change even though the effect is difficult to achieve. A special effect that serves the play, but unduly challenges a theatre, can lead to great frustration. The theatre may request changes to the scene including the special effect suggesting it isn't clear or doesn't work; when in truth they do not or cannot execute the effect. The active dramaturg helps the active playwright listen to the producing organization to discern where the true conflict lies and to identify a solution that works for everyone. The active dramaturg may prove indispensable in identifying when the challenge may be too great for that particular theatre, but not the story and other producing organizations. This information helps the active writer identify when to make a sacrifice to best support this production rather than discovering a solution that serves all subsequent productions.

When the Process Encounters Delays

Producers and theatres seek to avoid such last-minute adjustments and use the workshops and commission/rewrite process as an opportunity to identify a writer's ability to respond to criticism and to articulate and execute rewrites. Even so, delays due to limited resources or procrastination may prove inevitable. Many productions encounter this hurdle. When rewrites fail to arrive, the active dramaturg works with the director to uncover ways to mine what does exist and continues to collaborate with the writer. In these instances the team may have to wait until run-throughs and previews for the writer to see what needs to happen, but then little time remains to produce effective changes that the actors can absorb and execute well. Sometimes, the play never realizes its potential.

Sometimes solutions suddenly arrive during run-throughs and or even as late as previews. Some actors can accommodate these late arriving changes; others struggle. To ensure a strong production and a confident cast, changes to the script must stop and sometimes sooner than the creative team may like. However, the active writer and active dramaturg may continue to note where cuts may occur and how to improve the dialogue for the next draft and production. The writer may even continue to write the changes so that the director and active dramaturg can discuss them, but chooses to not deliver them to the cast.

When the Changes Do Not Occur

Not all actors can perform Shakespeare. Not all directors can direct musicals. Not all dramaturgs can work on new plays.

The truth is, not all playwrights can rewrite their work. Few want to say this aloud, but that is the truth: some writers cannot rewrite.

Sculpting and refining a scene based on what exists and what needs to be included to improve the story is an art in itself. It isn't about restraining the creative impulse, merely focusing it. To focus is to understand what works and why and then magnifying that in some instances and, in other instances, inserting it into other areas of the play. When the writer cannot see these changes, especially when working with a creative team that articulates why certain critical elements work and others work less well, the final draft will suffer. If the lack of rewrites significantly hampers the play, the producing theatre will sometimes table the production until later in the season; at other times the theatre must forge ahead.

The dramaturg has the responsibility of identifying whether the writer's response to rewrites or reshaping the work reveals someone with a slow, methodical approach; someone who is exploring with a purpose or simply exploring; someone who has no passion or connection for the work; or, someone who simply cannot make the rewrites. This unenviable position often places the dramaturg in the role of the "bad guy" and the focus of the writer's disappointment should the play be tabled to the next season or dropped entirely.

The active dramaturg faces much the same responsibility and response, but works to mitigate the writer's ire by presenting the playwright opportunities to step away or alter the process to accommodate the writer's needs. When postponing the production and moving opening day is not an option for the writer or the theatre, the active dramaturg listens for areas the writer wishes to change and focuses the work there. Sometimes this is enough to ignite a number of changes and the tide turns enough so that the play holds together. But remember: a dramaturg, active or otherwise, is not responsible for writing the play; in theatre that responsibility lies with the writer, and the writer alone. An active dramaturg can help facilitate a play's growth, which we hope leads to its success, but then we ask the eternal question: what defines success?

This may not be a bad question to ask a playwright: What would this process look like for you to call it a success? As the writer veers away from the goals or benchmarks that would result in a successful process—note the question does not involve the production elements or review—the active dramaturg may find it easier to help the writer return to the agreed upon path or identify how or why the path has changed. The writer may reveal that the play began as a writing exercise years ago and the reason and passion for the story no longer exists, thus providing the active dramaturg and the creative team a new approach for the process. Rewrites still may not arrive, but the reason for the delay is that the play itself no longer speaks to the writer, and not that the active dramaturg pushed the writer, that the actors aren't performing well, or that the director doesn't understand the story. No deflections, no excuses, no disintegrating relationships. The theatre may not have the play or production they want, but they still have an opportunity to salvage a relationship with the writer and in the end, that's what it's all about—relationships.

Final Thoughts

The goal when preparing a script for a premiere production is to obtain a text that works on stage. This differs greatly from workshop rehearsals, where the team works to clarify story, strengthen characters, and explore options—in short, build a better mousetrap. When preparing for the premiere production, the team looks for active solutions that work on stage. When plays move forward from workshop to pre-rehearsal production without answering the questions governing the critical elements, the writer, artistic team, and producers often experience conflict because each has a different idea regarding the play's strengths and areas for improvement. More often than not, theatres move ahead with a production when play development lives within this in between phase.

To move a production forward while juggling the needs of a theatre, the creative team, the active writer, and the play, can present the active dramaturg with considerable challenges. Identifying the elements that remain crucial for each artist and where the concerns overlap will serve the active dramaturg and the playwright's rewrite process well. Even so, the demands of rewriting for production often place tension on the process—writers may fear disrupting the balance of what works in the play and the producer's expectations. The dramaturg may be placed within the middle of this great tension. The active dramaturg seeks ways to keep communication open between the various parties and identifying ways to mitigate the fear of rewriting or stretching one's theatre to meet the play's needs. At the same time, active dramaturgs look to identify when procrastination and reluctance to move forward underscore something other than fear, a creative disconnect between the writer and the play's ideas, or preference to create over refining what exists.

Part III: The Dramaturgy Variations: Developing Play Development Skills

Introduction

The need for in-class exercises that allow all students to experience dramaturgy in action with some measure of safety exists. These exercises, like Sherlock Holmes' experiments, help focus the eye so that the active dramaturg learns to do more than see, and to observe; the active playwright, to engage fully and creatively; the actor and director, to contribute to the process. Even if one no longer takes or leads classes, engaging in an exercise or two keeps the mind sharp and allows new observational skills to develop and analytical skills to manifest. In truth, any artist interested in developing new work—director, actor, or playwright—will find these exercises useful.

The active dramaturg seeks opportunities that stretch and expand the dramaturgical skill set and, outside of numerous invitations to workshops and establishing relationships with new writers, exercises provide a great opportunity to delve more deeply into the craft or keep the skills sharp. Think of the dramaturgical exercise as equivalent to the actor's vocal exercises or warm-up; many actors may forgo these, but the best regularly use the exercises that work for and challenge them and for decades to come so that they can be heard in a theatre and/or on screen whether they yell or whisper.

The Dramaturgy Variations

The exercises in this section relate to each dramaturgy variation, and each provides options for three levels of challenge. Levels do not indicate just increased difficulty but also an expanded vision possibly requiring more people to complete the exercise. Even so, the active dramaturg can engage with each level alone or part of a group by choosing to consider the exercise as a problem set or as a scenario to prepare for as realistically as possible. The exercises create the opportunity to become comfortable with the active dramaturgical approach thereby improving one's artistic flexibility.

In general, the first level of the exercise helps active dramaturgs develop the basic skills needed for managing the first conversation with a playwright and posing open questions. The second provides an opportunity to learn the basics regarding moderating a discussion with actors. The third allows the active dramaturg to explore how to engage with a director and writer through improvisations to strengthen the scene. Each level builds upon the other while helping the active dramaturg, and those who use dramaturgical skills, to improve their future collaborations and in turn their ability to develop new work.

Of the four dramaturgy variations, only two include in-depth examples: Playing with Shakespeare and The Six- to Ten- to Fourteen-Line Scenes. These dramaturgy variations have a specific process that benefits from both narrative and in-process explanation. Each of the dramaturgy variations presents those interested in active dramaturgy, or any aspect of new-play work, an opportunity to become better acquainted with a specific role within play development work and the specific interplay between the playwright and the active dramaturg.

Final Thoughts

The temptation when crafting a game plan or entering into the frenzied pace of a new-play workshop is to establish a protocol and follow it to the letter. Although preparation will always serve the active dramaturg well, success comes when the work needed to formulate a game plan has been done, but willingness to follow the creative flow remains. Managing that collaborative evolution can sometimes appear chaotic or without structure. In truth, the plan that exists is based less on a predetermined course of action and more on flexibility informed by active listening for key words, phrases, or comments that connect to the major concerns the playwright and artistic team wish to explore during the workshop and connects to the identified areas of concern. The *art* of new-play dramaturgy comes about when balancing the critical elements, the key questions for development, and the writer's stated objectives and needs for the workshop, in ways that emanate naturally from conversations involving anyone participating in the workshop. The exercises throughout this section, but especially those based on the evolution of a Six-Line Scene into a Fourteen-Line Scene, help develop the creative muscles needed to navigate the development process throughout a strong creative thinker's entire career.

Dramaturgy Variation I: Improvisational Exercises for Play Development and Active Dramaturgy

Every once in awhile, the best way to help a writer envision the creative possibilities includes using improvisations to develop characters, crack open a scene, or explore the play's most significant question. If designed well, an improvised scene, moment, or character exploration, can unlock a writer's creativity in record time. Often the director, playwright, and dramaturg collaborate to design the givens of the improvisation and what the team wants to address or explore. Active dramaturgs also look at the unscripted explorations as opportunities to uncover clues to address the play's voice or overarching story.

A strong improvisation will capture everyone's attention and often end with someone exclaiming, "Did we film that?" or "We can just write this down and move on!" As great as the improvisation may be, it is just that—an in-the-moment solution to a set of questions by a particular group of actors who know things about the characters, play, and each other that may or may not exist in the play or future rehearsals. In other words, a short hand may exist to fuel the exercise but a word-for-word transcription often will rarely serve the play well because the actors' work that depended upon a short hand and other references that worked well in the moment, work less so on the page. Although the recorded improvisation may guide the writer, the playwright (active or not) needs to distill and shape the discoveries in order to ensure that the scene truly connects to the play's story, events, and voice.

The temptation to use the successful improvisation and its actor-generated exchanges will overwhelm the discussion, especially if the actors identify a way to connect and push the emotional limits of the scene through comic or dramatic dialogue and action. What the active dramaturg strives to identify is how or why the exchange or improvisation works. Simply claiming the dialogue without identifying and articulating the context and the crucial critical elements will not provide the play with a workable scene. Having the active dramaturg working with the playwright to identify these key moments can help the active playwright move through the development with greater efficiency.

Improvisations do shed light on challenging areas and at times they provide the exact solution or a way to solve a major problem. These complete solutions are rare. The active dramaturg and those who use dramaturgical skills in rehearsal, watch the improvised exercises with an eye to understand what works and why, rather than noting how to recreate it exactly.

Throughout, the active dramaturg not only notes potential solutions but identifies moments that might benefit from more exploration via an additional improvisation or discussion. Who participates in the discussions remains critical. Sometimes the director, playwright, and active dramaturg should consider how to use or further the improvisation. At other times, including the actors in the discussion greatly benefits the development and accelerates the process.

The Exercise: Improvisational Exercises for Play Development and Active Dramaturgy

Level I: Using a Set-Text Play to Build Experience

1. Identify a play with a challenging scene or question. For example, the proposal scene between Richard and Lady Anne in Shakespeare's *Richard III*.
2. Create a series of questions to explore. For example, how does Anne get to the point that she agrees to marry him?
3. Opt to create the improvisation in both the Elizabethan era and some other historical era or the current era.
4. Have the active dramaturg note key moments that indicate where shifts need to occur or what information needs to be revealed; remember, the necessary shifts may not include dialogue but stage directions or simply actors conveying meaning now that they are more familiar with the scene.

The improvisation can begin as an exercise to understand character motivation and then repeat to explore contemporary ways the characters might communicate or relate with one another. In either scenario, the active dramaturg listens for clues the team might use to strengthen the performance of the scene Shakespeare wrote. If using this exercise to fuel an adaptation of Shakespeare's play, the active dramaturg listens for the moments of tension, twists, or places where the team might explore these key elements of drama in the adaptation. The active dramaturg also listens for thematic ideas that buoy the adaptation.

Level II: Using Improvisation to Build a New Play

1. Have the group or individual create a brief scenario or question for exploration. Create a scenario or prompt that suggests an obstacle or tension. For example, a love story where no one is in love. As one gains experience, identify other stories or plots without identifying the obstacle or tension in the prompt so that the active dramaturg develops the skill of identifying a strong tension or theme that will inspire dramatic tension.
2. If necessary, introduce either a fact in a character's history or obstacle for each character or participant.
3. Have the active dramaturg listen for and identify the key questions or themes that evolve.
4. Discuss how the discoveries in Step 3 might grow into a scene or play.

To identify key elements or moments, listen for the Moments of Zen within the improvisation and the meditation moments, listen for repeated phases that transform in meaning, listen for the pauses and unusual ways of using language to communicate.

Level III: Using Images to Inspire an Improvisation

1. Have the group or individual build a world and story around an image. First use a representational photograph, image, or drawing. For a challenge, use a nonrepresentational image such as a Jackson Pollack or Kandinsky painting.
2. If necessary, introduce either a fact in a character's history or obstacle for each character or participant.
3. Have the active dramaturg listen for and identify the key questions or themes that evolve.
4. Discuss how the discoveries in Step 3 might grow into a scene or play.

To identify key elements or moments, listen for the Moments of Zen within the improvisation and the meditation moments, listen for repeated phases that transform in meaning, and listen for the pauses and unusual ways of using language to communicate.

As the improvised exercises progress, use the ideas for moderating discussions during rehearsal from Chapter 6 and reflections based on the critical elements to aid in expanding the story, character, and world to devise a solid scene or play.

Dramaturgy Variation II: The Manuscript-Based Improvisation

Most dramaturgy in the United States involves developing existing manuscripts rather than devising a play through improvisation. Whether the manuscript falls into the category of the ten-minute play, a one-act, or a ninety-minute or full-length (two acts or longer) play, the basic steps and approach remains the same. Developing the dramaturgical muscles needed for play development by working on a ten-minute play or short one-acts, provides the parallels an active dramaturg needs much like a playwriting student learns about form and structure by writing a ten-minute or one-act play, or a director or actor hones their craft through scene work. Every artist must start somewhere.

The key to this exercise is identifying unpublished manuscripts. Published plays appear finished on the page, making it difficult to engage with them as one would an untested manuscript. Even plays that are unpublished, but have a limited production history pose challenges for this set of exercises because individuals can use the Internet to learn more about the play. The benefit of using unproduced works—and redacting the playwright's name after securing permission to use the scripts in class—allows anyone studying how to apply dramaturgical skills to best mimic the process of reading and identifying new work for play development workshops or festivals.

The Heart of The Manuscript-Based Improvisation

The manuscript exercise focuses on building professional skills such as writing play reports and using those reports to lobby for that play's place in a new-play workshop, a festival of new work, and the initial development conversations. Through these activities, everyone gains insight into how directors, dramaturgs, and even playwrights use active dramaturgy daily. Participants learn by adopting the persona of either the active playwright or the active dramaturg for the manuscript—and then switching roles. Each participant experiences how the other approaches play development and responds to the critically creative process. The improvisational element lies within the willingness to adopt not only the role of dramaturg and playwright but an ability to delve deeply because of preparation and to invest fully in the exercise itself to assume the persona of the writer and the active dramaturg. Beyond basic skill-building exercises, The manuscript-based improvisation provides anyone studying dramaturgical approaches the opportunity to assume the persona of the active playwright and become more aware of the active playwright's process. Playwrights who participate in the exercise have the opportunity to engage in the work and development process from a creative distance (because they did not originate the work) and can take risks, and learn to hear and respond to critical comments with emotional distance. In short, when working with anonymous manuscripts, everyone can focus on developing collaboration skills safely and better understand the play's world, voice, and intent from a creative distance.

The freedom to approach the exercise so fully invites the active dramaturg (and anyone else participating) to become more acquainted with the writer's process, mindset, and passion. Finding ways to better identify or relate to the writer's process helps the active dramaturg facilitate the workshop and developmental process more effectively. Also, the active dramaturg quickly learns the importance of establishing a window into the work—discovering ways to reveal how the work speaks to, fuels, and supports a creative passion. Too often dramaturgs and others approach the new play as an object that simply exists. A play formed through passion, however, does more than exist (even if it needs work) it will, given the right attention and a playwright willing to do the work, continue to grow and evolve into a work of art not just an *objet d'art*.

The Challenge of the Dramaturgical Improvisation

Without question, the greatest challenge when completing this exercise comes when the dramaturg (or any participant) assumes the persona of the playwright. True, few dramaturgs consider themselves performers and even this minor foray into the land of make believe is enough to paralyze some with fear, but this is an improvisation and everyone, especially the active dramaturg, should engage with this process without the fear of doing it right. Yes, the exercise's success requires the use of certain acting muscles and a bit of imagination, but there are no right or wrong answers. Every action, answer, question, and emotional response presents a learning opportunity. Focusing on developing listening skills and the patience play development requires will help. No theatre student conquered *Hamlet* at the first read or the fiftieth. What the actor did learn is how the process works and how to develop performance and rehearsal processes that serve the play and the actor's skill set.

The second greatest fear many dramaturgy students experience during this exercise is the requirement that the person who assumes the writer's role must articulate an intent and passion for the story. Many remark that, even after studying the work, they do not know how to answer questions regarding passion for the work and the drive to write. Yes, a key tenet of dramaturgy is to not assume, to use the facts of the play to arrive at a logical conclusion or a plausible possibility that once discussed may be deemed more right than wrong. Fear not. If one uses the play's facts with a bit of imagination during this exercise, all of the correct habits are reinforced and muscles developed. In addition, to do so allows the active dramaturgy student to move closer to the playwright's creative spirit reducing the gulf between them, facilitating a more fulfilling collaboration.

To repeat: the exercise does not emphasize making assumptions. It depends upon and expects that the active dramaturg will use the play's facts and its critical elements to inform the dramaturgical improvisation. To become comfortable letting go and exploring the play from the inside out is crucial in becoming a truly active dramaturg. The dramaturgical improvisation lends itself to these discoveries and the challenges that accompany such an exploration.

When the active playwright assumes the role of the active dramaturg, a similar struggle occurs. The playwright who uses the critical elements to identify the play's facts will be successful and discover a way to understand both the play's skeleton and its outer flesh. In addition, the playwright exploring the active dramaturg's role must balance a desire to create and facilitate creation and revision.

A Note about Manuscripts: Professional Discretion Is Advised

- ◆ Always secure the writer's permission.
- ◆ Always remove the playwright's name for the exercise, especially in a class setting.
- ◆ Always have the manuscripts returned before moving to another activity or the end of the semester.

Because anonymity is key, no one should discuss the manuscripts outside the class or skill-building workshop. Once the exercise or class concludes, sharing the writer's identity and the play's production history (as well as any changes that occurred) may prove beneficial, but is not necessary.

If the exercise is executed outside a classroom environment, the same guidelines apply. Also, comments and thoughts about the manuscript (one's passion for or one's dislike of) should remain between the individuals involved in the manuscript-based exercise. If the manuscript truly excites you, look for opportunities to present it, and if an opportunity to work with the writer arises, remember to begin at the beginning without any assumption that the discoveries or solutions made during the improvisations will be appropriate for the actual writer's vision.

In other words: what happens in the classroom or rehearsal hall stays in the classroom or rehearsal hall.

The Dramaturgical Improvisation: The Manuscript-Based Improvisation

Level I: Active Dramaturgy and Literary Management

Create a reader response form.

1. What basic information might others in your company need to know about the play? Create areas on the form to address these areas of interest.

2. Consider the key elements needed for someone to best assess a script's viability for a reading or production at the theatre and be sure to include those elements on the form.
3. Consider: How many readers are there in your organization? How to ensure a balanced and fair review of the manuscript?

Use this form when engaging in other manuscript-based activities. How does this form differ from recording the reflection process for a creative team conversation?

Level II: Active Dramaturgy and Selecting Plays for a Festival

You are part of a two- to four-person team charged with creating a festival of new work.

1. Choose a festival producer and at least one other person to round out the team: a director, a literary manager, a playwright, a dramaturg. Each has a vote in deciding the festival. (Take turns assuming each role.)
2. Each member of the team should bring his or her top choices based on the play reports.
3. Consider the goals of your festival. For example: What does your festival/theatre seek to produce? Does your festival focus on devised-only work? Does your festival develop musicals? Does your festival look for work that is ready or almost ready for production?
4. How long will your workshop be? A three-day workshop; a four- to seven-day workshop; a fourteen- to thirty-day workshop?
5. Consider whether cast size impacts selection.
6. Consider how the festival will be presented and to whom—subscribers or invited guests or theatre professionals only.

Variation   Change the length of your festival: three-day workshop; four- to seven-day workshop; fourteen- to thirty-day workshop.

Variation   Create a budget for the festival. Consider who your artists are and where they come from—locally or will they travel to you—how much will actors be paid, and what are the housing needs.

Level III: Dramaturgical Improvisation

1. Find a partner.
2. Choose two manuscripts from your reader reports or festival lineup—one from your list, one from your partner's. Identify who will serve as the active playwright and the active dramaturg for one manuscript, Manuscript A. The pair will swap roles for the second manuscript, Manuscript B.

3. Read the two manuscripts in your respective roles—as the active playwright or the active dramaturg. Note how the reading process may or may not change.

4. Come together for the first meeting before the workshop. Both the active dramaturg and active playwright should prepare for this meeting according to their chosen roles. The preparation includes understanding the play and identifying goals for the conversation or workshop. DO NOT prepare the actual conversation in advance. Everything that occurs during the meeting should be spontaneous. The **only** preparation is individual homework. You may also prepare a back pocket question or two.

5. Have the conversation. During the conversation, the active playwright should feel free to respond fully and truthfully. If the active dramaturg poses an upsetting question or angers the writer, the active writer should say so and not feel the need to be tactful. **This is an exercise designed to identify areas to develop**. If the writer feels the need to walk out of the room, do so. Avoid being rude just to be rude; the goal is for each pair to become a better artist.

6. Conclude the meeting.

7. Each person should reflect on the meeting and craft notes and reflections on the conversation—for their role (active writer or active dramaturg) and the active dramaturg should craft dramaturgical notes for the playwright. This reflection may occur in front of the class or through privately crafted notes or a combination of both.

8. Come together for a second meeting. Discuss the dramaturgical notes for the playwright. Discuss any progress that has been made—lines written, sections cut or reordered, or a new plan—or has nothing happened. **Even though the active playwright for this exercise is not the actual writer, small changes or an outline of changes may be crafted—for the exercise only.**

9. Discuss the progress or lack thereof.

10. Conclude the second meeting.

11. Repeat Step #7.

Note: For the person adopting the role of active playwright, feel free to respond fully as a writer might. If a question strikes you as odd or insulting, respond so that the active dramaturg knows it. Also, if changes are made, be mindful that the goal is to discuss the intention and the direction the new work takes the play. Because this is not the actual writer, character voice may not match. This is less of a ghostwriting exercise and more of a way to practice navigating the active playwright/active dramaturg conversation and collaboration process.

Variation   Alter your personality: you may become quiet; you may become argumentative; you may keep a civil tone but insist on your point with passion.

Playwright Variation   Choose to be a difficult playwright who will not make one change.

Playwright Variation   Choose to be a playwright who is easily led and makes any change suggested.

Playwright Variation   Choose to be a playwright who acquiesces in the meeting, but has no intention of making a change.

Dramaturg Variation   Choose to be a dramaturg with an agenda—either personal or the theatre's.

Dramaturg Variation   Choose to be a dramaturg who agrees with the writer at any cost.

Dramaturg Variation   Choose to be a dramaturg who directs the writer.

Time   No more than 15 minutes for each active playwright/active dramaturg conversation.

Repeat, using the other manuscript, Manuscript B. Notice how the different personalities impact the play's evolution. Was it possible to strike a middle ground? Did either participant change their approach when the conversation appeared to stall or meander?

Level III: Dramaturgical Improvisation: Role Swap

Repeat Level II, but this time swap roles for each manuscript. The active dramaturg for Manuscript A is now the active playwright for Manuscript A, and the active playwright becomes the active dramaturg. Note how your former relationship to the play impacts (helps or hinders) your participation in this exercise.

Repeat both the role swap and the exercise in Level II for Manuscript B.

Time   15 minutes

Variation   Choose a scene to review during the conversation.

Variation   Present a major revision during the conversation (removing a character, changing the ending, etc.).

Dramaturgy Variation III: Playing with Shakespeare

Shaping a play through cutting lines presents unique challenges. As discussed earlier in Chapter 3, the process of eliminating lines in a set-text play to affect the running time allows the active dramaturg to become better acquainted with the text and to better understand the delicate balance between character and story. One line may appear superfluous or be cut in most productions, but upon closer examination those few words can reveal a new world order or shift in power. Taking the time to cut a few scenes in set-text plays attunes the new-play dramaturg's ear: to language; the ability to track character and story evolution; and to identify the skips in logic a minor or major cut presents as the writer discusses them.

The Exercise: Playing with Shakespeare

This exercise focuses exclusively on cutting a scene within a Shakespearean text and then adapting other full-length plays to achieve a shorter running time. An active dramaturg may adapt a Shakespearean text by placing the story in a new locale or era such as *Richard III* to Germany in the late 1930s/early 1940s or *Hamlet* to New York City near the millennium. Many adaptations require the artistic team and active dramaturg to identify how Shakespeare's lines might resonate more deeply or differently in these new contexts. In Richard Loncraine's *Richard III* set in the 1930s, the famous line, "A horse, a horse, my kingdom for a horse!" reveals Richard's desperation because in spite of this modern era, no cars, tanks, or trucks are at hand; Richard is at such a loss, he would gladly give away his kingdom for a horse to escape. Suddenly, an oft-quoted line sounds fresh because the context changed and brought the line's truest meaning back to both the play and character. In Michael Almereyda's *Hamlet* set in the late 1990s, Elsinore is a multinational corporation with its headquarters in New York rather than a Danish kingdom, which brings the story into the twentieth century well and shifts the relationship of a king to his people to an employer and his employees. The delicate balance between a line of dialogue's impact on the story becomes quite apparent during exercises with parameters similar to Loncraine's and Almereyda's adaptations. The exercise, Playing with Shakespeare, does not qualify as new-play development. However, the exercise, which focuses on cutting lines or eliminating characters while maintaining the story's integrity, does help hone play development skills.

As an example, take the scene where Macbeth first encounters the weird sisters in Shakespeare's *Macbeth*, act 1.3. Although some find it tempting to read for cuts while reading the scene (or play) for the first time (or the first time in a long while), avoid that temptation. When encountering any manuscript or scene, first read to simply understand the flow of action, story, and nature of the scene. Next, read through the scene to identify the basic plot points that must remain. For example, in Scene 1.3 we learn an important fact: the prophesy has come true, Macbeth has become the thane of Cawdor. Identify other facts that must remain and consider marking them in a way so that they stand out to avoid

> Dramaturgs who focus on new plays might never work on a Shakespearean drama. For these dramaturgs, skills needed to cut set-texts wane. Cutting new plays differs because the opportunity to request a few brief passages to connect the disconnected passages exists. When working on set-texts, the possibility for additional dialogue no longer exists, and it is possible to see how the cuts truly transform the story's shape.

accidentally cutting them. In the example that appears at the end of this section, the lines with essential storytelling facts are highlighted.

While marking these important passages, a few less obvious cuts pop out like lines 84 and 85, "Or have we eaten on the insane root / That takes the reason prisoner?" Avoid eliminating them during this pass. Yes, the lines describe the emotional landscape and, depending upon other lines that resonate with the creative team's vision, could reveal a lot about character and how Banquo and Macbeth interact easily with one another. But, because one might want to cut the lines or trim them in ways that allow for the characters' journeys to illustrate how aspects of their friendship were ruined as power corrupts Macbeth; wait until the second or third pass to actually cut or trim the lines. When reading for the facts, avoid eliminating lines that indicate the emotional landscape. Simply become better acquainted with the scene's facts and emotional landscape, and mark these areas so that during the next steps you remember to look at their impact on what the entire play becomes.

During the second pass, look to determine which lines reveal *critical* emotional journeys or character evolution or the emotional landscape. Consider underlining these lines in pencil to help differentiate and track them throughout the exercise. In the example that follows, some of the underlined lines present humor and show the weird sisters to have distinct personalities—for example, one is extremely long-winded. Other lines, 106–9, reveal Banquo and Macbeth's desire to proceed with caution.

MacBeth's soliloquy "This supernatural soliciting" begins at line 130 and presents an opportunity to set a rule for speeches—to cut or not to cut. During a first pass, the choice to retain the speech makes great sense no matter how well known the soliloquy is. After reading for critical emotional moments, the active dramaturg considers whether to trim a few lines and, after a quick read, whether to eliminate the speech altogether. Some speeches such as MacBeth's dagger speech or Hamlet's "To be or not to be" should never be removed from a production purporting to present the Bard's work. Lesser known speeches often do not appear in the final cut, but do not assume that because a speech is less well known it should be cut. In many ways, these lesser-known speeches present actors an opportunity to truly shine and a creative team a chance to highlight a unique approach in memorable ways. In short, take time to consider retaining the complete speech.

Following the next three or four passes, explore the elements of a scene. To do so, begin making cuts—in pencil—by eliminating some of the non-highlighted or underlined areas. As an exercise, provide yourself with a target such as thirty or forty lines (depending upon the length of scene). For the example that appears at the end of this section, let's start by cutting twenty lines. After cutting these twenty lines, audiences still learn that Cawdor is thought to be a traitor, the soliloquy remains, Banquo and Macbeth's reliance upon each other (they discuss ideas and share opinions) remains.

If the scene needs to be shortened further and the soliloquy is to remain uncut, the first weird sister's lines regarding the woman with chestnuts in her lap might be trimmed. This alters the perception of the weird sisters, but keeps the political intrigue intact. Should even more cuts be needed, look to Ross' and Angus' lines.

Take care when looking at comic sections or passages of quick repartee or rhyming patterns. These cuts need to balance the language pattern and the pause they often provide. The drunken guard's speech in *Macbeth* does more than present a soldier who impedes a power hungry warrior, the speech provides a great deal of levity within an otherwise dark and humorless world and grounds the supernaturally inspired action in the real world.

Here is what the completed process—with each exploratory step combined—looks like. Highlights for facts; underlined text for critical emotional moments; strikethroughs for cut lines.

First Witch	I myself have all the other,	
	And the very ports they blow,	15
	All the quarters that they know	
	I' the shipman's card.	
	I will drain him dry as hay:	
	Sleep shall neither night nor day	
	Hang upon his pent-house lid;	20
	He shall live a man forbid:	
	Weary se'n nights nine times nine	
	Shall he dwindle, peak and pine:	
	Though his bark cannot be lost,	
	Yet it shall be tempest-tost.	25
	Look what I have.	
Second Witch	Show me, show me.	
First Witch	Here I have a pilot's thumb,	
	Wreck'd as homeward he did come.	
	Drum within.	
Third Witch	A drum, a drum!	30
	Macbeth doth come.	
ALL	The weird sisters, hand in hand,	
	Posters of the sea and land,	
	Thus do go about, about:,	
	Thrice to thine and thrice to mine,	35
	And thrice again, to make up nine	
	Peace! the charm's wound up.	
	Enter MACBETH and BANQUO.	
MACBETH	So foul and fair a day I have not seen.	
BANQUO	How far is't call'd to Forres? What are these	
	So wither'd and so wild in their attire,	40
	That look not like the inhabitants o' the earth,	
	And yet are on't? Live you? Or are you aught	
	That man may question? You seem to understand me,	
	By each at once her choppy finger laying	

	Upon her skinny lips: you should be women,	45
	And yet your beards forbid me to interpret	
	That you are so.	

MACBETH   Speak, if you can: what are you?

First Witch   All hail, Macbeth! hail to thee, thane of Glamis!

Second Witch   All hail, Macbeth, hail to thee, thane of Cawdor!

Third Witch   All hail, Macbeth, thou shalt be king hereafter!   50

BANQUO   Good sir, why do you start; and seem to fear
                Things that do sound so fair? I' the name of truth,
                Are ye fantastical, or that indeed
                Which outwardly ye show? My noble partner
                You greet with present grace and great prediction   55
                Of noble having and of royal hope,
                That he seems rapt withal: to me you speak not.
                If you can look into the seeds of time,
                And say which grain will grow and which will not,
                Speak then to me, who neither beg nor fear   60
                Your favours nor your hate.

First Witch   Hail!

Second Witch   Hail!

Third Witch   Hail!

First Witch   Lesser than Macbeth, and greater.   65

Second Witch   Not so happy, yet much happier.

Third Witch   Thou shalt get kings, though thou be none:
                So all hail, Macbeth and Banquo!

First Witch   Banquo and Macbeth, all hail!

MACBETH   Stay, you imperfect speakers, tell me more: 70
                By Sinel's death I know I am thane of Glamis;
                But how of Cawdor? The thane of Cawdor lives,
                A prosperous gentleman; and to be king
                Stands not within the prospect of belief,
                No more than to be Cawdor. Say from whence   75
                You owe this strange intelligence? or why
                Upon this blasted heath you stop our way
                With such prophetic greeting? Speak, I charge you.
                Witches vanish.

BANQUO   The earth hath bubbles, as the water has,
                And these are of them. Whither are they vanish'd?   80

MACBETH   Into the air; and what seem'd corporal melted
             As breath into the wind. Would they had stay'd!

BANQUO   Were such things here as we do speak about?
             Or have we eaten on the insane root
             That takes the reason prisoner?   85

MACBETH   Your children shall be kings.

BANQUO   You shall be king.

MACBETH   And thane of Cawdor too: went it not so?

BANQUO   To the selfsame tune and words. Who's here?
             Enter ROSS and ANGUS.

ROSS   The king hath happily received, Macbeth,
             The news of thy success; and when he reads   90
             Thy personal venture in the rebels' fight,
             His wonders and his praises do contend
             Which should be thine or his: silenced with that,
             In viewing o'er the rest o' the selfsame day,
             He finds thee in the stout Norweyan ranks,   95
             Nothing afeard of what thyself didst make,
             Strange images of death. As thick as tale
             Came post with post; and every one did bear
             Thy praises in his kingdom's great defence,
             And pour'd them down before him.

ANGUS   We are sent   100
             To give thee from our royal master thanks;
             Only to herald thee into his sight,
             Not pay thee.

ROSS   And, for an earnest of a greater honour,
             He bade me, from him, call thee thane of Cawdor: 105
             In which addition, hail, most worthy thane!
             For it is thine.

BANQUO   What, can the devil speak true?

MACBETH   The thane of Cawdor lives: why do you dress me
             In borrow'd robes?

ANGUS   Who was the thane lives yet;
             But under heavy judgment bears that life   110
             Which he deserves to lose. Whether he was combined
             With those of Norway, or did line the rebel
             With hidden help and vantage, or that with both
             He labour'd in his country's wrack, I know not;
             But treasons capital, confess'd and proved,   115
             Have overthrown him.

MACBETH   *Aside.*
                   ~~Glamis, and Thane of Cawdor:~~
               ~~The greatest is behind.~~ *To ROSS and ANGUS.*
               ~~Thanks for your pains.~~
               To BANQUO.
               ~~Do you not hope your children shall be kings,~~
               ~~When those that gave the thane of Cawdor to me~~
               ~~Promised no less to them?~~

BANQUO   ~~That trusted home~~   120
               ~~Might yet enkindle you unto the crown,~~
               ~~Besides the thane of Cawdor. But 'tis strange:~~
               ~~And oftentimes, to win us to our harm,~~
               ~~The instruments of darkness tell us truths,~~
               ~~Win us with honest trifles, to betray's~~   125
               ~~In deepest consequence.~~
               ~~Cousins, a word, I pray you.~~

MACBETH   *Aside.*
                   ~~Two truths are told,~~
               ~~As happy prologues to the swelling act~~
               ~~Of the imperial theme. — I thank you, gentlemen.~~
               Aside.
               This supernatural soliciting   130
               Cannot be ill, cannot be good: if ill,
               Why hath it given me earnest of success,
               Commencing in a truth? I am thane of Cawdor:
               If good, why do I yield to that suggestion
               Whose horrid image doth unfix my hair   135
               And make my seated heart knock at my ribs,
               Against the use of nature? Present fears
               Are less than horrible imaginings:
               My thought, whose murder yet is but fantastical,
               Shakes so my single state of man that function   140
               Is smother'd in surmise, and nothing is
               But what is not.

BANQUO   Look, how our partner's rapt.

~~MACBETH~~   ~~*Aside*~~
               ~~If chance will have me king, why, chance may crown me,~~
               ~~Without my stir.~~

BANQUO   New honors come upon him
               Like our strange garments, cleave not to their mould   145
               But with the aid of use.

MACBETH   *Aside.*
               Come what come may,
               Time and the hour runs through the roughest day.

BANQUO   Worthy Macbeth, we stay upon your leisure.

MACBETH   Give me your favour: my dull brain was wrought
               With things forgotten. Kind gentlemen, your pains   150
               Are register'd where every day I turn
               The leaf to read them. Let us toward the king.
               Think upon what hath chanced, and, at more time,
               The interim having weigh'd it, let us speak
               Our free hearts each to other.

BANQUO   Very gladly.   155

MACBETH   Till then, enough. Come, friends.
               [*Exeunt*]

Here is the edited scene:

ACT I SCENE III

               A heath near Forres.
               Thunder. Enter the three Witches.

First Witch   Where hast thou been, sister?

Second Witch   Killing swine.

Third Witch   Sister, where thou?

First Witch   A sailor's wife had chestnuts in her lap,
               And munch'd, and munch'd, and munch'd:—
               'Give me,' quoth I: 5
               'Aroint thee, witch!' the rump-fed ronyon cries.
               Her husband's to Aleppo gone, master o' the Tiger:
               But in a sieve I'll thither sail,
               And, like a rat without a tail,
               I'll do, I'll do, and I'll do.   10

Second Witch   Show me, show me.

First Witch   Here I have a pilot's thumb,
               Wreck'd as homeward he did come.
               Drum within.

Third Witch   A drum, a drum!   30
               Macbeth doth come.

ALL	The weird sisters, hand in hand,
	Posters of the sea and land,
	Thus do go about, about:
	Thrice to thine and thrice to mine 35
	And thrice again, to make up nine.
	Peace! the charm's wound up.
	Enter MACBETH and BANQUO.

| MACBETH | So foul and fair a day I have not seen. |

BANQUO	How far is't call'd to Forres? What are these
	So wither'd and so wild in their attire, 40
	That look not like the inhabitants o' the earth,
	And yet are on't? Live you? or are you aught
	That man may question? You seem to understand me,
	By each at once her choppy finger laying
	Upon her skinny lips: you should be women, 45
	And yet your beards forbid me to interpret
	That you are so.

| MACBETH | Speak, if you can: what are you? |

| First Witch | All hail, Macbeth! hail to thee, thane of Glamis! |

| Second Witch | All hail, Macbeth, hail to thee, thane of Cawdor! |

| Third Witch | All hail, Macbeth, thou shalt be king hereafter!   50 |

BANQUO	Good sir, why do you start; and seem to fear
	Things that do sound so fair? I' the name of truth,
	Are ye fantastical, or that indeed
	Which outwardly ye show? My noble partner
	You greet with present grace and great prediction 55
	Of noble having and of royal hope,
	That he seems rapt withal: to me you speak not.
	If you can look into the seeds of time,
	And say which grain will grow and which will not,
	Speak then to me, who neither beg nor fear 60
	Your favours nor your hate.

| First Witch | Hail! |

| Second Witch | Hail! |

| Third Witch | Hail! |

| First Witch | Lesser than Macbeth, and greater.   65 |

| Second Witch | Not so happy, yet much happier. |

| Third Witch | Thou shalt get kings, though thou be none: |
| | So all hail, Macbeth and Banquo! |

First Witch   Banquo and Macbeth, all hail!

MACBETH   Stay, you imperfect speakers, tell me more: 70
By Sinel's death I know I am thane of Glamis;
But how of Cawdor? the thane of Cawdor lives,
A prosperous gentleman; and to be king
Stands not within the prospect of belief,
No more than to be Cawdor. Say from whence   75
With such prophetic greeting? Speak, I charge you.
Witches vanish.

BANQUO   The earth hath bubbles, as the water has,
And these are of them. Whither are they vanish'd?   80

MACBETH   Into the air; and what seem'd corporal melted
As breath into the wind. Would they had stay'd!

BANQUO   Were such things here as we do speak about?
Or have we eaten on the insane root
That takes the reason prisoner?   85

MACBETH   Your children shall be kings.

BANQUO   You shall be king.

MACBETH   And thane of Cawdor too: went it not so?

BANQUO   To the selfsame tune and words. Who's here?
Enter ROSS and ANGUS.

ROSS   The king hath happily received, Macbeth,
The news of thy success; and when he reads   90
Thy personal venture in the rebels' fight,
His wonders and his praises do contend
Thy praises in his kingdom's great defence,
And pour'd them down before him.

ANGUS   We are sent   100
To give thee from our royal master thanks;
Only to herald thee into his sight,
Not pay thee.

ROSS   And, for an earnest of a greater honour,
He bade me, from him, call thee thane of Cawdor: 105
In which addition, hail, most worthy thane!
For it is thine.

BANQUO   What, can the devil speak true?

MACBETH   The thane of Cawdor lives: why do you dress me
In borrow'd robes?

ANGUS   Who was the thane lives yet;
But under heavy judgment bears that life   110
Which he deserves to lose. Whether he was combined
With those of Norway, or did line the rebel
With hidden help and vantage, or that with both
He labour'd in his country's wrack, I know not;
But treasons capital, confess'd and proved,   115
Have overthrown him.

MACBETH   *Aside.*
    Glamis, and Thane of Cawdor:
The greatest is behind. *To ROSS and ANGUS.* Thanks
for your pains.
To BANQUO.
Do you not hope your children shall be kings,
When those that gave the thane of Cawdor to me
Promised no less to them?

BANQUO   That trusted home   120
Might yet enkindle you unto the crown,
Besides the thane of Cawdor. But 'tis strange:
And oftentimes, to win us to our harm,
The instruments of darkness tell us truths,
Win us with honest trifles, to betray's   125
In deepest consequence.
Cousins, a word, I pray you.

MACBETH   *Aside.*
    Two truths are told,
As happy prologues to the swelling act
Of the imperial theme. — I thank you, gentlemen.
Aside.
This supernatural soliciting   130
Cannot be ill, cannot be good: if ill,
Why hath it given me earnest of success,
Commencing in a truth? I am thane of Cawdor:
If good, why do I yield to that suggestion
Whose horrid image doth unfix my hair   135
And make my seated heart knock at my ribs,
Against the use of nature? Present fears
Are less than horrible imaginings:
My thought, whose murder yet is but fantastical,
Shakes so my single state of man that function   140
Is smother'd in surmise, and nothing is
But what is not.

BANQUO   Look, how our partner's rapt.

BANQUO New honors come upon him,
Like our strange garments, cleave not to their mould
But with the aid of use.

MACBETH *Aside.*
Come what come may,
Time and the hour runs through the roughest day.

BANQUO Worthy Macbeth, we stay upon your leisure.

MACBETH Give me your favour: my dull brain was wrought
With things forgotten. Kind gentlemen, your pains 150
Are register'd where every day I turn
The leaf to read them. Let us toward the king.
Think upon what hath chanced, and, at more time,
The interim having weigh'd it, let us speak
Our free hearts each to other.

BANQUO Very gladly. 155

MACBETH Till then, enough. Come, friends.
[*Exeunt*]

Level I: Tragedy

1. Find a scene within a Shakespearean tragedy
2. Read the scene for sense and understanding.
3. Read the scene a second time. Highlight the lines associated with major and essential plot points and dramatic events.
4. Read the scene a third time. Underline lines associated with revealing character or the tenor of the play's world.
5. Consider the impact of the speeches and humorous moments. Should they stay or go?
6. Cut twenty lines from the scene.

Variation Cut thirty lines.

Variation Reshape a soliloquy that occurs within the scene.

Level II: Comedy

1. Find a scene within a Shakespearean comedy
2. Read the scene for sense and understanding.
3. Read the scene a second time. Highlight the lines associated with major and essential plot points and dramatic events.
4. Read the scene a third time. Underline lines associated with revealing character or the tenor of the play's world.

5. Consider the impact of the speeches and humorous moments. Should they stay or go?
6. Cut twenty lines from the scene.

Variation   Eliminate thirty lines.

Variation   Reshape a soliloquy that occurs within the scene.

Level III: Playing with Other Set-Text Plays

1. Find a scene within a set-text play (see note below).
2. Read the scene for sense and understanding.
3. Read the scene a second time. Highlight the lines associated with major and essential plot points and dramatic events.
4. Read the scene a third time. Underline lines associated with revealing character or the tenor of the play's world.
5. Consider the impact of the speeches and humorous moments. Should they stay or go?
6. Cut twenty lines from the scene

Challenge   Transform a ninety-minute play into forty-five minutes.

Note: As the dramatic cannon evolves, the length of plays lessens. Cutting twenty lines from a Eugene O'Neill or Theodore Ward scene is easier (and more often done) than deleting lines from an Adrienne Kennedy or Caryl Churchill play. Even so, attempting to trim or cut a short contemporary play develops editing and analytical skills. A cut version of Kennedy's or Churchill's plays may never see the light of day, but the ability to trim even extremely tight dialogue will serve every artist well.

Dramaturgy Variation IV: The Six- to Ten- to Fourteen-Line Scenes

What follows are the three stages of a single activity: developing the six-line scene into a fourteen-line scene. For this dramaturgical variation, the initial six-line scene is workshopped and transformed into a ten, and then a fourteen-line scene. Although each step focuses on a different aspect of the development process, each highlights how a small, strategically placed dramaturgical question can lead to a change that can enhance or clarify the scene's story or facilitate the creative process. The exercise also illustrates how a poorly designed dramaturgical question can hinder a play's growth.

The six- to fourteen-line process closely mirrors the development process for new works of any length: the active writer writes; actors read the work aloud; active dramaturgs and others discuss the work and pose questions to help further exploration;

rewrites occur; and the work is read aloud again or presented. By closely exploring the evolution of six lines to fourteen, the basic structure and philosophy governing developments may be seen and ways to rehearse this process outside the workshop process revealed.

The Exercise: The Six- to Ten- to Fourteen-Line Scenes

This exercise challenges everyone interested in new plays from the active dramaturg to the active playwright to the actor and the director. When completed in a group setting, this exercise provides everyone insight into the play development experience. Because anyone can be the writer—and everyone should take a turn in each role—a true appreciation for the entire process emerges. When completed, each artist gains insight into the other's craft and responsibilities within the earliest phases of the workshop experience.

This exercise may be completed in the classroom or some steps at home (such as rewrites). Setting time limits for each step helps focus thoughts and develop the active dramaturg's ability to be flexible and limit the active playwright's need to perfect the writing; much the same may be said for the others participating in this exercise. Everyone learns how to focus their thoughts and questions in order to improve the work.

As in a number of other chapters, analysis and criticism accompanies first the dramaturg's notes and then an example of the active dramaturg's notes appears. Because these exercises mirror the creative conversation in a workshop process, one comment can lead the participants down a path with many twists and turns. To shape as realistic an example as possible, the creative conversations that model the dramaturg conversations, and then the active dramaturg conversations, do not align as closely as the bad notes to good notes or bad question into open question in previous chapters. Even though the modeled dialogues will not demonstrate how to change one less effective statement directly into a more effective one, the scripted creative conversations do wrestle with the same questions and concerns.

An In-Depth Look at the Six-Line Scene Exercise

Write a Six-Line Scene: Five to Seven Minutes   For this exercise, writing within a brief period of time allows the ideas to flow without too much editorializing or second-guessing. The goal of this initial step is to place ideas on the page. True, no one writing the six lines may have a true passion for the subject or the play, but this lack of attachment aids in helping writers find ways to either identify or re-identify and connect or re-connect with the creative impulse. Keep in mind that six lines of dialogue does not mean six sentences. A line of dialogue is defined as one character speaking and may be composed of many sentences or words approximating sentences.

The Dramaturg's Game Plan   When preparing to collaborate on a piece, an active dramaturg begins to assemble a game plan or an approach. With a six-line scene that no one has read aloud or heard, it may appear that no game plan will exist. Initially, the dramaturg's game plan is to simply listen.

The Active Dramaturg's Game Plan   The active dramaturg establishes a plan to listen carefully, identify repetitions or areas that might inspire repetitions, and uncover themes or large ideas that emerge and may be developed. The active dramaturg identifies the true subject by stripping away metaphor or actor inflection, in order to confirm which details are most important.

Prepare for the First Read   The writer wrote this piece with two characters designated as A and B. Before casting, the director and writer should discuss whether gender matters. For this exploration, the writer requests that a woman play A and a male, B. Nothing else regarding character is discussed for this first read.

The cast reads the play.

The goal of the six-line scene exercise is to develop the brief scene into a more substantial scene or possibly a ten-minute play (or longer). The game plan is simply to listen for possibilities using the seven critical elements as a frame.

Read the First Six Lines

A: So, what do you think it will be like this year? The flowers and music from last year were amazing. Best I've ever seen. But it was a bit over the top. I mean who's gonna rally behind that flag—extravaganza number five? Nope. I think we will see a simple—and because it is simple—an elegant but not ostentatious send off. Maybe a rustic look—branches and burlap—but done up in an elegant way. Burlap is very in this year. Agree? Disagree? No comment? What do you think? It would really help this conversation to know your thoughts. It would be less one-sided, which would, by extension, make this more of a conversation than a one-person monologue that feels as if it will never end. Seriously, I'm tired of talking. So, I will stop. But not before asking: What do you think it will be like this year?

And now, I'm done.

Really.

Done.

D-

B: —it will be the same.

A: —? The same? The same? It's never the same. Never. Last year, music and flowers; the year before that, a light show documenting the history of history; the year before that, all the children danced with that amazing singer what's her name; and the year before that, that magician made them disappear before their time—that was amazing. Amazing. But you think it will be the same! It's never the same. Never.

B: It is the same every year. They are called. They are commissioned. They go out. If we are lucky, they return. If not, two more are called. It is the same until it is finished.

A: Well, that's, that's the tradition. Of course that's the same. But who looks forward to that? It's what's different that matters.

B: What?! It's what's different that matters?! Not. One. Minute. Of that, that frivolous nonsense matters. Not. One. Minute. The call and the journey set them apart. That's the only thing that matters. The only thing! No journey, no success, no water, no you, no me, no us. Nothing.

What the Dramaturg and the Active Dramaturg Heard   During this read, the dramaturg may have heard a conversation that provoked a lot of questions and led to a bit of an argument. The dramaturg may have also heard that a journey is involved and that this happens a lot.

The active dramaturg heard that one character holds a great deal of excitement for the mystery surrounding the event and that another character sees the experience as dangerous if not grave. The purpose for the journey involves water and success means the end of everything. Failure is not an option for whoever is chosen to take on the journey.

The First Dramaturgical Discussion between the Dramaturg and Playwright   In an actual workshop setting, the dramaturg and writer begin to discuss the play following the first reading. This conversation would take place with the director and could occur with the cast listening or while the cast is on break. Because this is an exercise, the creative team is present and watching, but the conversation remains between the dramaturg and playwright alone.

The First Dramaturgical Discussion

Dramaturg: What draws you to this piece?

Writer: Um, a writing assignment to create six lines.

Dramaturg: Okay, well. Do you want to know anything more about these characters or where they are?

Writer: Sure, I think I'd like to know more. Maybe their names. I chose to write them as letters A and B because I just wanted to get something down. I think if I were to know their names I would have a greater sense of who they are and what they are doing or waiting for.

Dramaturg: Yes, I was also wondering where the characters were. Are they in a *Hunger Games*–like setting or talking about something akin to the holocaust depicted in Caryl Churchill's *Far Away*?

Writer: I don't know. I certainly didn't intend to bring us to the *Hunger Games*, although I happen to love that trilogy. Maybe. I will think about that. What can I say about the *Hunger Games*?

Dramaturg: An extension of the trilogy could be quite exciting. You could help us learn more about the world, especially the revolutionaries who turn out to be as horrid as the reigning government.

Writer: Okay. I'll look at working on a *Hunger Games*–like play. Thanks!

Unpacking the Dramaturg/Playwright Conversation

How successful was this brief conversation? Has the writer articulated a vision for the piece and identified a focused, personal approach to the work? Or, has the dramaturg articulated a personal response and used this to direct the writer to a particular path of creativity? Much of the above conversation suggests the latter, a dramaturg-led direction rather than one suggested by the playwright. Yes, the writer purports to agree with this *Hunger Games* approach, but does the impetus for writing such a story exist within the work? Does the artist ultimately responsible for setting words to paper have a strong enough connection with this dramaturg's suggestion?

Where does the dramaturg go awry?

Dramaturg: What draws you to this piece?

Writer: Um, a writing assignment to create six lines.

The dramaturg begins with an open, artist-based question: "What draws you to this piece?" However, in this instance the question suggests that the dramaturg is willfully ignorant of the process. The result, "Um, a writing assignment to create six lines," presents a response that draws the conversation to a close thus preventing the dramaturg from identifying key ideas that the writer may wish to explore and expand in future drafts.

The original conversation continued as follows:

Dramaturg: Okay, well. Do you want to know anything more about these characters or where they are?

Writer: Sure, I think I'd like to know more. Maybe their names. I chose to write them as letters A and B because I just wanted to get something down. I think if I were to know their names I would have a greater sense of who they are and what they are doing or waiting for.

The dramaturg needs to recover from the awkward opening and response that stops the creative conversation cold. The writer's response that this is an assignment may come across as a retort a dramaturg will hear in school only, but think again. Numerous writers seek and obtain commissions that respond to a prompt provided by a theatre or producing agency. Other writers (or theatres) obtain grants to fund the writing, and the grants have set ideas or topics the play must touch upon. True, these topics have considerable range and flexibility, but at the end of the day a writer funded by an art and science grant must merge those two ideas—art and science—into a dramatic work while retaining a significant connection and level of passion for the project's many phases. Otherwise, rewrites will prove impossible and the play will flounder, leading to either a series of readings or only one production, if that. In the end, identifying a way to elicit a writer's passion for a topic or subject remains an active dramaturg's key responsibility in service of the art.

During this brief dialogue, the dramaturg asks the writer, as if stating a last resort, "Do you want to know anything more about these characters or where they are?" This question further propels the conversation off-kilter and the dramaturg sounds a bit accusatory if not exasperated because the dramaturg uses "you" in a way that suggests no one else wants to know about these characters. The pronoun "you" can cause a sentence's meaning to shift in ways no artist intends or wants. Using the pronoun "you" sparingly will improve communication. The dramaturg's question also implies the writer doesn't want to pursue the scene and, although this may be true, the dramaturg allowed this negativity toward the project to color the conversation. If such a comment makes its way into the conversation, the *active* dramaturg takes a moment to acknowledge it and then moves on. For example, "Yes, this assignment is quick with the challenge of entering new worlds with just six interesting lines of dialogue. Maybe there is more here to mine."

Instead of a writer who is excited and willing to explore, this writer responds to the dramaturg's questions in a bit of a defensive manner, "Sure, I think I'd like to know more." The decision to know the characters' names comes across as a half-ditch attempt to please the dramaturg—play the game and discuss something that will do little to move the scene's evolution along. Once the writer knows the characters' names, if they have names, where will the writer go from there? How has the dramaturg facilitated this process in a positive way? The dramaturg could have asked how will knowing the names provide insight into the characters. The dramaturg might learn more about the playwright. The writer might discover that this response will not help the process or has a chance to focus on why or how the names drive or connect to the play's action.

As the conversation progresses, the dramaturg works to facilitate creative discovery by grounding the world in a preexisting setting by using *The Hunger Games* or *Far Away* as points of reference.

> Dramaturg: Yes, I was also wondering where the characters were. Are they in a *Hunger Games*–like setting or talking about something akin to the holocaust depicted in Caryl Churchill's *Far Away*?

These references did not come from the playwright. Because the ideas came solely from the dramaturg, the ideas may connect only superficially with the playwright. What's more, the writer may be placed in an untenable situation of having to create a version of these post-apocalyptic societies that the dramaturg or director agrees with and wants, but does not relate to the writer's creative impulse. No one on this creative team will succeed because the basic tenets of each world—*Hunger Games* or *Far Away*—have yet to be discussed and embraced by the team and specifically the playwright.

> Writer: I don't know. I certainly didn't intend to bring us to the *Hunger Games*, although I happen to love that trilogy. Maybe. I will think about that. What can I say about the *Hunger Games*?

Now, the writer has shifted to asking the dramaturg to create a writing assignment. And the dramaturg falls into the trap to become a teacher by doling out an assignment and defining how it should function. The writer may be posing a rhetorical question regarding commenting on the *Hunger Games* or may be expressing a sense of exasperation.

> Dramaturg: An extension of the trilogy could be quite exciting. You could help us learn more about the world, especially the revolutionaries who turn out to be as horrid as the reigning government.

> Writer: Okay. I'll look at working on a *Hunger Games*–like play. Thanks!

Either way, the result is a writer who has ceded all control by agreeing to work on a *Hunger Games*–like play. Looking ahead, the tension will grow and the collaboration will sour and no one will understand why.

The Active Dramaturg/Active Playwright Conversation   Although most active dramaturgs choose to begin the conversation with a question related to the writer's passion for the subject, the active dramaturg accepts that when writing a short scene during a timed situation, a writer may not begin writing from a place of passion but of assignment. Therefore, the active dramaturg looks to begin with a question grounded in an observation following the first read so that the conversation might begin in a similar place of passion and deep connection.

The Active Dramaturg/Active Playwright conversation might open as follows:

> Active Dramaturg: What struck you most or jumped out while listening to this reading?

> Active Writer: I definitely want one character to be male and one to be female. It's a bit predictable and stereotypical that the female character in this round was A. A is concerned about look and remembers the past celebrations. I'm not sure I like casting A as a female.

To collaborate well any artist needs to pick up on cues and delve deeply into those that may help deepen a connection. Sometimes the cues suggest discomfort and the collaborative response is to shift the conversation by reframing the comment or tabling the discussion altogether. In this instance, the active dramaturg chooses to delve more deeply and explore the active playwright's concern regarding gender and dialogue.

> Active Dramaturg: Are there ways to keep A as a female but shift her from using what you consider stereotypically female references?

> Active Writer: I'm not sure. Maybe reading it with B as a female and A as a male will help.

> Active Dramaturg: Maybe the casting will help highlight words and phrases that land as uniquely female or male?

> Active Writer: Yeah, that would be helpful. I think I'm looking more for balance—a bit of female language for him and male language for her—to keep everyone guessing as to who the leader is—as if leaders must be male. I'm not sure either will be the leader but that together they will succeed. I really want them to be equals at the core and for there to be strong hints of that from the very beginning. Right now, I haven't helped the actors find that because I haven't quite put my finger on it. But that's the goal.

> Active Dramaturg: A good goal to have!

Rather than stopping cold as in the previous conversation, the Active Dramaturg's conversation promotes an environment where the active writer can explore not knowing answers in a comfortable setting. The revelations help both the active dramaturg and the active playwright learn an amazing goal for the play and how the characters should interact as the story unfolds. In just two or three exchanges, one of the active playwright's driving questions has been revealed: how to show that when leading or solving problems together neither gender exhibits stereotypical male or female qualities. To know that the active writer will be looking at the language and sentence structure that helps paint a less stereotypical picture of each gender is fantastic. To discuss how to do this—at this stage in the creative process—would distract the active writer from the goal of understanding the scene and the characters. Also, to dwell on how to change A's language or what it means to render a stereotypical female character for the stage would lead to the development of only one character, A. The goal of this development process is to move the entire scene forward. Given the presence of actors, presenting the possibility of shifting who plays whom allows the writer to explore changes without changing language. Shifting who plays whom also allows the writer to hear where language can shift to lessen or increase gender differences.

There are other points to discuss regarding story and how it unfolds. The scene introduces a great deal of mystery and allows the audience to guess what will be different, successfully placing the audience just behind the story while making them feel they are ahead or right in step with the actors. An artistic team never wants the audience to be ahead of the play's story.

Active Dramaturg: Outside of the gender of each character, what might help us know more about the world they occupy? For example, are these characters old or young?

Active Writer: One is certainly aware of the world. I'm not sure if that means one is old as in a parent, or an adult or just a more mature young adult. I think B is old enough be concerned.

Here, the playwright indicates that whatever the situation is, it is serious enough that a person must possess a certain level of maturity to fathom it—partially or completely. The goal is to spark some thoughts rather than isolate an answer of eighteen years old or forty-three. At this point in the process, a specific age may not provide a window to creativity. Too little is known about the world to ground how a specific age directs action and behavior. But the active dramaturg works to facilitate that discovery.

By posing an open question earlier, "Are these characters old or young?" the active dramaturg presents the opportunity for both characters to be similar in age or not. Were the active dramaturg to narrow the question and ask if one is older than the other, it is possible that the play's development would lead to an adult character and a younger character. If the active writer begins to wrestle with that scenario—and it later proves wrong—creativity hasn't been accelerated. If, however, the simple open question of, "consider the age of the characters" is posed, the active writer can quickly explore the pros and cons of various ages or place the question on the back burner as others are explored. An open question can often come across as an invitation to consider an idea; prescriptive questions often come across as thinly veiled directives to create along a particular line of thought.

To avert the misstep of unintentionally disempowering the playwright, the active dramaturg looks to ground explorations of text by using the critical elements. In this particular case, the active dramaturg may look to explore time as a structural device—a strong fallback position because time provides the form for all plays. Time is a broad concept, and in this instance is used to define the characters' age. By defining the characters as old or young, the active writer has an opportunity to raise the stakes within the scene and for the characters.

Active Dramaturg: B is concerned about what? Does age or experience force what happens to the characters?

Active Writer: I think so. Yes, being called. B will either be called, or could be called, or has friends in the pool. It would be interesting if both A and B were the same age, but something doesn't feel right. Maybe A is older, not B's mother, but older.

The open question brought about a discussion of B's role in the larger scene—he may be called. Suddenly, B's age is clear: whatever the actual number, B is old enough that this year's summons can and does involve him (or her, if B is cast as a female). In addition, the open question regarding age allows the active writer to articulate what feels more true to the story—at this time—and the active dramaturg does not press the writer for a more concrete description of time or age because this scene is early in its development. The active dramaturg does, however, present possibilities.

However, sensing that the writer may be focusing too much on age, the active dramaturg presents another possibility—that choice (actor or director) can help the active writer make adjustments.

> Active Dramaturg: Maybe she's distracting B. Maybe the choice that informs the line makes it less stereotypical.
>
> Active Writer: Hmmm. Maybe.

This may be something the active dramaturg chooses to present to the director the next time the actors read the scene or the rewrites the active writer makes.

> Active Dramaturg: Where are A and B? In place or time?
>
> Active Writer: The time is some time in the future. The world or where they live is organized around this single, annual event where two young people are called to travel out of the compound and retrieve a set amount of water and bring it back to the group to ensure life for another year.

The active writer has a clear sense of time for this scene: the future. In the next draft, the "future" needs to be defined more clearly and indicated within the text, but the active dramaturg needn't focus on that for this first and early draft. In subsequent drafts, should details that define time and place be absent, a reminder that these clues need to be in the script should suffice, for it is clear the writer is attuned to time as a structural element.

As the allotted conversation time winds down, the active dramaturg attempts to bring about a discussion regarding place and defining it within the scene.

> Active Dramaturg: And place? If place is important, how can we weave in a sense of place for the conversation or place as in the world?
>
> Active Writer: Place is important. I think I know where they are now. I didn't when I was writing, but now, now I think I do.

It seems as if the many questions unrelated to place have helped the writer answer the question; how exactly we will discover in the next draft.

The First Active Dramaturg/Active Playwright Conversation

> Active Dramaturg: What struck you most or jumped out while listening to this reading?
>
> Active Writer: I definitely want one character to be male and one to be female. It's a bit predictable and stereotypical that the female character in this round was A. A is concerned about look and remembers the past celebrations. I'm not sure I like casting A as a female.
>
> Active Dramaturg: Are there ways to keep A as a female but shift her from using what you consider stereotypically female references?

Active Writer: I'm not sure. Maybe reading it with B as a female and A as a male will help.

Active Dramaturg: Maybe the casting will help highlight words and phrases that land as uniquely female or male?

Active Writer: Yeah, that would be helpful. I think I'm looking more for balance—a bit of female language for him and male language for her—to keep everyone guessing as to who the leader is. I'm not sure either will be the leader but that together they will succeed. I really want them to be equals at the core and for there to be strong hints of that from the very beginning. Right now, I haven't helped the actors find that because I haven't quite put my finger on it. But that's the goal.

Active Dramaturg: A good goal to have! Outside of the gender of each character, what might help us know more about the world they occupy? For example, are these characters old or young?

Active Writer: One is certainly aware of the world. I'm not sure if that means one is old as in a parent, or an adult, or just a more mature young adult. I think B is old enough be concerned.

Active Dramaturg: B is concerned about what? Does age or experience force what happens to the characters?

Active Writer: I think so. Yes, being called. B will either be called, or could be called, or has friends in the pool. It would be interesting if both A and B were the same age, but something doesn't feel right. Maybe A is older, not B's mother, but older.

Active Dramaturg: Maybe she's distracting B. Maybe the choice that informs the line makes it less stereotypical.

Active Writer: Hmmm. Maybe.

Active Dramaturg: Where are A and B? In place or time?

Active Writer: The time is some time in the future. The world or where they live is organized around this single, annual event where two young people are called to travel out of the compound and retrieve a set amount of water and bring it back to the group to ensure life for another year.

Active Dramaturg: And place? If place is important, how can we weave in a sense of place for the conversation or place as in the world?

Active Writer: Place is important. I think I know where they are now. I didn't when I was writing, but now, now I think I do.

A Side-by-Side Comparison of the Conversations	
Dramaturgy/ Playwright Conversation	**Active Dramaturgy/ Active Playwright Conversation**
Dramaturg: What draws you to this piece? Writer: Um, a writing assignment to create six lines. Dramaturg: Okay, well. Do you want to know anything more about these characters or where they are? Writer: Sure, I think I'd like to know more. Maybe their names. I chose to write them as letters A and B because I just wanted to get something down. I think if I were to know their names I would have a greater sense of who they are and what they are doing or waiting for.	Active Dramaturg: What struck you most or jumped out while listening to this reading? Active Writer: I definitely want one character to be male and one to be female. It's a bit predictable and stereotypical that the female character in this round was A. A is concerned about look and remembers the past celebrations. I'm not sure I like casting A as a female. Active Dramaturg: Are there ways to keep A as a female but shift her from using what you consider stereotypically female references? Active Writer: I'm not sure. Maybe reading it with B as a female and A as a male will help.
Dramaturg: Yes, I was also wondering where the characters were. Are they in a *Hunger Games*–like setting or talking about something akin to the holocaust depicted in Caryl Churchill's *Far Away*? Writer: I don't know. I certainly didn't intend to bring us to the *Hunger Games*, although I happen to love that trilogy. Maybe. I will think about that. What can I say about the *Hunger Games*? *(Cont. on next page.)*	Active Dramaturg: Maybe the casting will help highlight words and phrases that land as uniquely female or male? Active Writer: Yeah, that would be helpful. I think I'm looking more for balance—a bit of female language for him and male language for her—to keep everyone guessing as to who the leader is. I'm not sure either will be the leader but that together they will succeed. I really want them to be equals at the core and for there to be strong hints of that from the very beginning. Right now, I haven't helped the actors find that because I haven't quite put my finger on it. But that's the goal. Active Dramaturg: A good goal to have! Outside of the gender of each character, what might help us know more about the world they occupy? For example, are these characters old or young? Active Writer: One is certainly aware of the world. I'm not sure if that means one is old as in a parent, or an adult, or just a more mature young adult. I think B is old enough be concerned. *(Cont. on next page.)*

A Side-by-Side Comparison of the Conversations (cont.)	
Dramaturgy/ **Playwright Conversation**	**Active Dramaturgy/** **Active Playwright Conversation**
	Active Dramaturg: B is concerned about what? Does age or experience force what happens to the characters? Active Writer: I think so. Yes, being called. B will either be called, or could be called, or has friends in the pool. It would be interesting if both A and B were the same age, but something doesn't feel right. Maybe A is older, not B's mother, but older. Active Dramaturg: Maybe she's distracting B. Maybe the choice that informs the line makes it less stereotypical. Active Writer: Hmmm. Maybe.
Dramaturg: An extension of the trilogy could be quite exciting. You could help us learn more about the world, especially the revolutionaries who turn out to be as horrid as the reigning government. Writer: Okay. I'll look at working on a *Hunger Games*–like play. Thanks!	Active Dramaturg: Where are A and B? In place or time? Active Writer: The time is some time in the future. The world or where they live is organized around this single, annual event where two young people are called to travel out of the compound and retrieve a set amount of water and bring it back to the group to ensure life for another year. Active Dramaturg: And place? If place is important, how can we weave in a sense of place for the conversation or place as in the world? Active Writer: Place is important. I think I know where they are now. I didn't when I was writing, but now, now I think I do.

Rewrite the Six Lines. You May Expand to Ten. Take the original six-line scene and make corrections, adjustments (additions, deletions, order, etc.) to the original lines. To aid in answering questions and clarifying the story, the writer may add four additional lines of dialogue thus taking the original six to ten lines.

The Dramaturg's Game Plan To see how this play continues the *Hunger Games* theme, which characters and story lines are continued. How does this world resemble or differ from the world depicted.

The *Active* Dramaturg's Game Plan   To listen for new details that outline the story, but also ground the story. What additional details has the playwright added? How do these details expand and deepen the story?

Prepare for the Second Read Around the Table.   The director should confer with the writer to discuss any casting changes (additions or deletions) or other adjustments. In this instance, the writer requires one additional actor and chose to retain the initial casting.

Because this is the same cast and the second reading, the director may want to suggest how the cast approaches the text. Should they try to read it with fresh eyes and make no acting choices, or should the cast approach the script with the knowledge of the first read and the information gleaned from the conversation between the dramaturg and the playwright?

In this instance, the director asks the cast to read the script with fresh eyes and to avoid making any specific choices. The creative team simply wants to hear the changes the playwright has made.

The director should encourage the actors to simply read the text and avoid any specific choices at this time.

Read the Ten-Line Scene

> **Imura:** So, what do you think it will be like this year? The flowers and music from last year were amazing. Best I've ever seen. Yes, it was a bit over the top. I mean who's gonna rally behind that flag? Nope. I think we will see a simple—and because it is simple—an elegant but not ostentatious send off. Maybe a rustic look—branches and burlap—but done up in an elegant way. Burlap is very in this year. Agree? Disagree? No comment? What do you think?
>
> . . .
>
> Do you think they'll work with the concrete grey or mask it entirely? Maybe they'll begin at the slip of the evening. No better time of day. The quiet before everything starts. Sometimes I sneak out before everyone is up just to catch a glimpse of the sun before it slips behind the mountain and the moon looms large. Don't get me wrong, I love the moon; worship at its feet. But there is something about the glaring white light of the sun. It's blinding. Yeah, you're right about that. But it masks an entire world in light so bright we can't see; we can only hear, unless we use those special goggles, but who can afford those?
>
> . . .
>
> It would really help this conversation to know your thoughts. It would be less one-sided, which, by extension, would make this more of a conversation than a one-person monologue that feels as if it will never

end. Seriously, I'm tired of talking. So, I will stop. But not before asking: What do you think it will be like this year?

And now, I'm done.

Really.

Done.

D–

Tavor: —it will be the same.

Imura: —?

The same? The same? It's never the same. Never. Last year, music and
flowers; the year before that a light show documenting the history
of history; the year before that all the children danced with that
amazing singer what's her name; and the year before that that magician made them disappear before their time—that was amazing. A.
may. zing. But you, you think it will be the same. It's never the same.
Never.

Tavor: (*Sits very still.*) It is the same every year. They are called. They are
commissioned. They go out. If they are lucky, they return. If not, two
more are called. It is the same until it is finished.

Imura: Well, that's, that's the tradition. Of course it's the same. But who
looks forward to that? It's what's different that matters.

Tavor: (*He tenses but still sits very, very still.*) It's what's different that matters?!
Not. One. Minute. Of that, that frivolous nonsense matters. Not. One.
Minute. The call and the journey set them apart. That's the only thing
that matters. The only thing! No journey, no success, no water, no you,
no me, no us. Nothing.

Imura: Yeah, that's right. And we either dwell on that and fall prey to the
mind games, or we keep a clear head and think about what's different.
Possibility lies in difference not what's the same. Redundancy brings
about nothing new.

Tavor: Look around you. What do you see? A door to freedom? No. A
window to the future? No. A waiting room. We are in the waiting
room. Waiting. We cannot leave. We won't be staying here either. We
are waiting. Until we are summoned and moved on to the next step.
We have no control. We must do what they tell us to do when they
tell us to do it: wait or not wait; walk the long walk or not. We are not
who we were. I am not me and you are not you. We are merely vessels
set forth to do their bidding. We are without possibilities.

Imura: Yeah, with that bit of thinking, no question the possibilities are the
exact opposite of endless. But if we're called after the frivolous doings
as you call them, we have to get up and walk and serve the people,

brave the world beyond and bring back the goods. I know I can do it. Not because I'm an optimist or naïve, but because I refuse to lock myself into thinking about how difficult it all is. You either enjoy the puzzle and the challenge or you don't.

Voice: Imura and Tavor. Step to the middle of the room. (As they step to the middle, a platform appears and they begin to descend.) You have been called.

What the Dramaturg Heard   The dramaturg heard little mention of the sporting events or revolution associated with the *Hunger Games*. Although the female character displays a great sense of self-awareness, she is not pursuing a cause for others or for herself or a sense of duty. The male character remains focused on the travails that await whomever is chosen. The piece moves closer to a thought piece rather than a journey and self-discovery play. Unusual names. They suggest a futuristic time. How were these names chosen? Do they hold meaning for the writer or the world?

What the Active Dramaturg Heard   The active dramaturg heard greater details regarding the current environment, a cold room where people wait—more than suggesting that this pair housed together will form something of a team. The need for the two of them to come together and find a way to collaborate may need to reveal itself soon. How can the tension regarding Imura and Tavor's role in searching for water infuse the dialogue and action sooner, given the brevity of these scenes/this work?

Second Discussion between Dramaturg and Playwright

Dramaturg: Very different from the *Hunger Games*. This isn't a wholly new chapter in the saga, separate from what currently exists. After our conversation, I expected to see how you expand the story to draw us or you further into the *Hunger Games*. Maybe seen as your passion for this piece?

Writer: When I went to write, I realized my sketch was looking to do something different rather than simply take the *Hunger Games* and create a sequel.

Dramaturg: Oh, yes. Although the characters are being called, the process is different. And we see how the characters respond to waiting differently. I think we are starting to see her, Imura, as less stereotypically female even though she is a bit of a cheerleader. You have done a lot to differentiate their speech patterns and perception of the event. That's quite effective.

Writer: Thanks.

Dramaturg: And we know a bit about the world and the importance of this journey that citizens are called to do. What else might we know about it? How long do they have? What is expected?

Writer: I don't know. I'm not even sure what it means to be called yet. But I'm starting to become curious. I'm kinda psyched to know what happens next.

Dramaturg: So am I. So am I.

Dissecting the Second Dramaturg/Playwright Conversation

How is this conversation the least bit dramaturgical? How has the dramaturg identified creative questions that help the writer hone in on areas or questions that help transform what currently exists into an even more dynamic exchange?

The first comment, "Very different from the *Hunger Games*" reveals the dramaturg's comments as completely unresponsive. No level of analysis exists. The dramaturg reveals a bias while listening; the dramaturg expected to hear a new installment of the *Hunger Games* and what the writer shared did not meet those expectations. Enough with the *Hunger Games*. The dramaturg's comment more than suggests that the dramaturg did not listen to what the writer wrote. The dramaturg looks to check off accomplishments or additions against the established list the dramaturg drew up during the previous conversation. Because little meets these short-sighted expectations, the scene comes across as less successful.

Had the playwright participated in establishing the objectives for the project and written a scene full of a similar amount of surprises, the dramaturg might refrain from comparing what was submitted against the list. This dramaturg fails to respond to what the playwright wrote. Responding to what comes remains key. It may be that the writer has a wholly new vision. It may be that the writer thought the new lines met the questions the group decided upon during the creative conversation. Taking the time to identify what the writer wants to write and why helps clarify whether the writer wants to rewrite or can rewrite, and whether the writer is connected to the material or still discovering which creative path to take and question to pursue.

The dramaturg for this process continues to reveal a bias and an extreme inability to embrace the writer's vision with the remark, "This isn't a wholly new chapter in the saga, separate from what currently exists. After our conversation, I expected to see how you expand the story to draw us or you further into the *Hunger Games*. Maybe seen as your passion for this piece?" To continue to describe what the dramaturg expected rather than what the writer offered, places the writer on the defensive and in the position of having to defend creative choices rather than explore how to strengthen or clarify them. No artist should have to defend a choice. "When I went to write, I realized my sketch was looking to do something different rather than simply take the *Hunger Games* and create a sequel." The dramaturg then back pedals and begins to comment on what was written. Unfortunately, the dramaturg wasted a significant amount of time focusing on the wrong entities—the dramaturg and the *Hunger Games* rather than the writer and this scene.

The dramaturg attempts to transition the conversation but holds on to the *Hunger Games*. "Oh, yes. Although the characters are being called, the process is different. And we see how the characters respond to waiting differently." It isn't clear whether the dramaturg thinks the characters respond to waiting differently—from each other or in comparison to characters depicted in the *Hunger Games*.

The inelegant transition into the discussion regarding female stereotypes appears connected to the conversation and dramaturgical in nature, but only superficially. "I think we are starting to see her, Imura, as less stereotypically female even though she is a bit of a cheerleader. You have done a lot to differentiate their speech patterns and perception of the event. That's quite effective." The comments simply chart some of the writer's accomplishments and responds as a teacher might. Nothing in the comments helps the writer identify how elements work and might expand in subsequent drafts. And the writer has nothing to add, so simply responds with, "Thanks."

The next exchange attempts to move the writer forward, "And we know a bit about the world and the importance of this journey that citizens are called to do. What else might we know about it? How long do they have? What is expected?" The dramaturg's questions are too broad. The writer also wonders what else we might know about the journey and the attending details. Nothing in these questions helps the writer identify a specific path for this scene. When the conversation concludes, the writer admits to wondering what the next steps will be as does the dramaturg. This creative relationship is stalled. Whatever transformation the scene undergoes will be entirely due to the writer's self-driven creative conversation not a creative collaboration.

Discussion between the Active Dramaturg and the Active Writer   The active dramaturg begins the conversation with observations of changes and how they land or impact perception. Noting changes between the two drafts by identifying how the changes work and propel the story or character forward can help everyone involved make changes quickly—be they acting choices or changes in dialogue. The active dramaturg may have also chosen to begin the conversation by repeating the question, "What jumped out during this reading? What landed or interested you most?"

> Active Dramaturg: Quite a different world! We know their day is our night, the sun is too bright to support human life, assuming they are human. And the two, Imura and Tavor, have been called. I assume they will be sent on the journey. As I replay the scene in my head, she seems more nervous than comforting. Or maybe she is excited. Either way, she certainly stands up for herself, and that begins to take away the stereotypical depiction of a talkative female. What are you seeing coming out in this draft that you might want to explore further?

The active dramaturg also briefly discusses a concern the writer had initially—that the female character spoke and behaved in a stereotypical manner.

Now that the idea is less new, the active dramaturg can begin to broach the idea of what drives the active writer to continue writing; to look for ways to discuss where the passion for the piece lies.

> Active Writer: They need to be balanced. Their fear needs to be balanced as well as their intellect. I want to write a piece that keeps the two a team. I don't need them to go through the typical Hollywood "I hate you now I love you" journey. I need them to be smart enough to understand how

to survive this harrowing journey and that they are equals even though their strengths are in very different areas. The decision to pair them was purposeful. I'm just not sure how that will play out.

The active writer responds with two key ideas: the characters need to appear as equals even if during specific moments their relationship is anything but balanced. The active writer is still exploring questions of how the pair functions throughout the story and what sort of relationship they will develop.

> Active Dramaturg: Writing to discover is great. The world is beginning to make apparent how their differing approaches to this experience will provide tension. They have managed to avoid alienating the other so far, but their different approach does provide tension and can lead to conflict. It's holding my interest so far. As you become more familiar with the world, what idea inspires you or drives the writing?

At first, the active dramaturg confirms the writer's concern that the answers are not totally clear yet. By providing such reassurance, the pressure to create perfection is lessened and hopefully the ability to create continues.

> Active Writer: Well, I hadn't thought about it, but now that you ask . . . I think I'm interested in exploring what sort of courage or strength it takes to assume the responsibility to serve and protect others when one is called up rather than volunteering.

Using these comments that reference how the rewrites begin to successfully address one of the active writer's goals—increasing tension—allows the active dramaturg to move the conversation toward a discussion of The Sentence.

> Active Dramaturg: So, in a sentence, a play dealing with . . .

> Active Writer: Maybe I'd say a play dealing with assuming or taking control of a situation where none exists—for the time being.

The Sentence provides the active playwright with more material to fuel the creative process and keeps the active dramaturg's game plan in play—keeping the process moving forward, but with direction and a purpose. In addition, the play continues to grow to contain active moments that realize the play's themes and ideas. The active dramaturg and active playwright do more than trade compliments or hold personally gratifying or intellectually stimulating conversations.

The active writer begins to put ideas into words and the active dramaturg helps shape what's offered into The Sentence without dictating what The Sentence should be—at any stage but especially at this early stage in the creative process (this piece is merely twenty minutes old). A solid sentence is not necessary just yet and what the writer offers will continue to move this process forward. When the play is further along and the writer finds it difficult to form a more complete and satisfying Sentence, the active dramaturg should pause the process and allow the writer more time to craft a solid Sentence during the collaborative conversation.

Active Dramaturg: Sounds good. I do wonder about how long they have been
together or in the same place waiting. Is it important to the story to know
how long they've been waiting? Do they know how long the journey will be?

The active dramaturg's second step is to pose a few questions that help to focus the
continuing exploration. In this instance, key questions regarding the relationship
between the characters and space as regulated by time.

Active Writer: And I'm starting to wonder if they know each other or if
this pairing in the waiting room is their first introduction.

A true collaborative conversation begins as the active writer offers additional questions rather than just solutions. The active writer and active dramaturg are beginning to explore the questions together. If time permits, they might begin to explore
the possible solutions as well; but beginning with an exploration of questions helps
propel the creative process.

Active Dramaturg: And they haven't introduced themselves to each other.
They really are simply waiting together. What propels her to start talking to him? How easy it is may be a directorial question, but it's worth
thinking about from a writing standpoint, too.

The active dramaturg has the opportunity to point out what hasn't yet happened
through questions grounded in the exploration of relationship and character introduction. Rather than bluntly stating they haven't done this and they haven't done
that, the active dramaturg wonders why certain formalities have been avoided.
What's the story to explore there?

Active Writer: Yeah. I'm wondering if it matters how they got there.

Active Dramaturg: It may. The play doesn't necessarily need to start there.
We might learn about it while they are on their journey. Or not. What
I wonder is how they leave the waiting room. Do they descend to their
mission or simply to the pomp and circumstance? How do they move
forward? How does the world they live in interact with them during the
journey? How long do they wait before they give up and send another
team? What are the rules for the team and the world they live in?

Active Writer: Yeah, it's a question of monitoring and success without
making the experience appear contrived for everyone's entertainment.
This excursion is extremely important and given to two people annually. The question is: Why?

Here the active dramaturg has an opportunity to introduce a theme-based critical
question or comment that flows directly from the conversation. By grounding the
comments in specific moments or lines from the scene, the active dramaturg demonstrates a connection to the work, pinpoints where the play currently informs the thematic discussion and moves the creative conversation beyond what currently exists.

Active Dramaturg: One character mentions service specifically while another
talks about maintaining society's life. How does service to the people

come about and what does it give other than life for an additional year. Does each individual person know about and understand the service concept or just the elite few? And are those who are finalists to be chosen among the elite few? What separates those who are called from the other young men and women—is the team always one man and one woman?

Active Writer: And how does all of that connect to survival—of the human race and the hero and heroine?

Active Dramaturg: Yup.

The active writer presents even more options for the play's growth. These storylines stem from what exists as well as the creative conversation. Although the comments are broad and often take the form of questions rather than specifically map out the next draft, these ideas will propel the work forward. Questions can feed the work more than specifics that dictate what to do in one or two moments. Questions feed the evolution.

The Active Dramaturg/Active Playwright Conversation

Active Dramaturg: Quite a different world! We know their day is our night, the sun is too bright to support human life, assuming they are human. And the two, Imura and Tavor, have been called. I assume they will be sent on the journey. As I replay the scene in my head, she seems more nervous than comforting. Or maybe she is excited. Either way, she certainly stands up for herself, and that begins to take away the stereotypical depiction of a talkative female. What are you seeing coming out in this draft that you might want to explore further?

Active Writer: They need to be balanced. Their fear needs to be balanced as well as their intellect. I want to write a piece that keeps the two a team. I don't need them to go through the typical Hollywood "I hate you now I love you" journey. I need them to be smart enough to understand how to survive this harrowing journey and that they are equals even though their strengths are in very different areas. The decision to pair them was purposeful. I'm just not sure how that will play out.

Active Dramaturg: Writing to discover is great. The world is beginning to make apparent how their differing approach to this experience will provide tension. They have managed to avoid alienating the other so far, but their different approach does provide tension and can lead to conflict. It's holding my interest so far. As you become more familiar with the world, what idea inspires you or drives the writing?

Active Dramaturg: Well, I hadn't thought about it, but now that you ask . . . I think I'm interested in exploring what sort of courage or strength it takes to assume the responsibility to serve and protect others when one is called up rather than volunteering.

Active Dramaturg: So, in a sentence, a play dealing with . . .

Active Writer: Maybe I'd say a play dealing with assuming or taking control of a situation where none exists—for the time being.

Active Dramaturg: Sounds good. I do wonder about how long they have been together or in the same place waiting. Is it important to the story to know how long they've been waiting? Do they know how long the journey will be?

Active Dramaturg: I do wonder about how long they have been together or in the same place waiting. Is it important to the story to know how long they've been waiting? Do they know how long the journey will be?

Active Writer: And I'm starting to wonder if they know each other or if this pairing in the waiting room is their first introduction.

Active Dramaturg: And they haven't introduced themselves to each other. They really are simply waiting together. What propels her to start talking to him? How easy it is may be a directorial question, but it's worth thinking about from a writing standpoint, too.

Active Writer: Yeah. I'm wondering if it matters how they got there.

Active Dramaturg: It may. The play doesn't necessarily need to start there. We might learn about it while they are on their journey. Or not. What I wonder is how they leave the waiting room. Do they descend to their mission or simply to the pomp and circumstance? How do they move forward? How does the world they live in interact with them during the journey? How long do they wait before they give up and send another team? What are the rules for the team and the world they live in?

Active Writer: Yeah, it's a question of monitoring and success without making the experience appear contrived for everyone's entertainment. This excursion is extremely important and given to two people annually. The question is: Why?

Active Dramaturg: One character mentions service specifically while another talks about maintaining society's life. How does service to the people come about and what does it give other than life for an additional year. Does each individual person know about and understand the service concept or just the elite few? And are those who are finalists to be chosen among the elite few? What separates those who are called from the other young men and women—is the team always one man and one woman?

Active Writer: And how does all of that connect to survival—of the human race and the hero and heroine?

Active Dramaturg: Yup.

A Side-By-Side Comparison of the Second Conversation

Dramaturg/ Playwright Conversation	Active Dramaturg/ Active Playwright Conversation
Dramaturg: Very different from the *Hunger Games*. This isn't a wholly new chapter in the saga, separate from what currently exists. After our conversation, I expected to see how you might expand the story to draw us or you further into the *Hunger Games*. Maybe seen as your passion for this piece? Writer: When I went to write, I realized my sketch was looking to do something different rather than simply take the *Hunger Games* and create a sequel. *(Cont. on next page.)*	Active Dramaturg: Quite a different world! We know their day is our night, the sun is too bright to support human life, assuming they are human. And the two, Imura and Tavor, have been called. I assume they will be sent on the journey. As I replay the scene in my head, she seems more nervous than comforting. Or maybe she is excited. Either way, she certainly stands up for herself, and that begins to take away the stereotypical depiction of a talkative female. What are you seeing coming out in this draft that you might want to explore further? Active Writer: They need to be balanced. Their fear needs to be balanced as well as their intellect. I want to write a piece that keeps the two a team. I don't need them to go through the typical Hollywood "I hate you now I love you" journey. I need them to be smart enough to understand how to survive this harrowing journey and that they are equals even though their strengths are in very different areas. The decision to pair them was purposeful. I'm just not sure how that will play out. Active Dramaturg: Writing to discover is great. The world is beginning to make apparent how their differing approaches to this experience will provide tension. They have managed to avoid alienating the other so far, but their different approach does provide tension and can lead to conflict. It's holding my interest so far. As you become more familiar with the world, what idea inspires you or drives the writing? *(Cont. on next page.)*

A Side-by-Side Comparison of the Conversations (cont.)

Dramaturgy/ Playwright Conversation	Active Dramaturgy/ Active Playwright Conversation
Dramaturg: Oh, yes. Although the characters are being called the process is different. And we see how the characters respond to waiting differently. I think we are starting to see her, Imura, as less stereotypically female even though she is a bit of a cheerleader. You have done a lot to differentiate their speech patterns and perception of the event. That's quite effective. Writer: Thanks. *(Cont. on next page.)*	Active Writer: Well, I hadn't thought about it, but now that you ask . . . I think I'm interested in exploring what sort of courage or strength it takes to assume the responsibility to serve and protect others when one is called up rather than volunteering. Active Dramaturg: So, in a sentence, a play dealing with . . . Active Writer: Maybe I'd say a play dealing with assuming or taking control of a situation where none exists—for the time being. Active Dramaturg: Sounds good. I do wonder about how long they have been together or in the same place waiting. Is it important to the story to know how long they've been waiting? Do they know how long the journey will be? Active Writer: And I'm starting to wonder if they know each other or if this pairing in the waiting room is their first introduction. Active Dramaturg: And they haven't introduced themselves to each other. They really are simply waiting together. What propels her to start talking to him? How easy it is may be a directorial question, but it's worth thinking about from a writing standpoint, too. Active Writer: Yeah. I'm wondering if it matters how they got there. Active Dramaturg: It may. The play doesn't necessarily need to start there. We might learn about it while they are on their journey. Or not. What I wonder is how they leave the waiting room. Do they descend to their mission or simply to the pomp and circumstance? How do they move forward? How does the world they live in interact with them during the journey? How long do they wait before they give up and send another team? What are the rules for the team and the world they live in? *(Cont. on next page.)*

A Side-by-Side Comparison of the Conversations (cont.)	
Dramaturgy/ Playwright Conversation	**Active Dramaturgy/ Active Playwright Conversation**
Dramaturg: And we know a bit about the world and the importance of this journey that citizens are called to do. What else might we know about it? How long do they have? What is expected? Writer: I don't know. I'm not even sure what it means to be called yet. But I'm starting to become curious. I'm kinda psyched to know what happens next. Dramaturg: So am I. So am I.	Active Writer: Yeah, it's a question of monitoring and success without making the experience appear contrived for everyone's entertainment. This excursion is extremely important and given to two people annually. The question is: Why? Active Dramaturg: One character mentions service specifically while another talks about maintaining society's life. How does service to the people come about and what does it give other than life for an additional year. Does each individual person know about and understand the service concept or just the elite few? And are those who are finalists to be chosen among the elite few? What separates those who are called from the other young men and women—is the team always one man and one woman? Active Writer: And how does all of that connect to survival—of the human race and the hero and heroine? Active Dramaturg: Yup.

Second Rewrite; Add Four Lines   Take the ten-line scene and make corrections, adjustments (additions, deletions, order, etc.) to the current scene. To aid in answering questions and clarifying the story, the writer may add four additional lines of dialogue thus taking the current ten lines to fourteen.

The Dramaturg's Game Plan   To listen and discover whether the writer has adjusted to the original plan of crafting a story akin to the *Hunger Games*. Has the groundwork been laid for a romance to blossom between Imura and Tavor? Can this writer rewrite?

The Active Dramaturg's Game Plan   To listen to what's been written. To discover how the writer has begun to address the questions of forging a bond between Imura and Tavor. Has the world and the challenge facing the characters been described further?

Prepare for the Reading: The Director's Approach   Because no new
characters appear, the director may choose to either read the scene with fresh eyes
and no choices or encourage the cast to explore choices and characterizations,
especially during the first half of the scene.

Read the Fourteen-Line Scene

Imura: So, what do you think it will be like this year? The flowers and
music from last year were amazing. Best I've ever seen. Yes, it was a bit
over the top. I mean who's gonna rally behind that flag? Nope. I think
we will see a simple program—and because it is simple—an elegant
but not ostentatious send-off, it will be the best ever. Maybe a rustic
look—branches and burlap—but done up in an elegant way. Burlap is
very in this year. Agree? Disagree? No comment? What do you think?

. . .

Do you think they'll work with the concrete grey or mask it entirely?
Maybe they'll begin at the slip of the evening. No better time of day.
The quiet before everything starts. Sometimes I sneak out before
everyone is up just to catch a glimpse of the sun before it slips behind
the mountain and the moon looms large. Don't get me wrong, I love
the moon; worship at its feet. But there is something about the glaring
white light of the sun. It's blinding.

. . .

Yeah, you're right about that. But it masks an entire world in light
so bright we can't see; we can only hear, unless we use those special
goggles, but who can afford those?

. . .

It would really help this conversation to know your thoughts. It would
be less one-sided, which would, by extension, make this more of a
conversation than a one-person monologue that feels as if it will never
end. Seriously, I'm tired of talking. So, I will stop. But not before asking: What do you think it will be like this year?

And now, I'm done.

Really.

Done.

D-

Tavor: (*Sits very still.*) – It will be the same.

They are called.

They are commissioned.

They go out.

If they are lucky, they return. If not, two more are called.

It is the same until it is finished.

It is the same every year.

Imura: Well, that's, that's the tradition. Of course that's the same. But who looks forward to that? It's what's different that matters. It's different. It's never the same. Never. Last year, music and flowers; the year before that a light show documenting the history of history; the year before that all the children danced with that amazing singer what's her name; and the year before that that magician made them disappear before their time—that was amazing. A. may. zing. But you, you think it will be the same. It's never the same. Never.

Tavor: (*He tenses but still sits very, very still.*) It's what's different that matters?! Not. One. Minute. Of that, that frivolous nonsense matters. Not. One. Minute. The call and the journey set them apart. That's the only thing that matters. The only thing! No journey, no success, no water, no you, no me, no us, no nothing.

Imura: Yeah, that's right. And we either dwell on that and fall prey to the mind games, or we keep a clear head and think about what's different. Possibility lies in difference not what's the same. Redundancy brings about nothing new.

Tavor: Look around you. What do you see? A door to freedom? No. A window to the future? No. A waiting room. We are in the waiting room. Waiting. We cannot leave. We won't be staying here either. We are waiting. Until we are summoned and moved on to the next step. We have no control. We must do what they tell us to do when they tell us to do it: wait or not wait; walk the long walk or not. We are not who we were. I am not me and you are not you. We are merely vessels set forth to do their bidding. We are without possibilities.

Imura: Yeah, with that bit of thinking, no question the possibilities are the exact opposite of endless. But if we're called after the frivolous doings as you call them, we have to get up and walk and serve the people, brave the world beyond, and bring back the goods. I know I can do it. Not because I'm an optimist or naïve, but because I refuse to lock myself into thinking about how difficult it all is. You either enjoy the puzzle and the challenge or you don't.

Voice: Imura and Tavor. Step to the middle of the room. You have been called.

As they step to the middle, a platform appears and they begin to descend.

Tavor: And so it begins. Come on.

Imura: No. Not yet, we need a plan. We can't just appear at the top, if we're chosen we will have just minutes before we're sent forth. You know what happens. So what's the plan? Request two packs with goggles, five days of goop, silver pad, first aid kit, and twelve rations of water?

Tavor: Make it six days of goop. Add a pair of gloves—an all-weather jacket, a fifty-foot rope, hiking boots, survival clothes, a torch— for both of us. And the two things no one ever asks for: *The Book of All Things*, a paperback copy will do, and the original decree that makes this all possible: *The Act of Journey* including the preamble.

Imura: Are you nuts? Books? We should ask for a horse or a transport or a vehicopter. Everyone asks for these things. Even the losers.

Tavor: Where are the victors now? You either succeed or you disappear. I've never seen the victors either. When does it all end? I'd like to know why, wouldn't you? Before we disappear. Besides, we need a map. They have always denied the request for paper and pencils and a compass; haven't you ever wondered why? I want to know why.

As they near the arena, the sounds of the audience grow louder and more ecstatic.

End of Scene

What the Dramaturg Heard   The dramaturg heard a scene that continues to move away from *The Hunger Games*. What does the writer wish to explore? What are the characters wanting to do? How do they relate to one another? Why is this world so bleak? What is it about this journey the characters are called to do that is so terrifying and difficult?

What the Active Dramaturg Heard   The active dramaturg heard a scene that reveals how the two characters might function as a team. Not as adversaries but as two people who contribute to each other's ideas. Perhaps not true collaborators, but their relationship could evolve into a strong collaboration. Tavor has a bit of a rebellious streak, although it's quite calculated. Imura is a bit more of a free spirit, but she shares her ideas and plans and thinks about her moves. They are a well-matched team. As a scene, it begins and ends in a mysterious fashion and leaves you wanting to know more. The two are so well matched and need to establish an alliance so quickly the tension between them does not appear as high. Given the nature of a survival game—the extreme dependency on others—the interpersonal tension may not be possible, leaving the tension to exist between the characters and their foes or obstacles. Is the tension between the characters and their obstacles clear? Could the tension be increased?

The Dramaturg Moderating a Table Discussion with Actors

Director: That was a great read. We're going to discuss the scene before moving ahead with the rehearsal. Our dramaturg will be helping with this discussion. Take it away, Dramaturg.

Dramaturg: Thanks, Director! Yes, let's start talking about this amazing play. What do you think of the piece? Let's start with the playwright.

Playwright: Um, well, I'd really like to hear what the actors think. Yeah, if we could just start with the actors. I'll chime in if I have anything to add, but I'd like to listen as much as possible.

Dramaturg: Okay. Actors, what are your impressions of the piece so far? Imura? Tavor? Voice?

Actor Imura: I think it's a great piece so far. Imura is a fun, spirited character. Yeah, she's fun to play. And Tavor is quiet, but he thinks a lot.

Dramaturg: Tavor? Your thoughts on your character or the play?

Actor Tavor: Well, I had some thoughts on Imura, but I guess I'll talk about the play.

Dramaturg: Oh, if you want to talk about Imura, go right ahead. What are your thoughts?

Actor Tavor: Well, she does talk a lot. A lot of inane chatter. I think it's too much and it should be cut. Like the section where she goes on and on. I liked it better when we had the first paragraph only.

Dramaturg: Well, the other paragraphs tell us a lot about the world and past events. Does your character want her to stop talking or do you, the actor want her to stop?

Actor Tavor: I think Tavor the character thinks girls talk too much.

Dramaturg: Okay. So has the writer's choice to have her talk a lot hurt the story or simply upset Tavor?

Actor Tavor: It's too long. Tavor needs to cut her off and they need to get on the same page sooner.

Actor Voice: And if the Voice came in sooner, the outside tension would make her stop talking and force the plan.

Dramaturg: Well, that's for the playwright to decide. We are just providing feedback to what's written. Does the story grab you? Do you know where it's going or are you surprised?

Actor Imura: Well, we know they are waiting to be called. I'm not sure what that means, but I'm willing to find out. I think Imura is more interested in thinking about the spectacle. It kind of reminds me of *The Hunger Games*.

Dramaturg: It does, doesn't it? Any more thoughts about that, the way this reminds you of the *Hunger Games*?

Actor Imura: No, not really.

Dramaturg: I see that *Hunger Games* idea and wonder how the two characters might come together. Is there a romance? What are their skills? We know nothing about their skills.

Actor Tavor: True. Well, we know Tavor is a thinker and Imura is attracted to shiny things.

Laughter

Dramaturg: So knowing more about their gifts might balance the play's current tilt toward a girl who likes to talk too much and needs sparkly spectacle in her life?

All actors: Yeah, sounds like it.

Dramaturg: Playwright, do you have any thoughts?

Playwright: So, I need to cut a lot and add more skills? I'm not sure that serves the story. I'm not sure what drives the story, but I think I'm less interested in romance and more interested in how the characters respond to the situation they're in.

Dramaturg: Isn't it the story of two young people on a journey to find water for their community? I think we have that. What we don't have is how they will get there and who these characters are alone and together. Okay. Thanks everyone for this feedback. The writer looks to have hit the limit.

Director: Yes, let's take a ten-minute break. Thank you, everyone.

The Dramaturg's Conversation   An unwillingness to respond to the play written remains this dramaturg's challenge and shapes how the actors respond to the scene. When the conversation opens to include the cast, this steadfast refusal to serve the play leads to a battle of wills between the actor playing Tavor and the dramaturg. Such a display never serves the playwright, the play, or the process. The post-reading conversation goes awry with the dramaturg's first statement

Dramaturg: Thanks, Director! Yes, let's start talking about this amazing play. What do you think of the piece? Let's start with the playwright.

Complimenting the piece or the reading the actors give will always be positive and a great place to begin; however, the dramaturg follows this compliment with an extremely vague question, "What do you think of the piece?" Anyone could respond by commenting on its length, the language characters use, the lack of lines each has. More importantly, the question asks for opinions exclusively. The dramaturg, perhaps unknowingly, invites the actors to ground their comments well outside the scene's action, which will not serve the development process.

Before turning to the actors, the dramaturg abruptly transitions to the writer and asks for the writer's thoughts on the piece. This writer responds in ways that reveal a lack of empowerment.

> Playwright: Um, well, I'd really like to hear what the actors think. Yeah, if we could just start with the actors. I'll chime in if I have anything to add, but I'd like to listen as much as possible.

The writer's words suggest a desire to hide from the conversation and asking for permission to listen. This language shows that this process has not empowered the writer and, quite possibly, the writer no longer enjoys this development and creative process, and has developed a negative thought regarding the development process in general.

The dramaturg does have a second opportunity to start the discussion so that the actors provide insights that reveal how the dialogue informs their character choices or provides clues into how the world impacts the characters. Instead the dramaturg chooses to say,

> Dramaturg: Okay. Actors, what are your impressions of the piece so far? Imura? Tavor? Voice?

Again, the dramaturg asks for opinions over informed responses. The result: actors who share basic responses where they lobby for changes to their own characters at the detriment of others and fail to push the actors to probe the play deeply.

> Actor Imura: I think it's a great piece so far. Imura is a fun, spirited character. Yeah, she's fun to play. And Tavor is quiet, but he thinks a lot.

Then the dramaturg attempts to transition the conversation. For the first time the dramaturg focuses the question, but in doing so excludes an option, the opportunity to comment on Imura. This rough transition stops the discussion and the dramaturg must back pedal to keep the conversation moving forward.

> Dramaturg: Tavor? Your thoughts on your character or the play?

> Actor Tavor: Well, I had some thoughts on Imura, but I guess I'll talk about the play.

> Dramaturg: Oh, if you want to talk about Imura, go right ahead. What are your thoughts?

> Actor Tavor: Well, she does talk a lot. A lot of inane chatter. I think it's too much and it should be cut. Like the section where she goes on and on. I liked it better when we had the first paragraph only.

The actor playing Tavor begins to share opinions that reveal a personal response to the material and a specific way to change the material. His comments come across as directives to the playwright rather than observations or constructive criticisms that the writer can choose to respond to or ignore.

The dramaturg's choice to identify whether the comments exist as personal comments or the character's responses will serve the process well. Sadly, as the dramaturg works to shift the conversation, the statement that immediately follows appears factual, but actually manages to incite the actor playing Tavor, resulting in an unproductive exchange that pits the dramaturg against the actor thereby undermining any collaborative spirit in the rehearsal hall.

Dramaturg: Well, the other paragraphs tell us a lot about the world and past events. Does your character want her to stop talking or do you, the actor want her to stop?

Actor Tavor: I think Tavor the character thinks girls talk too much.

Dramaturg: Okay. So has the writer's choice to have her talk a lot hurt the story or simply upset Tavor?

Actor Tavor: It's too long. Tavor needs to cut her off and they need to get on the same page sooner.

Actor Voice: And if the Voice came in sooner, the outside tension would make her stop talking and force the plan.

Not every actor believes the workshop discussion presents an opportunity for the cast to request or suggest rewrites that serve their individual interests, however, this actor does, and he lobbies for his character in the worst possible way. To the dramaturg's credit, this line of commenting stops with the remark reminding the cast that the writer controls the play and that the discussion process should present feedback only. The dramaturg redirects the conversation with two questions that sound like strong open questions, but in the end close the conversation and continue to ask for opinions grounded outside the play's world.

Dramaturg: Well, that's for the playwright to decide. We are just providing feedback to what's written. Does the story grab you? Do you know where it's going or are you surprised?

It appears as if the dramaturg's questions succeed because the actress reading Imura reveals some insights into the character's thought process based on the play's facts. She even shares her thought on the scene's similarities to known works. If an actor or any artist chooses to share connections to films or music or books or plays no one can find fault; however, the choice to shape the new work into the template created by the pre-existing work can disempower a writer and the new work's promise.

Actor Imura: Well, we know they are waiting to be called. I'm not sure what that means, but I'm willing to find out. I think Imura is more interested in thinking about the spectacle. It kind of reminds me of *The Hunger Games*.

Dramaturg: It does, doesn't it? Any more thoughts about that, the way this reminds you of *The Hunger Games*.

Actor Imura: No, not really.

Dramaturg: I see that *Hunger Games* idea and wonder how the two characters might come together. Is there a romance? What are their skills? We know nothing about their skills.

In shifting the conversation away from *The Hunger Games*, the dramaturg fails to open the conversation to larger critical questions and remains fixated on specifics that may (or may not) support the writer's vision. The dramaturg wants to explore a romantic storyline and to know specifics regarding skills. Although the notion of a romance may present a frame for a large portion of the story, the introduction of skills can be introduced simply and quickly. The dramaturg may not realize it, but the writer once again has only specific tasks to accomplish rather than large questions to ponder and possible places to introduce the information.

> Actor Tavor: True. Well, we know Tavor is a thinker and Imura is attracted to shiny things.

> *Laughter*

> Dramaturg: So knowing more about their gifts might balance the play's current tilt toward a girl who likes to talk too much and needs sparkly spectacle in her life?

> All actors: Yeah, sounds like it.

> Dramaturg: Playwright, do you have any thoughts?

> Playwright: So, I need to cut a lot and add more skills? I'm not sure that serves the story. I'm not sure what drives the story, but I think I'm less interested in romance and more interested in how the characters respond to the situation they're in.

> Dramaturg: Isn't the story about two young people on a journey to find water for their community? I think we have that. What we don't have is how they will get there and who these characters are alone and together. Okay. Thanks everyone for this feedback. The writer looks to have hit the limit.

No question the writer appears to have hit the wall. The dramaturg ignores the writer's growing sense of aggravation and confusion. "So, I need to cut a lot and add more skills? I'm not sure that serves the story. I'm not sure what drives the story, but I think I'm less interested in romance and more interested in how the characters respond to the situation they're in." The writer has a sense of what the play should or could explore further, but because the dramaturg fails to listen actively, neither the play nor the writer is served.

Next, the dramaturg further ignores the writer by imposing what The Sentence should be. "Isn't the story about two young people on a journey to find water for their community? I think we have that." Although it's good to strive to capture the play's story in a sentence, to dismiss the work and the writer and the creative process is both wrong and extremely hurtful. The dramaturg has not asked the playwright for The Sentence at any point during this development process. Here, the dramaturg tells the writer what the story is. Rather than offering what comes across. Remember, what's written and what's intended are not always in line, especially in early drafts. Ignoring the writer is bad enough, but here, with this imposed sentence, the dramaturg dismisses the work and the writer and demonstrates little respect for the development process. Nothing in this conversation reveals collaboration or respect for the writer not even the bit of laughter and consensus among the actors. The dramaturg and actors may believe that their laughter conveys creative connection, but in this situation it suggests an imbalance of power and a rehearsal hall where the writer feels outmatched and unsupported. In the end, the director calls the conversation to a close in an attempt to salvage some semblance of camaraderie and order.

The Active Dramaturg/Active Playwright Conversation   When the Active Dramaturg begins the conversation, the welcome provides a subtle yet clear frame for the comments while acknowledging the writer's efforts throughout the process.

> Active Dramaturg: Thanks, Director! And thanks to our playwright. This piece continues to deepen the characters and the world with every draft.

The air of welcome coupled with a focused yet open question continues with the questions:

> Active Dramaturg: Do you, Writer, have any thoughts you'd like to share with the group following this read? What struck you most during this reading?

The active playwright may choose to respond or to simply listen. In addition, the active writer, and in turn the cast, hears that focusing on what struck them or stood out most during this reading will serve the conversation (at least in its initial phase) best. Although "'what struck you most'" does call for an opinion, the opinions must focus on this reading and draft and specific images or passages. Because this question follows the comment regarding a draft that deepens the characters and world, the suggestion to focus responses here first and then branch out impacts the writer and cast.

The air of welcome and general sense of listening and support the active dramaturg cultivated throughout the process inspires the writer to decline to speak in a way that creates distance but remains connected to and excited by the process:

> Active Playwright: Thanks! I'm really curious to hear what everyone else thinks. I really did enjoy hearing the actors' spin on the characters. This is the best part of a workshop—hearing your words read immediately after writing them—and having them read by talented people. Thank you. But right now, I'd just like to listen to the group's thoughts.

The active dramaturg moves the conversation to the actors with a question that clearly frames the most important aspects of this discussion's initial phase—a sense of how the scene's evolution impacts the actors' knowledge of the characters and the world:

> Active Dramaturg: Actors, what struck you about this piece? You've seen it evolve from six lines to almost twenty. What have you learned about the characters and the world?

The actress playing Imura begins with a response that reveals a personal opinion and then moves to articulating how the character behaves and why. Such comments would not be possible had the writer not added more character details.

> Actor Imura: Well, I'd like to begin. I think Imura's a fun, spirited character. Underneath all of her chatter, I think she is quite anxious, and that she'd like a partner. She can only push Tavor so much because if she goes too far she will have to fend for herself, and if they are called she will not succeed on her own.

The active dramaturg knows that the playwright doesn't want Imura to come across as stereotypically female, and in this case it means talkative. The actress playing Imura mentions chatter/chattiness, and the active dramaturg uses this as an opportunity to explore the writer's concerns:

> Active Dramaturg: Do you feel that she is too girly? That her chatter is stereotypically female?

Again, the actress responds with an answer based partly in opinion and the rest in the play's facts and the actor's need to forge a character based in the play's reality. When the actor playing Tavor offers his insight, the active dramaturg works to separate the character from the actor to ensure that the scene's development serves the story and characters rather than an individual actor's opinions without engaging in an argument:

> Actor Imura: I don't think so. She's got a good reason for talking and trying to make a new friend or teammate.

> Actor Tavor: I think she is a bit too chatty. Not too much though. I agree that it seems to come from a place other than overly girliness, but at times it felt excessive—which is good—and then went on a bit too long. Not too often, though.

> Active Dramaturg: Does Tavor the character think this?

> Actor Tavor: Tavor the character thinks she talks too much.

> Active Dramaturg: Okay. What about you the actor? Is there a balance between her chattiness and Tavor's reserved speech? Or does it feel slanted too much in one direction?

> Actor Tavor: I guess some might think it's balanced, but I still feel it's too much. I will say this though, I love the Voice. I can hear it coming from nowhere with reverb instilling terror within both of them. They feel alone and lulled into complacency and then—bam!—they are forced to face reality.

Because the active dramaturg uses questions to focus on specific elements in the scene, the actor playing Tavor remains engaged in the process and freely expresses confusion. No one around the table believes that a lack of understanding reflects poorly on them as actors, the active writer's talent, or the scene's structure; everyone believes that confusion presents an opportunity to clarify a moment, nothing more nothing less.

> Actor Voice: And what a reality. An amazing amount of pressure for two young people who know nothing of each other or the situation they are to face and are expected to succeed. I especially love that they descend to meet the Voice rather than ascend.

> Tavor: That confused me, actually. Why descend? Why sink lower?

> Active Dramaturg: What images does descending call to mind that causes this confusion?

Again, the active dramaturg poses specific questions that engage the actors in discussing possibilities within the character, the play's world, or both without questioning or challenging the actors.

> Actor Tavor: Well, I guess I think of Imura and Tavor as heroes, and heroes rise.

> Active Dramaturg: What if they aren't heroes?

> Actor Imura: I'm not sure I'd root for them or be interested in their journey if they weren't heroic. I'm not sure I care if they rise or sink, just the notion that they assemble their plan quickly. Everything else seemed to take time, but this, this happened fast.

Throughout the conversation, the active dramaturg looks to pose questions that directly reference the critical elements. Here, the question focuses on time because the actors have begun to discuss how the rhythm of the scene changes when the Voice interrupts the action.

> Active Dramaturg: So, throughout the scene, time passed in ways that made the waiting seem to be the only point?

> Actor Voice: Yes, and then they weren't waiting and things began to happen quickly. As if they—Imura and Tavor—were no longer in control.

> Active Dramaturg: How were Imura and Tavor controlling time and other things before the Voice was heard?

> Actor Imura: They gave us everything we needed—

> Actor Tavor: What they wanted us to hear—

> Actor Imura: Right. And then suddenly, the Voice came in and it was about what others needed.

The active dramaturg's game plan included identifying moments of tension and possibly increasing the conflict within the scene. The active dramaturg moves from time to expectations because the cast begins discussing the Voice and what the

Voice represents—the world outside the waiting room and its demands on Imura and Tavor. Stating this idea explicitly would transform the discussion into a class-room lecture, and so the active dramaturg opts for a simple question:

Active Dramaturg: What is expected of them other than getting the water?

Imura: I'm not sure.

Actor Tavor: Me neither.

Active Dramaturg: Do we need them to have more expectations placed upon them?

Actor Tavor: I think they'll have more obstacles as they seek the water and that's where we will see more expectations placed upon them.

The active playwright adds a comment because the cast begins to speculate what might occur, but in ways that do not specify actions or deeds, but point to general turning points within the story. Discussing the scene in such a focused yet broad manner respects the writer's role as the creator, but honors the development process as a place where many voices collaborate to explore and help build something new.

Active Playwright: Would you want to know more about the possible tensions or obstacles before they set off on their journey or as they encounter them?

Actor Imura: Hmm. Surprises are always nice, but there is something to having more than one goal on the journey as you set out.

The active dramaturg continues to pursue the original game plan—identifying more opportunities for tension and obstacles—by presenting a clear example grounded in a known work, *The Wizard of Oz*. Rather than pushing the active writer to recreate *The Wizard of Oz* or making clear connections between the film and the writer's scene, the active dramaturg highlights the key dramaturgical element the scene might benefit from and identifies how it functions in the film's story.

Active Dramaturg: Yeah, look at the *Wizard of Oz*; one main goal and then three additional goals that are just as important to the three new characters—the Scarecrow, the Tinman, and the Lion—as returning home is to Dorothy. I'm not suggesting that this become the *Wizard of Oz*, but those needs are revealed early and the conflict—returning home and battling the Wicked Witch of the West—even earlier. Right now, this play has a journey in a barren, challenging environment and no other known challenges or foes, yet.

Active Playwright: Yeah, with the characters on a better path it's easier to see that the need for obstacles and foes will add a number of layers to the story. Time to think!

In the end, the active writer listens to a conversation that remains positive and inspirational even when actors voice concern or dislike for certain moments. The active dramaturg facilitates a conversation that avoids taking a personal tack, allowing all involved the freedom to hear the comments without feeling defensive. The result: the active writer remains engaged with the work and eager to explore it further.

The Active Dramaturg Moderating a Table Discussion

Director: Wonderful reading everyone. To help the writer further develop the piece, we—the dramaturg, the writer, and I—thought a discussion with the actors, those of you who were listening, and us would benefit from the process. Our active dramaturg will be moderating the discussion. Take it away, active dramaturg!

Active Dramaturg: Thanks, Director! And thanks to our playwright. This piece continues to deepen the characters and the world with every draft. Do you, Writer, have any thoughts you'd like to share with the group following this read? What struck you most during this reading?

Active Playwright: Thanks! I'm really curious to hear what everyone else thinks. I really did enjoy hearing the actors spin on the characters. This is the best part of a workshop—hearing your words read immediately after writing them—and having them read by talented people. Thank you. But right now, I'd just like to listen to the group's thoughts.

Active Dramaturg: Actors, what struck you about this piece? You've seen it evolve from six lines to almost twenty. What have you learned about the characters and the world?

Actor Imura: Well, I'd like to begin. I think Imura's a fun, spirited character. Underneath all of her chatter, I think she is quite anxious and that she'd like a partner. She can only push Tavor so much because if she goes too far she will have to fend for herself, and if they are called she will not succeed on her own.

Active Dramaturg: Do you feel that she is too girly? That her chatter is predictably female?

Actor Imura: I don't think so. She's got a good reason for talking and trying to make a new friend or teammate.

Actor Tavor: I think she is a bit too chatty. Not too much though. I agree that it seems to come from a place other than overly girliness, but at times it felt excessive—which is good—and then went on a bit too long. Not too often, though.

Active Dramaturg: Does Tavor the character think this?

Actor Tavor: Tavor the character thinks she talks too much.

Active Dramaturg: Okay. What about you the actor? Is there a balance between her chattiness and Tavor's reserved speech? Or does it feel slanted too much in one direction?

Actor Tavor: I guess some might think it's balanced, but I still feel it's too much. I will say this though, I love the Voice. I can hear it coming from nowhere with reverb instilling terror within both of them. They feel alone and lulled into complacency and then—bam!—they are forced to face reality.

Actor Voice: And what a reality. An amazing amount of pressure for two young people who know nothing of each other or the situation they are to face and are expected to succeed. I especially love that they descend to meet the Voice rather than ascend.

Actor Tavor: That confused me, actually. Why descend? Why sink lower?

Active Dramaturg: What images does descending call to mind that causes this confusion?

Actor Tavor: Well, I guess I think of Imura and Tavor as heroes, and heroes rise.

Active Dramaturg: What if they aren't heroes?

Actor Imura: I'm not sure I'd root for them or be interested in their journey if they weren't heroic. I'm not sure I care if they rise or sink, just the notion that they assemble their plan quickly. Everything else seemed to take time, but this, this happened fast.

Active Dramaturg: So, throughout the scene, time passed in ways that made the waiting seem to be the only point.

Actor Voice: Yes, and then they weren't waiting and things began to happen quickly. As if they—Imura and Tavor—were no longer in control.

Active Dramaturg: How were Imura and Tavor controlling time and other things before the Voice was heard?

Actor Imura: They gave us everything we needed—

Tavor: What they wanted us to hear—

Actor Imura: Right. And then suddenly, the Voice came in and it was about what others needed.

Active Dramaturg: What is expected of them other than getting the water?

Actor Imura: I'm not sure.

Actor Tavor: Me neither.

Active Dramaturg: Do we need them to have more expectations placed upon them?

Actor Tavor: I think they'll have more obstacles as they seek the water and that's where we will see more expectations placed upon them.

Active Playwright: Would you want to know more about the possible tensions or obstacles before they set off on their journey or as they encounter them?

Actor Imura: Hmm. Surprises are always nice, but there is something to having more than one goal on the journey as you set out.

Active Dramaturg: Yeah, look at the *Wizard of Oz*; one main goal and then three additional goals that are just as important to the three new characters—the Scarecrow, the Tinman, and the Lion—as returning home is to Dorothy. I'm not suggesting that this become the *Wizard of Oz*, but those needs are revealed early and the conflict—returning home and battling the Wicked Witch of the West—even earlier. Right now, this play has a journey in a barren, challenging environment and no other known challenges or foes, yet.

Active Playwright: Yeah, with the characters on a better path it's easier to see that the need for obstacles and foes will add a number of layers to the story. Time to think!

A Side-by-Side Comparison of the Moderated Discussions

The Dramaturg Moderating a Table Discussion	The Active Dramaturg Moderating a Table Discussion
Director: That was a great read. We're going to discuss the scene before moving ahead with the rehearsal. Our dramaturg will be helping with this discussion. Take it away, dramaturg.	Director: Wonderful reading everyone. To help the writer further develop the piece, we—the dramaturg, the writer, and I—thought a discussion with the actors, those of you who were listening, and us would benefit the process. Our active dramaturg will be moderating the discussion. Take it away, active dramaturg!
Dramaturg: Thanks, Director! Yes, let's start talking about this amazing play. What do you think of the piece? Let's start with the playwright.	Active Dramaturg: Thanks, Director! And thanks to our playwright. This piece continues to deepen the characters and the world with every draft. Do you, Writer, have any thoughts you'd like to share with the group following this read? What struck you most during this reading?
Playwright: Um, well, I'd really like to hear what the actors think. Yeah, if we could just start with the actors. I'll chime in if I have anything to add, but I'd like to listen as much as possible.	
Dramaturg: Okay. Actors, what are your impressions of the piece so far? Imura? Tavor? Voice?	
(Cont. on next page.)	*(Cont. on next page.)*

| A Side-by-Side Comparison of the Moderated Discussions (cont.) ||
The Dramaturg Moderating a Table Discussion	The Active Dramaturg Moderating a Table Discussion
Actor Imura: I think it's a great piece so far. Imura is a fun, spirited character. Yeah, she's fun to play. And Tavor is quiet, but he thinks a lot. Dramaturg: Tavor? Your thoughts on your character or the play? Actor Tavor: Well, I had some thoughts on Imura, but I guess I'll talk about the play. Dramaturg: Oh, if you want to talk about Imura, go right ahead. What are your thoughts? Actor Tavor: Well, she does talk a lot. A lot of inane chatter. I think it's too much and it should be cut. Like the section where she goes on and on. I liked it better when we had the first paragraph only. Dramaturg: Well, the other paragraphs tell us a lot about the world and past events. Does your character want her to stop talking or do you, the actor want her to stop? Actor Tavor: I think Tavor the character thinks girls talk too much. Dramaturg: Okay. So has the writer's choice to have her talk a lot hurt the story or simply upset Tavor? Actor Tavor: It's too long. Tavor needs to cut her off and they need to get on the same page sooner. Actor Voice: And if the Voice came in sooner, the outside tension would make her stop talking and force the plan. Dramaturg: Well, that's for the playwright to decide. We are just providing feedback to what's written. Does the story grab you? Do you know where it's going or are you surprised? *(Cont. on next page.)*	Active Playwright: Thanks! I'm really curious to hear what everyone else thinks. I really did enjoy hearing the actors spin on the characters. This is the best part of a workshop—hearing your words read immediately after writing them—and having them read by talented people. Thank you. But right now, I'd just like to listen to the group's thoughts. Active Dramaturg: Actors, what struck you about this piece? You've seen it evolve from six lines to almost twenty. What have you learned about the characters and the world? Actor Imura: Well, I'd like to begin. I think Imura's a fun, spirited character. Underneath all of her chatter, I think she is quite anxious and that she'd like a partner. She can only push Tavor so much because if she goes too far she will have to fend for herself, and if they are called she will not succeed on her own. Active Dramaturg: Do you feel that she is too girly? That her chatter is predictably female? Actor Imura: I don't think so. She's got a good reason for talking and trying to make a new friend or teammate. Actor Tavor: I think she is a bit too chatty. Not too much though. I agree that it seems to come from a place other than overly girliness, but at times it felt excessive—which is good—and then went on a bit too long. Not too often, though. Active Dramaturg: Does Tavor the character think this? Actor Tavor: Tavor the character thinks she talks too much. Active Dramaturg: Okay. What about you the actor? Is there a balance between her chattiness and Tavor's reserved speech? Or does it feel slanted too much in one direction? *(Cont. on next page.)*

A Side-by-Side Comparison of the Moderated Discussions (cont.)

The Dramaturg Moderating a Table Discussion	The Active Dramaturg Moderating a Table Discussion
Actor Imura: Well, we know they are waiting to be called. I'm not sure what that means, but I'm willing to find out. I think Imura is more interested in thinking about the spectacle. It kind of reminds me of *The Hunger Games*.	Actor Tavor: I guess some might think it's balanced, but I still feel it's too much. I will say this though, I love the Voice. I can hear it coming from nowhere with reverb instilling terror within both of them. They feel alone and lulled into complacency and then—bam!—they are forced to face reality.
Dramaturg: It does, doesn't it? Any more thoughts about that, the way this reminds you of the *Hunger Games*.	Actor Voice: And what a reality. An amazing amount of pressure for two young people who know nothing of each other or the situation they are to face and are expected to succeed. I especially love that they descend to meet the Voice rather than ascend.
Imura: No, not really.	
Dramaturg: I see that *Hunger Games* idea and wonder how the two might come together. Is there a romance? What are their skills? We know nothing about their skills.	
Actor Tavor: True. Well, we know Tavor is a thinker and Imura is attracted to shiny things.	Actor Tavor: That confused me, actually. Why descend? Why sink lower?
Laughter	Active Dramaturg: What images does descending call to mind that causes this confusion?
Dramaturg: So knowing more about their gifts might balance the play's current tilt toward a girl who likes to talk too much and needs sparkly spectacle in her life?	Actor Tavor: Well, I guess I think of Imura and Tavor as heroes, and heroes rise.
All Actors : Yeah, sounds like it.	Active Dramaturg: What if they aren't heroes?
Dramaturg: Playwright, do you have any thoughts?	Actor Imura: I'm not sure I'd root for them or be interested in their journey if they weren't heroic. I'm not sure I care if they rise or sink, just the notion that they assemble their plan quickly. Everything else seemed to take time, but this, this happened fast.
Playwright: So, I need to cut a lot and add more skills? I'm not sure that serves the story. I'm not sure what drives the story, but I think I'm less interested in romance and more interested in how the characters respond to the situation they're in.	
Dramaturg: Isn't it the story about two young people on a journey to find water for their community? I think we have that. What we don't have is how they will get there and who these characters are alone and together. Okay. Thanks everyone for this feedback. The writer looks to have hit the limit.	Active Dramaturg: So, throughout the scene, time passed in ways that made the waiting seem to be the only point.
	Actor Voice: Yes, and then they weren't waiting and things began to happen quickly. As if they—Imura and Tavor—were no longer in control.
	Active Dramaturg: How were Imura and Tavor controlling time and other things before the Voice was heard?
(Cont. on next page.)	Actor Imura: They gave us everything we needed—
	(Cont. on next page.)

A Side-by-Side Comparison of the Moderated Discussions (cont.)	
The Dramaturg Moderating a Table Discussion	The Active Dramaturg Moderating a Table Discussion
Director: Yes, let's take a 10-minute break. Thank you, everyone.	Tavor: What they wanted us to hear—
	Actor Imura: Right. And then suddenly, the Voice came in and it was about what others needed.
	Active Dramaturg: What is expected of them other than getting the water?
	Actor Imura: I'm not sure.
	Actor Tavor: Me neither.
	Active Dramaturg: Do we need them to have more expectations placed upon them?
	Actor Tavor: I think they'll have more obstacles as they seek the water and that's where we will see more expectations placed upon them.
	Active Playwright: Would you want to know more about the possible tensions or obstacles before they set off on their journey or as they encounter them?
	Actor Imura: Hmm. Surprises are always nice, but there is something to having more than one goal on the journey as you set out.
	Active Dramaturg: Yeah, look at the *Wizard of Oz*; one main goal and then three additional goals that are just as important to the three new characters— the Scarecrow, the Tinman, and the Lion—as returning home is to Dorothy. I'm not suggesting that this become the *Wizard of Oz*, but those needs are revealed early and the conflict—returning home and battling the Wicked Witch of the West—even earlier. Right now, this play has a journey in a barren, challenging environment and no other known challenges or foes, yet.
	Active Playwright: Yeah, with the characters on a better path it's easier to see that the need for obstacles and foes will add a number of layers to the story. Time to think!

Level I: The Active Dramaturg/Active Playwright Conversation

When executing this in a class, create groups of six to eight—a playwright, director, active dramaturg, and three to four actors—and allot approximately twenty-five to thirty minutes for each phase of the workshop.

This exercise challenges everyone interested in new plays from the active dramaturg to the active playwright to the actor and the director.

Time Allotments

> 5 minutes to write a six-line scene
> Reading the scene aloud (no preparation by the actors)
> 8 minutes for the dramaturgical discussion
> 10 minute to rewrite the scene based on the workshop comments
> 3 minutes to discuss the changes and impact of the rewrites

1. If using this exercise in a class, divide into groups of six to eight people. Invite everyone to write a six line scene—that is six lines of dialogue of any length; not necessarily six sentences. The time allotted for writing is no more than five minutes.

2. If in groups, each active writer should be paired with an active dramaturg and director, and those remaining are the actors. Each group member should experience each role at some point during the rotation; in a group of six, there will be six active dramaturgs, active playwrights and directors. If using this exercise alone or in pairs to develop skills, prepare to read the scene. If working alone, consider reading the scene aloud to yourself to ensure each line of dialogue resonates.

3. The active playwright and director should cast the scene (simply choose actors) from those in the small group. Scenes may be read around a table.

4. The active dramaturg and active playwright will begin the dramaturgical discussion. The active dramaturg begins posing open questions with an eye to clarifying moments. Consider the critical elements when formulating questions. If focusing on one scene per group per class, no more than five minutes for the conversation. If working on the entire small group, three minutes per conversation.

5. Once each play has been discussed, provide each active playwright eight minutes to rewrite the scene. The active playwright may *add* four additional lines of dialogue in addition to tweaking any of the existing six lines.

6. Revist the scene and add additional lines.

7. Re-read the scenes aloud.

8. The active dramaturg then moderates a brief discussion of the changes—their impact on the overall story and scene. If working alone, use the critical elements to expand and critique the work.

9. Share both the original six-line scene and the rewritten scene with the larger class. Also, share the dramaturgical questions that proved most helpful.

These activities may take place in small groups or each reading and conversation may take place before the entire class.

Level II: Active Dramaturgy: Moderating a Discussion at the Table

This exercise builds on the basic questions and requires the active dramaturg to build a game plan for the workshop as well as manage the post-reading discussion with the creative team.

If using this exercise in a class, divide into groups of six to eight people. The groups may be different or the same as those in Level I. If using this as an out-of-class experience, have each group member note the process in general with attention to success and challenges. One of the actors should time the process. This process will take thirty to thirty-five minutes per scene.

Time Allotments

    5 minutes to write a ten-line scene
    5 minute pre-reading active playwright/active dramaturg conversation
    3 minutes to create a game plan
    Reading the scene aloud (no preparation by the actors)
    8 minutes for dramaturgical discussion
    10 minute to rewrite the scene based on the workshop comments
    3 minutes to discuss the changes and impact of the rewrites

1. Invite everyone to bring their ten-line scene to class and consider ways to further shape the ten lines. Additions, edits, and cuts may be made, but the lines of dialogue may not exceed ten lines.
2. For this level, the active dramaturg should meet with the active playwright before the reading to continue the conversation, and identify areas the writer wishes to explore. The active dramaturg should also identify areas to explore and introduce to the discussion.
3. The active dramaturg should create a game plan to serve the writer's vision and the scene. The playwright may wish to consider how to best listen for the questions raised during the conversation with the active dramaturg and director.
4. If in groups, each active writer should be paired with an active dramaturg and director and those remaining are the actors.
   Extra challenge: change the active dramaturg paired with the active playwright to create a second workshop atmosphere.
5. The playwright and director should cast the scene (simply choose actors) from those in the small group.
6. Have the actors read the scene. The director may introduce some thoughts or ask the actors to simply read the scene without making choices.

7. Discuss the scene with the active dramaturg moderating. The active dramaturg may organize this discussion any way that best serves the writer and the scene. This should be an active conversation with the active playwright contributing comments or questions to help shape the rewrite process.

8. The rewrite for the ten-line scene should respond to the insights gained during the readings and conversation around the table. The playwright's rewrites should tighten the current lines. The active writer has the option to add four additional lines of dialogue.

9. Time permitting, read the entire scene again and discuss the changes with the active dramaturg moderating.

Return to the table and have the actors first read the original ten-line scene and then read the rewritten scene aloud to the larger group. These activities may take place in small groups or each reading and conversation may take place before the entire class.

Level III: Active Dramaturgy: Moderating the Audience Discussion for a New Work

This exercise explores what a discussion following a workshop with an actor and directors might be like. If using this exercise in a class, divide into groups of six to eight people. The groups may be different or the same as those in Level I or Level II. If using this as an out-of-class experience, have each group member note the process in general with attention to success and challenges. One of the actors should time the process. This process may take up to fifty minutes per scene.

Time Allotments

10–15 minutes for reading the scene aloud (no preparation by the actors)
10–15 minutes for the dramaturgical discussion
10 minutes to explore a scene or moment
10 minutes to discuss the process

1. Hold a mini workshop as in Level II. If appropriate, the active playwright has the opportunity to add an additional four lines. A goal may be to ensure the scene has a true sense of conclusion (as if the end of a brief play or merely the end of a scene in a larger work).

2. Present the scene to the class or group. Directors should present a script-in-hand reading of the scene, which means that actors are not expected to memorize any lines. Directors may choose to present the reading in chairs at the table or music stands or stage the reading. *Do not discuss what happened during the workshop process before the small group or class.*

3. When the scene concludes, the active dramaturg begins to moderate a post-reading discussion. The active dramaturg works throughout this

5–10 minute discussion (the length depends on the length of the scene and how many participate in the discussion) to elicit comments from the audience and engage the creative team in the discussion.

Prior to the discussion the active dramaturg works to identify key questions the director and playwright have or wish to have the audience discuss. It is possible to use one of the fourteen-line scenes created for the active dramaturgy variation.

4. The active dramaturg should open the discussion, prepare back pocket questions, identify questions the playwright or creative team would like to have answered, identify someone to take notes during the conversation, and craft a conclusion.
5. When the post-reading discussion concludes, invite the active dramaturg to first comment on the process—challenges and successes—and then invite others to identify how they experienced the discussion.

Rather than tell the dramaturg you did well here or poorly there, participants should share their experiences. For example, which questions were clear or made them feel truly invited to participate; which responses engaged or pushed them away.

Challenge   Invite someone to pose difficult or inapprproiate questions to the active dramaturg to improve the dramaturg's ability to field difficult questions. Or, instruct the writer to leave the discussion in a fit of anger, disgust, or a state of emotional disarray at some point during the discussion to help the dramaturg manage the discussion following a disruption.

Part IV: Thoughts to Consider

Introduction

Sherlock Holmes met his challenges with confidence culled from research and accomplishment. Sometimes, he engaged Dr. Watson in conversation to prepare for or to better understand and then frame the central question, to ensure a successful outcome. Similarly, the active dramaturg develops and strengthens skills through practice and then debates the underlying thoughts governing what is done and why in service of moving the discipline, art, and field forward. In short, the active dramaturg cultivates conversations that help reshape the field.

To that end, many of the key challenges that thwart the efforts of those involved in developing new work are funding resources, audience reception, and critical response. A rarely discussed fourth hurdle is the inherent, unacknowledged bias each person brings to the table when first considering and then developing new work. As much as it is nice to think that education, a passion for giving voice to the voiceless, a desire to transform society or the art form itself, and personal experience negates all bias, they do not. Sadly, we all have bias. Happily, we have the ability to acknowledge our biases and behave in ways that render them invisible, if not innocuous.

Whether encountering work that speaks to various cultural or ethnic experiences or developing a language to discuss those works and their playwrights, an active dramaturg will, at some point, need to ask the questions of how bias from the field, society, and oneself impacts or informs the development process of culturally specific theatre. The active dramaturg plays a key role in shaping the artistic conversations that mitigates the limiting effect any bias, and in particular cultural bias, has on identifying, honing, and accepting new work and new artistic voices. Similarly, when collaborating, the active dramaturg wishes to identify a language and physical behavior (its own language) to enable a true collaborative conversation rather than adopt an inappropriate role of teacher or leader.

Because the specific answers defining how to best avoid the pitfalls bias dictates change with each artistic generation, but the informing circumstances rarely do, it behooves the active dramaturg to identify the historical zeitgeists to better prepare for his or her generation's conversation that will enhance collaborations. Too often creative conversations concerning differences and bias address the timeless questions and offer time-bound solutions that might work for today's artists and concerns, but fail to move the field forward if they do not acknowledge the solution's intended and unintended impact on tomorrow. The active dramaturg works to foster dialogues that explore the processes that currently keep many artistic communities and conversations separate. Active dramaturgs are active curators concerned about the future. This section seeks to prepare active dramaturgs for the conversations they will be called upon to facilitate, dialogues that confront personal, artistic, and societal biases fueled by provocative questions.

The Active Dramaturg and the Conversation Concerning Cultural or Ethnic Difference

Language frames perception. Words can liberate an idea and heighten awareness or constrain thinking even among the most pioneering and avant-garde. Linguistic limits occur largely because of the questions certain phrases and categories allow people to ignore. Vocabulary can prevent the birth of an alternative creative route or thought path because the terms chosen embrace a host of assumptions that have perpetuated for so long. These facile words or phrases allow us to comfortably not know, not see, or not think of the implications of using such language.

Active dramaturgs know that during the creative process, using exclusionary or deficit language, a language of *no* and *not* stifles creativity. The active dramaturg knows that positive or neutral language proves more motivating and welcoming. Similarly, negative and exclusionary words allow many conversations to remain imbalanced when discussing those of different ethnic or cultural backgrounds and even gender. With these thoughts in mind, the active dramaturg asks how skewed conversations detrimentally impact the process for selecting the mainstage season, the scripts selected for development at workshops or festivals, and the conversations concerning the hiring of the artistic team.

To avoid this potential linguistic pitfall, the radical choice for the active dramaturg would be to change the language that frames the discussion and informs the solutions needed to increase and diversify the number of those represented and participating in as well as cultivating a more balanced conversation.

It takes chutzpah to buck a trend (let alone a national linguistic code) when considering how to discuss writers as unique crafters of story rather than as a mere extension of a particular group responsible for giving voice to everyone's story and truth.

In particular, the active dramaturg accepts that the understanding of the 'other' as an individual within a cultural context, rather than as a wholesale example of the culture, improves collaboration. The term *cultural competency*, commonly used in health care education, looks beyond a limited definition of ethnicity and expands to include religious culture, sexual orientation, and gender to encourage a deeper familiarity and respect for the other. The term excels in its attempt to include and provide space for the whole person and that person's entire experience.

An example of shallow language that binds rather than liberates is the word *minority*. Most in my generation have used the word to introduce a conversation regarding people of color or when writing grants or collecting audience data. 'Minority' is also a numerical term that means lesser than.

Whenever the term *minority* is used to refer to someone who is not Caucasian (the current majority group within the United States), the effect is to push the conversation toward deficit rather than additive thinking. To move beyond less precise, hindering language is to consider the implication of repeated use on collaboration and the individual. Consider how one word historically shapes thoughts and the hurdles its continued, unconscious use creates. At least this is the argument Ricardo Kahn, the artistic director for the nation's only African-American regional theatre, Crossroads Theatre Company in New Brunswick, NJ, offered when I used the word *minority* while discussing playwrights. Kahn, who also served as Theatre Communications Group's first African-American Board President, gently admonished me with, "Lenora, minority means lesser than and no person is lesser than anyone else. We don't use the term *minority* here."

I was flustered. I did not and do not believe anyone is lesser than and didn't want to be seen as insulting any one person (including myself) each time I spoke. In addition, I didn't think that any industry or person who used the term set out to declare anyone lesser than anyone else. Neither was Ricardo. His point was to listen to the word and consider the implication of repeated use. Consider the word's subtext. Consider how one word shapes thoughts and the hurdles its continued, unconscious use creates.

I've never forgotten this conversation with Rick or the explosions that took place in my brain following the exchange, because it has forever altered the way I see people and language. It must be something akin to the moment someone truly questioned the phrase "separate but equal."

The need to adjust my language began. During the early 1990s, few people used the phrase "writers of color," now, in 2014, it is quite common. But as the millennium approached, I began to question a lot including where to begin the change and what language to use.

To change my language, I had to first actively acknowledge that language frames thoughts. Secondly, I had to accept the unpleasant fact that by using the term *minority*, I was unintentionally embracing the notion that I considered people lesser than others, and because I am an African-American woman, that by using the term I also considered myself lesser than, and was blithely proclaiming that fact to the world. Consistent use also suggests that I was happy to be seen as such. Rest assured, that was not an opinion that I have ever held of myself or others.

Noticing and then working to alter one's language inevitably reveals how language confines as well as liberates people, even among those with the best intentions. Using the vocabulary (or embracing an image) that most accept as appropriate, conveys tacit agreement and erects walls between collaborators. An active dramaturg acknowledges that language frames thoughts and that using certain words, albeit unintentionally, can lead to the assumption that a person embraces a belief contrary to what she or he holds true. Adopting new language changes how individuals, circumstances, and actions were previously and are currently seen. The revelations linguistic change brings inevitably strengthens relationships and collaborations.

As an active dramaturg shifts his or her personal language, and in turn the language of his or her collaborators, the opportunity to alter the way one collaborates with writers exists. As language evolves, the active dramaturg has the opportunity to help narratives by writers of various backgrounds move beyond the expectations that direct stories to adhere to a predetermined form; adopting a shape and voice uniquely their own.

Active dramaturgs regularly consider whether limiting language denies every artist the opportunity to be fully seen and to share varied experiences, especially those accomplishments or challenges the majority group considers the exception when there is a very real possibility these are closer to the norm. It is possible that looking to embracing the ideas put forth in cultural competence would improve how new works by female writers and writers of color are identified, developed, and supported.

The American theatre purports to provide a creative outlet for all well-told stories regardless of subject and all writers (or artists) regardless of creed, color, class, or sexual orientation. Many in the theatre embrace this mission and work to realize it professionally and personally. Even so, this mission has been called into question, most particularly the field's attitude toward female artists and its ability to support female writers and directors, as well as a culturally and ethnically diverse artistic population who seek regular outlets for their voices. The field is primed for active dramaturgs to guide a conversation focused on reframing the dialogue concerning difference.

A key challenge writers of color face, and one an active dramaturg can reshape through a questioning dialogue, is fostering a writer of color's freedom to craft a world that reflects their experiences or their imagination. Many writers of color confess that there is an expectation that their work must address topics in ways that support a predetermined point of view. An active dramaturg also has the challenge of regularly (and vigorously) asking the theatre community whether it opts for the story it can sell or prefers depictions of experience their audience can relate to, rather than (or at the expense of) supporting images and narratives that address the writer's true voice, vision, and perspective. The artist of color must adjust to accommodate the audience's perspective rather than vice versa.

Active dramaturgs acknowledge the impact one's cultural reference has on shaping and filtering perception and support a dialogue that works to expand these known cultural touchstones in myriad ways, so that audience and writer can meet each other at least half way. Most of the artists who read the submitted manuscripts and subsequently collaborate with writers of color often have little to nothing in common with the writer's life experiences. And that's fine. How many people of color have anything in common with the plays assigned in most classes and produced on most stages? In truth, even artists of color may have little in common with each other, for the experiences within the African American, Latino, Native American, and Asian communities are diverse. Throughout the development process, active dramaturgs strive to cultivate an environment that acknowledges the reality that similar experiences of personal or cultural exclusion may provide common discussion points, but never renders these characters of color interchangeable. No question a key reason to create and attend theatre is to learn, to experience something new, to become more aware, and to grow emotionally. Active dramaturgs play a crucial role in supporting these learning experiences. Active dramaturgs foster conversations and debates that engage and educate communities—so that audiences are prepared for the artist's point of view as well as the unique way the artist presents the earth-shattering idea.

Too often, however, theatres fail to fully and honestly engage and prepare for change—for themselves and their audiences. This is why many plays about people of color continue to have Caucasian characters who narrate or lead the audience through the story. In other words, the play's principle story, its basic frame and lens, is rooted in a familiar Caucasian perspective and voice. And here is where many artists of color find their developing plays at a crossroads: when the play's world moves beyond what some audiences and some collaborators know, the creative push is to either reshape it into one that is known—thereby de-emphasizing the characters of color, or the writer finds a development process with little questioning and rigorous development.

Or, artists with keen vision and talent are invited to participate in the development process, but in spite of the fact they were hired, they are unknown by their collaborators and relegated to a position of silence; or, the new collaborator shares information that although true, falls well outside what's expected and is, therefore, ignored. For example, when I worked on a piece about a well-known African American, I found a number of images of the subject's childhood home in biographies and autobiographies. When copies of the images were shared with the group, the director questioned how nice the houses looked, how well kept they were, and wanted different images. Even when confronted with the fact that these were the actual images of the African American's home, the decision was to underplay the figure's privileged upbringing in the face of what appears to be a biased view of African-Americans, their housing, and neighborhoods.

The active dramaturg cultivates a process that supports the active playwright's cultural and artistic vision and the new-to-the-group collaborator's voice.

This is not always easy. Sometimes active dramaturgs must counter a level of unwelcomeness from the theatre that hired them for the workshop. If, for example, the artistic director delays the start of the playwright's reading or has no intention of attending the reading, but provides no warning or excuse for this quite notable absence (or simply fails to show up, and yes, I have seen this happen), a playwright might ask why spend the energy to cultivate a relationship and reputation as a great collaborator? Or, a playwright may question why wrestle with the active dramaturg's difficult, yet rewarding, creative questions if the theatre has secured only limited rights for an adaptation and demonstrates little interest in delving deep into the material?

In situations such as this, the active dramaturg has the opportunity to encourage the writer to work beyond the theatre's low expectations. The active dramaturg has the opportunity and duty to nurture the play and support the writer's artistic voice, as fully as possible, regardless of the theatre's visible lack of interest. Even if the writer believes the work has a limited life due to the play's subject matter, the active dramaturg must approach the development process with full rigor. Why? Because you never know what the future holds. And who wants to be part of the problem?

Artists of color have a great deal to say regarding the American experience and the human experience. Their contributions have and will continue to greatly shape the landscape of American theatre. Currently, however, the American theatre still relegates the work of artists of color to a specific box. When artists push beyond these boundaries a few are allowed outside the bounds, but most are expected to remain in the place of what is perceived as correct; a supposition built on stories and images crafted for decades of people of color, but not by people of color. The active dramaturg works to create a welcoming environment for these voices and visions.

We have seen how homosexuals have moved beyond fey stereotypes to amazingly nuanced beings. Women have begun to emerge from the shadows both on stage and behind the scenes. Artists of color continue to pursue places for their stories on stage and opportunities to contribute to stories written by anyone for everyone. To become a culturally competent community of artists, the American theatre must improve its language around difference and how it actively acknowledges the diversity within each cultural and ethnic group, and the artistic visions of said groups should be supported even when these depictions fall well outside what's expected. An active dramaturg who embraces the concepts of cultural competency remains poised to better advocate for all writers and the various experiences culture and ethnicity provide.

The Active Dramaturg and the Conversation Concerning Labeling Playwrights

Just as the active dramaturg will be expected to shape and inform the conversation regarding the inclusion of a variety of voices on the American stage and supporting the artists' growth and audiences' reception, the active dramaturg will be constantly called upon to label and categorize writers according to the writer's evolution and potential as an artist.

The current vernacular used to identify a writer's artistic development and achievement involves terms that provoke more debate and derision than universal agreement. The current terms—emerging, mid-career, established/veteran—attempt to establish a writer's relationship to the theatre in units of time that imply rather than explicitly define production history and skill. Because foundations, grant applications, or theatres rarely define what constitutes *emerging, mid-career*, or *established/veteran*, the field or the applicant must discern its own meaning, which leads to confusion rather than clarity.

Why? The reasons are many.

At first glance, *emerging* seems a simple enough designation—a writer who is new or relatively new to writing for the professional theatre. If emerging has little to do to with a writer's chronological age, how does one define *relatively new to writing or the professional theatre world*? For example, is a recent graduate from an MFA playwriting program an emerging writer? What if said writer received professional productions before (or perhaps during) graduate school? What if Samuel French or Dramatists Play Service licenses the writer's work? Is the playwright still an emerging writer? Each question begets another resulting in confusion rather than clarity.

The term *veteran* presents similar challenges. Initially, veteran seems easy to define—someone who has many years and many professional productions and perhaps some awards. Equating awards with veteran status causes some problems, however, for although the world and profession understand the prestige of certain awards and nominations, there are more long-established writers than awards. Suddenly, numbers of production as well as a writer's age becomes a significant factor. But if age wasn't a factor in determining a writer's emerging status how could it apply to the term *veteran*?

And then there is mid-career.

How does anyone know they've arrived at the middle of their artistic career? People leave the field, journey over to television or film, and then return to theatre. What markers indicate the middle of a career? In general, most believe the label fits a writer who has been around for a while, but what constitutes *a while*? And what about the writers who remain stuck at the mid-career mark?

The active dramaturg recognizes the rabbit hole of questions and contridictions these labels present, as well as the exceptions like the mysterious Jane Martin, who seemed to avoid the status of emerging writer, or Sarah Ruhl, who also burst onto the theatrical scene as a strong playwright with numerous productions and awards. Which label did Lynn Nottage, a published and often-produced playwright with a career beginning in the late 1980s, find herself wearing before *Ruined*? Veteran or mid-career or established? Perhaps she was labeled as all simultaneously depending upon which theatre or foundation initiated the conversation.

Without question the descriptors *emerging, mid-career,* and *veteren* fail. The terms fail because they cause confusion, unintentionally insult the artist, and are applied without transparency or equity, especially when discussing writers of color.

The most significant reason these labels prove unsuccessful is because they limit how institutions and collaborators discuss writers by ignoring what matters most when discussing artistry: originality in rendering a subject, artistic voice, vision, and artistic mission or voice (the political writer—think Caryl Churchill—the memoirist Adrienne Kennedy or the genre-defying José Rivera). Not to mention a writer's professional production experience, professional workshop experience, and the writer's impact on the field.

The active dramaturg considers whether the field benefits from reframing the question of experience with craft and art. What if the field asked how many new-play development experiences a writer has had and with whom, and move on from there? Yes, stated that way the question and process sounds a bit perfunctory and indecent, but no more than forcing a writer into a category without a consistent set of guidelines. But at least the conversation focuses on the writing.

When considering development workshops, choosing to abandon the aforementioned labels and asking a different set of questions altogether helps an active dramaturg respond to work objectively and, most specifically, choose questions related to the work and experience. For example, how many workshops has the writer participated in? For what length of time? If a writer has had twelve two-day workshops and no two-week workshops, the lengthy development process will be a first, and negotiating the workshop may prove challenging. These specific facts change the conversation. Rather than putting forth a coded system that depends on comparing the artist to others the emphasis is now on understanding actual and specific experiences. In the end, such a framework purports to compare the writer to him or herself and creates greater transparency.

A strong follow-up question an active dramaturg might pose is: Has the writer experienced a high-stress environment where the workshop dictates the play's production future or have the workshops been exploratory in nature (for the theatre and for the writer)?

The labels might be reformed as: Emerging (versus a writer with one to five non-Equity productions; one to three Equity productions); Mid-Career (versus a writer with five to ten non-Equity productions; five to seven Equity productions at LORT theatres); Established (versus ten or more non-Equity or Equity productions); Veteran (versus multiple regular productions and possibly an award or two). (For Theatre for

Young Audiences, the labels would be much the same except the LORT designation may not apply and international and touring productions may be added.)

An active dramaturg might ponder the possibility of forgoing labels entirely and simply discuss the merits of the work in reference to the work itself. To achieve this would mean to place greater weight on the writing—storytelling, language, subject matter, artistic daring—and weigh productions and workshops differently because female writers and writers of color will fail to compete because of the significant lack of workshop invitations and production opportunities, if all things are considered equally and honestly.

In truth, when a writer has difficulty elevating the first two points—telling a story in an inventive and original manner without succumbing to more simplistic scene structure or using language in straightforward, unsurprising ways—the writer's career often stalls early on.

That said, it is important to note that some writers purposefully choose a more simplistic and predictable dramatic form coupled with the use of semi-adventurous dialogue and language because they favor uncomfortable or unpopular topics. For politically dense theatrical work to excel, writers often need to consider a simpler, less daring form. An active dramaturg acknowledges such a truth and shifts the conversation to favor the advances an active playwright makes with each subsequent script.

In other words, an active dramaturg considers all of the critical elements when discussing a writer and his or her thearical evolution. Sadly, our current system of labels and boxes rarely allows for such a refined approach. Labeling artists extends beyond achievement to include subject matter (AIDS or women) or presentation style (avante-garde or traditional). The entire practice lulls us into falsely believing we understand the writer's career trajectory and ability and that the writer's artistic sensibility remains stagnant.

With a renewed look at how the field categorizes writers and theatre artists, it may become apparant that the current labels work against many female playwrights and writers of color. Reexamining the languge used to discuss writers may lead seasons to transform in spectacular fashion.

The active dramaturg needn't wait for the field to change to shift the language around defining playwrights' professional progress. The active dramaturg need only be proactive and begin blazing a trail of unlimited discovery by eschewing labels and finite definitions.

The Active Dramaturg and the Conversation Concerning Dramaturgs versus Teachers versus Active Dramaturgs

At some point in an active dramaturg's career the creative conversation will be misconstrued and seen as pedagogical, that of teacher and pupil. Usually the age difference between dramaturg and playwright introduces this challenge into the relationship. Although dramaturgs may serve as playwriting teachers in various academic and professional settings, during a play development workshop a dramaturg should not begin to function as or be seen as a teacher. Active dramaturgy places considerable demands upon dramaturgs and those who function as dramaturgs throughout the play development process. To add the expectation or the spector of the responsibility of teaching the basics and art of writing drama, confuses and confounds the creative and collaborative process. In addition, the didactic method that some find in classrooms rarely works in rehearsal halls and never works in play development scenarios. Nevertheless, such behavior exists due to a misunderstanding of what active dramaturgs do when collaborating.

In the most basic sense, teachers and dramaturgs manage the creative process. To function as a teacher, one not only critiques writing but gives assignments, provides parameters for those assignments, sets deadlines, and institutes rewards and penalties when goals are, or are not, achieved. To function as a dramaturg, one serves as a sounding board—to respond to ideas a writer presents, or to pose questions designed to deepen the story and strengthen the writer's vision. Dramaturgs may also set deadlines in line with the rehearsal process, but only in relation to the demands of the process, not indiscriminately and not to exert control over the situation. (A process-defined deadline might be that a writer wants to have pages available for the next rehearsal that begins at 10 a.m. The active dramaturg may require that the new pages be sent by 9 a.m. so the stage manager or literary department can copy and distribute the pages.).

The goal of an active dramaturg, however, is to first lead the process and then manage the comments and critiques by crafting questions based on the critical elements that are designed to identify and clarify so that they work with the play's voice and the writer's vision. The active dramaturg doesn't shield the writer from challenging critical comments but works to frame and ground these critiques so that they inspire rather than detract from the creative process.

The active dramaturg invites the playwright to set a work agenda and establish deadlines that use or keep rehearsal deadlines in mind.

Unlike a teacher who may assign many plays for homework, the active dramaturg may refer to other playwrights or specific works as ways to illuminate a point or idea, but avoids assigning texts to read (no time exists during a play development workshop). The active dramaturg also refrains from comparing or identifying the new work undergoing development with pre-existing plays as a way to describe how this new piece works (this may come across as dismissive or belittling). Yes, an active dramaturg may inform a playwright about the way processes generally unfold, but avoids presenting the process as a series of hard and fast events as a teacher might.

Even the dramaturg's physical behavior when discussing the play or notes following a reading can disrupt the collaborative balance in favor of the less desired teacher and student dynamic. When the dramaturg remains seated behind a desk with the writer opposite, the inevitable conclusion, rightly or wrongly, is that the commitment to team work has changed.

An active dramaturg leads the process, because to lead is to clear away the obstructions and the distractions so that the individual is free to think clearly, identify the most important goals and creative hopes, and achieve those goals. To collaborate is to help frame the vision—rather than impose the vision—and to then get out of the way.

In Conclusion

Understanding how a game plan helps lead a play development process toward the successful attainment of its goals can transform a dramaturg into an active dramaturg, but do not be confused: active dramaturgs do not work miracles. In the end, the active writer must write; the director, direct; and an engaged, active dramaturg can help shape an inspirational process that leads to solutions and rewrites, but these are not miracles, these evolutions in story are the product of old-fashioned hard work.

The development process demands that everyone participate fully and grapple with the difficult questions of why and how and what. Why this play? How to best capture the emotion and tension? What can remain unsaid and what remains crucial to providing the audience enough information that it remains engaged and at the tipping point—not knowing too much or too little? Active dramaturgs help most in tracking and realizing the delicate balance between tension and mystery, especially as plays evolve and sections move, lines of dialogue disappear, and characters transform.

During a workshop, the active dramaturg engages in identifying moments to explore further or change or enhance because they are unclear. Through specific active questions and notes, the active dramaturg provides options and ways to approach the rewrites. Although the active dramaturg never writes or rewrites a portion of a play, it is the active dramaturg's responsibility to make suggestions and articulate ways to approach areas to explore that help to accelerate the rewrite or writing process. Anyone may be able to give a note, but only an active dramaturg (or an artist with extremely strong dramaturgical skills) can craft a note (oral or written) that serves as a roadmap to creation. Active notes fuel rewrites, whereas, notes simply open eyes and may spur some writing changes, but nothing sustained.

When building a game plan, the active dramaturg looks for and assesses the project's needs based on an evaluation of the critical elements that suggests a macroscopic or a microscopic approach. A macroscopic (or big picture approach) informs the game plan that deals with a play with an unclear story or character journey, or with the play that does not correspond with the writer's expressed vision. A macroscopic approach also serves the process when the writer needs to become reacquainted with the play or key characters, because a considerable amount of time has passed between writing and workshopping the play. A microscopic approach serves a process when the play is clear—most character journeys connect with the story and the writer's vision jibes with the play's vision. During such a process, the creative team focuses on specific scenes, character concerns—journey, language—or storytelling devices such as how to incorporate flashbacks (what triggers them, what causes them to dissolve) or masking tropes such as a ghost in a play like *Mariela and the Desert* or *Proof*.

Nothing challenges the active dramaturg more than the question of what to ask when. If a dramaturg calls a scene or story point into question too soon, the playwright may balk, shut down, or try to rewrite to address the specific point raised by the question rather than the overall concern the question heralds. The best way to discern when to ask what is to listen. Listen for a writer's commitment or lack thereof. A writer who waivers needs time to more fully grasp the play's power and intent. A writer too willing to shift will acquiesce to the collaborators and lose control of the story and everything that made the play attractive in the first place. When an active dramaturg collaborates with a team that fails to directly invite comments from the dramaturg, the active dramaturg listens to the discussion to determine the team's priorities and, when appropriate, chooses to voice the observation. A failure to include doesn't mean the dramaturg should remain quiet, merely bide one's time and engage slowly, purposefully.

Too much is at stake during a workshop or development process for an active dramaturg to relinquish his or her role in the creative/collaborative process and remain silent because some collaborators opt to exclude an artistic voice. Even outside the rehearsal hall, the active dramaturg plays a crucial part in shaping the conversation for creating a welcoming environment for all writers and their stories. The active dramaturg's position in American theatre, though often misunderstood because so much of the work remains invisible and intangible, has never been more crucial. It is the active dramaturg who shapes and nurtures the conversation surrounding cultural competency. It is the active dramaturg who clears the way for the adventurous writer's work to move from page to the production process.

Art is the repository of a society's soul; art captures not only the current zeitgeist but the consistent challenges to a society, its cultural' integrity, and overall vision of itself. Because of these responsibilities, the discipline must welcome all voices and allow those stories to flourish as fully and richly as possible, especially those charged with shaping the landscape so that all innovative artistic voices flourish. The language that defines, elevates, and expands the repertoire of American theatrical stories must morph along with our changing definitions of dramatic form or acceptable play length. The active dramaturg facilitates this radical approach to curating theatrical art for posterity.

Those who listen actively can distinguish between collaborations that pretend to—rather than actually—invite all artists to participate fully in creating a work where every voice is welcomed, valued, considered vital, and incorporated.

Language matters.

Curate well.

Appendix

How The Sentence Shapes the Rewrite Process and Informs the Game Plan

Rewriting can be exciting. The characters begin to come into focus and share surprises. The scenes have more detail and this means the play becomes richer and less predictable.

Rewrites can also be difficult. Sometimes the characters stop talking during the writing process. The conflicts and circumstances that come to mind don't always help clarify the character's journey or the play's central story. Sometimes the ideas just stop coming.

Here are a few tips that help when the rewriting or first-round writing process becomes a bit difficult. These can also help when the rewrites are going well and can add a little more nuance and drama to the play.

A Brief Checklist

1. Write down the play's story. The play's story or the action of the play should take the play's action from the first moment to the last. This should be written in one sentence, 'not to reduce the play, but to help focus the thoughts and provide a roadmap when rewriting.
2. Use The Sentence to create a roadmap for the play.
3. The Sentence tells where the conflict may enter the play
4. Use The Sentence to shape the characters.
5. Think about the new insights the process brings about. For instance, if the character is mentally ill, think about whether The Sentence supports that the character is mentally ill from the beginning, or becomes mentally unwell/unstable over the course of the play.
6. Remember, discoveries may lead to changing the order of the play's scenes or events, but not necessarily new characters.
7. Conflict is the essence of drama. In other words, don't make it easy for the characters to get what they want.
8. Details *or* specifics matter.
9. Make sure what's imagined is on the paper.

Here are some examples of suggestions 1–5.

The Sentence   If we had to tell the story of *The Hunger Games* in one sentence it could be: "This story explores what happens to young people forced to assume the responsibility of fighting for others as they discover that the glamour and popular support for warriors does little to sustain their humanity throughout the battle." This reveals that:

1. The story is about young people.
2. That young people fight for others—the surprise of the play is that most are forced into battle, but one person, Katniss, volunteers to fight.
3. That the warriors are treated like celebrities.
4. That the perks of living like a celebrity don't last when the battle starts.
5. That the warriors have to make decisions and do things that make them less like the persons they were when the story began.

The Roadmap

1. The Sentence for *The Hunger Games* provides five major events for the play. (See the five points under The Sentence.)
2. These five major events impact *every* character
3. There are places for surprise—someone volunteers; someone tries to remain more human and kind than others (or not).

The Conflict

1. Do these young people want to fight? Are they happy about this?
2. Do they react well to the person who volunteers?
3. Do they all enjoy the celebrity treatment? Do they enjoy it the same way?

To Shape Characters

1. Make a chart for each character
2. Put each point that The Sentence dictates is important for the play in one column and write how this character reacts in the other column.
3. Use The Sentence to pose questions
4. Use The Sentence and the chart to describe the character
5. Use the chart and the questions to create detail

To further explore: Take Character #1: Come up with a name and biography.

Possible Chart for Character #1:
Further Exploration Using The Sentence

Information Learned from The Sentence	Character Information The Sentence Yields
This is about young people	This character is fourteen years old. A young warrior.
Fighting for others	This character doesn't want to fight. This character thinks fighting is wrong. This character is also physically weak. (This character presents a lot of conflict to the play's central theme.)
Warriors treated like celebrities	This character loves the celebrity treatment. This character enjoys the attention more than training. This character can sing and is really popular because she sings better than Beyoncé. (Oh, yeah, the warriors are trained. Gotta include that. I need another column for that. This character loves the clothes.)
Celebrity perks don't continue during the battle	Singing doesn't help her fight. She is hungry because no one brings food to her. She regrets not paying attention to the training. (Hmmm . . . what challenge in battle does she face that leads her to think about her training or lack thereof?)
Warriors make decisions that lead them to question their humanity	She thinks fighting is wrong, but is attacked and must fight back. Does she become a super warrior or does she die? (How is she attacked? What does she think? How badly does she want to live? When does she realize this is about life and death, not just a game?)

BIBLIOGRAPHY

Brown, Lenora Inez. *The Art of Active Dramaturgy: Transforming Critical Thought into Dramatic Action*. Newburyport, MA: Focus Publishing, 2011.

Doyle, Sir Arthur Conan. "A Scandal in Bohemia." *The Complete Adventures of Sherlock Holmes*. Edited by Julian Symons. London: Martin Secker & Warburg, 1981.

Doyle, Sir Arthur Conan. "The Adventure of the Abbey Grange." *The Complete Adventures of Sherlock Holmes*. Edited by Julian Symons. London: Martin Secker & Warburg, 1981.

Lerman, Liz, and John Borstel. *Liz Lerman's Critical Response Process: A Method for Getting Useful Feedback on Anything You Make, from Dance to Dessert*. Takoma Park, MD: Dance Exchange, 2003.

Shakespeare, William. *The Tragedy of Macbeth*. Edited by Annalisa Castaldo. The New Kittredge Shakespeare, edited by James H. Lake. Newburyport, MA: Focus Publishing, 2008.

Shakespeare, William. *The Tragedy of Hamlet*. Edited by Bernice W. Kliman and James H. Lake. The New Kittredge Shakespeare, edited by James H. Lake. Newburyport, MA: Focus Publishing, 2009.

Plays Mentioned

William Shakespeare	*Macbeth, Hamlet,* and *Richard III*
Sarah Ruhl	*Eurydice*
Caryl Churchill	*Far Away*
Lynn Nottage	*Ruined*
Lynn Nottage	*Las Meninas*
Karen Zacarías	*Mariela and the Dessert*
José Rivera	*Boleros for the Disenchanted*
Tony Kushner	*Angels in America*
David Ives	*All in the Timing*
David Auburn	*Proof*

Films Mentioned

Shakespeare, William. *Hamlet*. Directed by and screenplay by Kenneth Branagh. With Kenneth Branagh, Richard Briers, Julie Christie, Derek Jacobi, Michael Maloney, and Kate Winslet. 242 minutes. Castle Rock Entertainment, 1996. DVD.

Shakespeare, William. *Hamlet*. Directed by and screen adaptation by Michael Almereyda. With Ethan Hawke, Kyle MacLachlan, Bill Murray, Liev Schreiber, Sam Shepard, Julia Stiles, and Diane Venora. 112 minutes. Miramax, 2000. DVD.

Shakespeare, William. *Richard III*. Directed by Richard Loncraine. Screenplay by Richard Loncraine and Ian McKellen. With Annette Benning, Jim Broadbent, Robert Downey Jr., Nigel Hawthorne, Ian McKellen, Kristin Scott Thomas, Maggie Smith, and John Wood. 104 Minutes. MGM Home Entertainment, 1995. DVD.

Lenora Inez Brown is the author of *The Art of Active Dramaturgy: Transforming Critical Thought into Dramatic Action* (Focus, 2011), as well as numerous articles, essays, and book chapters focused on dramaturgy and dramatic criticism. She is a former Head of Dramaturgy and Dramatic Criticism at The Theatre School, DePaul University and has served as a dramaturg at numerous world premiere productions. She has also served as a dramaturg at numerous new-play workshops and festivals including The Sundance Theatre Labs 2000 and 2001, South Coast Repertory's The Pacific Playwrights Festival, The Goodman Theatre's New Stages Series, The Bonderman Festival at Indiana Repertory Theatre, and New Visions/New Voices at The Kennedy Center. She helped initiate Madison Rep's new play festival, which included the premiere of Sarah Ruhl's *Eurydice*. She was the Director of New Plays at the 1999 Tony Award® regional theatre Crossroad Theatre Company and the dramaturg for the 1999 Tony® nominated musical *It Ain't Nothing But the Blues*. She continues to develop new work with MPAACT in Chicago and other theatre companies focused on new work. She is a past president of Theatre for Young Audience/USA. Ms. Brown holds an MFA in Dramaturgy and Dramatic Criticism from the Yale School of Drama.